PAST TIMES

A Social History of Singapore

Chan Kwok Bun and Tong Chee Kiong (eds)

TIMES EDITIONS

© 2003 Times Media Private Limited

Published by Times Editions
An imprint of Times Media Private Limited
A member of Times International Publishing Group
Times Centre
1 New Industrial Road
Singapore 536196
Tel: 6213 9288 Fax: (65) 6285 4871
E-mail: te@tpl.com.sg
Online Bookstore: http://www.timesone.com.sg/te

Times Subang
Lot 46, Subang Hi-Tech Industrial Park
Batu Tiga, 40000 Shah Alam
Selangor Darul Ehsan, Malaysia
Fax & Tel: (603) 56363517
E-mail: cchong@tpg.com.my

All rights reserved. No part of this publication may be reproduced,
stored in a retrieval system or transmitted, in any form or by any means,
electronic, mechanical, photocopying, recording or otherwise, without
the prior permission of the copyright owner.

National Library Board (Singapore) Cataloguing in Publication Data
Past times :– a social history of Singapore /– Chan Kwok Bun and Tong
Chee Kiong (eds.). – Singapore : Times Editions,– 2003.
p. cm.

ISBN : 981-204-916-9

    1. Singapore – History. 2. Singapore – Social conditions.
I. Chan, Kwok Bun. II. Tong, Chee Kiong.

      DS610.4
959.57 — dc21   SLS2002047199

Printed in Singapore by Utopia Press Pte Ltd

Contents

Preface by Professor Paul Hockings — *4*

Introduction : A Place in Times Past — *9*
Tong Chee Kiong & Chan Kwok Bun

Chapter 1 : Moulding a Nation: Education in Early Singapore — *17*
Maribeth Erb

Chapter 2 : Silent Witnesses: The 'Woman' in the Photograph — *33*
Nirmala PuruShotam

Chapter 3 : From Dispersed to Localised: Family in Singapore — *57*
Selina Ching Chan

Chapter 4 : Coming into Being: Birth and a Nation's Growth — *69*
Maribeth Erb

Chapter 5 : Erased Tropical Heritage: Residential Architecture and Environment — *87*
Chua Beng Huat

Chapter 6 : Gathering Speed: Transport and the Pace of Life — *103*
Roxana Waterson

Chapter 7 : Consuming Food: Structuring Social Life and Creating Social Relationships — *123*
Selina Ching Chan

Chapter 8 : It's Us Against Them: Sports in Singapore — *137*
Alexius Pereira

Chapter 9 : Leisure, Pleasure and Consumption: Ways of Entertaining Oneself — *153*
Yung Sai Shing & Chan Kwok Bun

Chapter 10 : Triads and Riots: Threats to Singapore's Social Stability — *183*
Alexius Pereira

Chapter 11 : Believing and Belonging: Religion in Singapore — *199*
Lily Kong & Tong Chee Kiong

Conclusion : Theatre of Four Corners: Photographers, Subjects, Sociologists and Readers — *233*
Zaheer Baber & Chan Kwok Bun

Preface

An ethnography is a descriptive account of a particular society, and that is just what this book attempts to be: it offers a picture of Singaporean life, past and present — and in a literal sense, with many photographs too. Each chapter adds to our insight into what it has meant to countless thousands to live in the villages, the townships, the city, the state and now the republic of Singapore. Our accumulating knowledge depends on the careful choice of topics and pictures in each chapter of the book, covering everything from teachers to triads.

Maribeth Erb's chapter, on the educational institutions of the past, is obviously a good way to begin. It introduces us to both the multiple ethnicities of the population and also the multiple sponsors of schooling: the former British colonial government, the Christian missionaries, Chinese businessmen, and others, each group with their own agenda for the children's upbringing and hence for the future of Singapore as they envisioned it. Children are central to cultural change, for they only learn selectively what is made available for them by older generations; and these in turn choose what they consider appropriate or relevant to pass on to the young.

Nirmala PuruShotam starts with a new and necessary reading of mid-20th century photographs of Singaporean social situations. All of the pictures she asks us to look at depict women in a patriarchal society. The unspoken pressures from fathers, husbands, even concubines and co-wives, are reflected in the expressions of women in many of the selected photographs. The nascent politicisation of working and middle-class women is well documented in this chapter, too. From the very beginning of Singapore, women have been a major part of the colony's workforce, and not only within household contexts.

The delightful family photographs that Selina Ching Chan has assembled, posed as they no doubt are, speak eloquently of the varied family structures that marriage was intended to promote. In the early days, however, Chinese and Indian working men came to Singapore by themselves, creating a gross disparity between the two genders which only slowly was remedied by the practice of having their marriages arranged. These tended to be with women from the hometown or home region, and resulted in the establishment of nuclear households in Singapore even when households would have been joint ones back home. Later on, with increased affluence, the Chinese in particular tended to develop these homes into extended households, since the sons were being encouraged to stay at home, for economy's sake, even after marriage.

The crucial act for increasing the population of Singapore, that of giving birth, is thoroughly explored by Maribeth Erb in the fourth chapter. Here she documents both similarities and differences in the traditional birthing practices of the three main ethnic communities, and then goes on to show the slow but steady rise in modern scientifically-based maternity facilities from 1889 onwards. Over a century later, in 1996, the KK Hospital was featured in the *Guinness Book of Records* as having supervised the record number of 39,835 births in one year, the world's largest number for a single maternity centre.

But if reproduction is the mainstay of any community, then housing is just as basic. In Singapore Chua Beng Huat discerns four kinds of house, and describes the local history and characteristics of each kind, illustrating them with well-chosen photographs. These four sorts of residence are the traditional Malay house, the southeastern Chinese house, the urban shophouse (also mainly Chinese), and the expansive bungalow surrounded by verandas of the privileged colonial class. Those readers interested in a more detailed discussion of Singapore architecture should look at Lee Kip Lin's excellent book, *The Singapore House: 1819-1942* (Singapore, 1988), or at another well-illustrated Times publication, *Portraits of Places: History, Community and Identity in Singapore,* edited by Brenda S.A. Yeoh and Lily Kong (Singapore, 1995).

Roxana Waterson offers here a fascinating account of the evolution of transportation in Singapore and indeed many similar colonies in Asia. It is a story not just of transition from one form to a more efficient one, and a more costly one, but a story of intermingling of technological influences from a variety of places — Europe certainly, but also China, Japan, Malaya and India. Price, convenience, government control, labour, speed, and passenger numbers all interacted to bring Singapore's transportation to its present efficient level. Ox-carts, gharries, litters and rickshaws have disappeared, it is true, but their less colourful replacements are now moving a vast population around the island-state with efficiency such as could only have been dreamt about a hundred years ago. Today a ring road circles the main island, and to the east lies a major international airport.

Selina Ching Chan in Chapter 7 demonstrates how much of public social interaction occurs at eating places. With such a multi-ethnic population, it is inevitable that Singapore is and always has been a fine place for dining on the most diverse kinds of food, and seafood especially. Perhaps less expectable is Chan's observation that people of one ethnic group, especially when young, were very willing to eat and drink whatever other ethnicities were consuming.

This inter-ethnic *camaraderie* was much less apparent, however, in the local development of team sports, as Alexius Pereira shows. He surveys a broad range of modern sports, all of them introduced to Singapore by Europeans except for the Malay boating events; and what stands out in the earlier history of all these sports is how they were associated with and restricted to a particular class, a particular 'race,' and indeed the more energetic part of the male population. The pettiness of colonial racism is illustrated by the way Eurasian men (of whom there were many) formed their own sporting club when they found themselves barred from the European one; but then Eurasian women had to create their own sporting club too when they found themselves excluded from the male Eurasian one! In various of the team sports there were clubs specifically for the British, Indians, Chinese, Malays, and Sikhs. Only since Independence have these barriers lessened somewhat — though not yet for women. Football has proved to be especially popular in recent decades, and broad-minded in its player-recruitment too.

Team sports, Alexius Pereira suggests, can be viewed as an expression of ritualized conflict. But he grapples with more life-threatening conflicts when, in another chapter, he explores the Chinese triads and the riots. A picture soon emerges which has not even been hinted at in all the preceding parts of the book. Singapore for much of its history was like a Wild West town transposed to the East, full of criminal gangs (and individuals) making their living through gambling, cock-fighting, protection rackets and brothels. The triads were especially impenetrable because so few of the colonial police were Chinese. The British officials preferred Malays, Indians and Eurasians as their policemen.

Much of the crime before World War II and the rioting that followed it were attributable to the failure of any social force, be it police, school or church, to integrate the community effectively. Every poor immigrant found himself in a small, strange land, with only the norms and practices of the homeland's culture as a steadying reference point. Only after Independence did the threat of criminal or communist violence subside, but by then Singapore was largely a Chinese self-governing republic. Neither the British nor the Malays were any longer in power.

The delightful chapter by Yung Sai Shing and Chan Kwok Bun deals with quite a variety of forms of leisure, pleasure and consumption. As they point out, people in Singapore were amusing themselves by 'flying kites, playing chess, cock-fighting, hunting, story-telling, rolling marbles, playing bubbles, theatre-going, dancing, listening to music, collecting sea-shells, riding bicycles, reading, going to the circus, and so on' (p.153). But this was not all: there had also been a background of crude 'ethnic vices,' namely gambling, smoking opium, drinking, prostitution, even crime and delinquency (ibid). Overshadowing in popularity many of these pastimes in the days before television were, first, the various Chinese opera troupes, whether on the streets or in the theatres, performing not just Peking operas but also the dialectal forms from Hokkien, Teochew, Canton and Macau; and secondly, the public storytellers and puppeteers. During the interwar years, these too were being eclipsed by musical revues, featuring many popular dance groups; and then by radio broadcasting. The account of various storytellers, dancers, broadcasters gives fascinating insights into the work of the artists that most readers will never have encountered.

The chapter by Lily Kong and Tong Chee Kiong pulls much of the preceding social history together by putting it into a context of varied faiths. From the earliest days of Singapore's settlement, the migrants who arrived there never thought of giving up their diverse religions. Thus, as the 19th century progressed, one could find the observances of Islam, Christianity, Hinduism, Zoroastrianism, Buddhism and the various forms of Chinese worship being pursued along the same city streets. Of course, the very act of migration and of surviving in a strange environment led to untold individual stresses and uncertainties which were addressed in a variety of ways, from fortune-tellers and spirit mediums to the Catholic confessional. Yet, as has always been true in multi-ethnic societies, religions could at the same time offer individuals a sense of belonging and also divide people into rioting communities, as has sometimes happened in Singapore's past. Even today, modernism has not promoted secularism much, and the great majority of the population still adheres to one named faith or another. The Republic has however seen a certain individualism develop in worship, with people taking practical short-cuts in the less essential parts of their observances. Churches, mosques and temples are increasingly functioning as community centres, too, with a variety of social facilities in place.

Implied in several of these chapters is the existence of the prominent Singaporean concept of *kiasu*, 'afraid to lose.' Its pervasiveness has led to a high level of competitiveness not only in sports but in education and the workplace too. This has proved to be a double-edged sword, for while it arguably keeps standards high in a great variety of endeavours, it also gives the behaviour of many the appearance of 'pushiness.'

It is a truism that Singapore is a place which, like every other place we know of, has a unique history. This place is distinctive because of the meanings which people ascribe to it. The authors of this book (as was also true in a previous one) are thus 'exploring the nature of place meanings through an understanding of the nexus between place, history, community and identity' (Yeoh and Kong 1995: 23). The nature of the photographic record in achieving this end has been explored in sociological terms in the concluding chapter by Zaheer Baber and Chan Kwok Bun, in such a way as to put the visual resources surveyed throughout the book into a larger context, the discourse about the relationships between photograph and its object/subject. This chapter should prove of value to historians of photography as well as to those trying to comprehend Singapore's colourful history.

The editors have brought together in this new volume chapters which outline and illustrate the historical sociology of Singapore. The nexus that they collaboratively explore conjoins colonial history with tropical domestic architecture, childbirth and family organisation, work and sport, rioting and religion, crime and country, to show us how the Republic of Singapore has come to be the way it is and to look the way it does today.

It is a small place, and doubtless it felt even smaller in colonial times when the total population could be numbered in the tens of thousands. Even now (2002) it only totals 4,452,732, of whom 76.7 percent are Chinese. Yet it is a place that is home to Hindus and Sikhs, Muslims and Catholics, Buddhists and Taoists, Parsis and Protestants, 'shenists' and Confucianists. Each faith supports a string of places of worship, and a calendar of festivals, which serve to give a distinctive identity to a certain community in each case.

The high quality of the photographic record of Singapore's history is surely evident from the many black-and-white illustrations that grace the pages of this book. It is something which social historians and anthropologists, residents and visitors, will all find enjoyable to read.

Paul Hockings

Professor Emeritus of Anthropology, University of Illinois;
and Adjunct Curator, Field Museum of Natural History, Chicago;
and Editor, *Visual Anthropology*.

A Place in Times Past

Tong Chee Kiong & Chan Kwok Bun

The 1950s and 1960s in Singapore were turbulent, formative years: a time of political upheaval, social dislocation, ethnic strife and nascent nationalism on the one hand, and burgeoning urbanisation and economic development on the other. Singapore today may seem like a different place altogether.

Yet, much of what has been written about those years is political and economic history. The intention of this book is to give glimpses of how people went about living their everyday lives. How did people amuse themselves? What was family life like and how has it changed? How did people perform religious rituals and what were their customs? What kinds of homes did they live in? What and how did they eat? What was school life like? How did they get around? To answer these questions, the chapters in this book cover a range of activities, from leisure and entertainment to major life transitions such as birth, marriage and death.

The photographs in this volume record a way of life that is quickly vanishing or already gone: the vegetable farms in Potong Pasir, which are now occupied by rows of uniform, monolithic Housing and Development Board (HDB) flats, and fishermen in the *kampungs* repairing their nets, in an area that is now bisected by the East Coast Parkway. Many photographs in this book depict scenes that are now scarce or no more: a Magnolia ice-cream cart on its rounds; young schoolgirls, fresh-faced, listening to radio broadcasting, smilingly, all in one room; the Indian milk seller plying his trade on a bicycle; cows grazing in open fields; the *satay* man carrying his baskets on a long wooden pole — setting up shop wherever he felt like it and without a hawker's licence; the *tongkangs* on Boat Quay, now replaced by pubs and alfresco dining establishments. In a sense, a more idyllic period that only older Singaporeans remember, though often nostalgically, conveniently forgetting the difficult socio-economic and political environment and the poor hygiene of the time.

The impetus for this book began with a chance meeting of the then head of the Department of Sociology at the National University of Singapore, Ong Jin Hui, and an editor of the Times Media, who mentioned that the National Archives had an impressive collection of photographs and showed him a sample. Ong then asked us to assemble and edit a collection of photo essays. We contacted a multi-disciplinary group of scholars who specialise in subject matters covered in this book. Photographs from the National Archives were made available to them. Other photographs were from private collections. Some authors supplemented their work with interviews and fieldwork. The brief given to the authors was simple: write a think piece with sociological and anthropological insights, and interweave it with archival photographs to inform the general public on the living cultures of Singapore society during past times. As Zaheer and Chan wrote in the concluding chapter, 'the interweaving of written and visual accounts captures the social history, or the details of the daily routines of individuals and institutions, the nitty-gritty of daily life and experiences.' Photographs lend themselves readily and comfortably to the narration of the mundane, the ordinary.

Many of the chapters focus on social and cultural change, and people's adaptation to it. For instance, Erb discusses how birth rituals in Singapore have undergone transformation. When hospital births became more prevalent than home births, the proper disposal of the placenta, which is an important ritual for both Chinese and Malays, became a problem, not simply in how the rituals are performed, but also in terms of women's control of the reproductive process. Similarly, Selina Chan's chapter on marriage and family demonstrates, both from an individual and a structural perspective, how people had to innovate and adapt to new circumstances in choosing a marriage partner. Chan also suggests that there has been a process of localisation, a growing cultural attachment to the local community as opposed to the migrants' home countries.

This sense of disengagement from home countries and increased identification with the local community and society is a theme in many chapters. Singapore was and still is an immigrant society. Migrants of all kinds came to the 'South Seas' throughout the eighteenth and early nineteenth centuries as sojourners. Until the 1950s and 1960s, the immigrants — under a British colonial government which was uninterested in them and discriminated against them — did not see Singapore as home. Uprooted, they were in Singapore to make their fortune and then quickly return home.

The immigrant character of Singapore society, with its people having close ties to their homelands, is depicted throughout this book. Selina Chan describes the practice of sending letters and, more importantly, remittances back home. Parents often sent their children back to the homeland to be educated. Similarly, in early Singapore, it was common to return to the homeland to seek a marriage partner. However, events in the home countries, such as the communist takeover of China in 1949, as well as political developments in Singapore, resulted in a reorientation towards Singapore as home. This is most clearly articulated in the chapter on education by Erb. She shows that there has been a movement towards an educational system that is Singapore-oriented, rather than China-oriented, and notes the development of a bilingual curriculum. She demonstrates the contrast between colonial educational policies, where the emphasis was 'divide and rule,' and those of the newly-formed Singaporean government, where education came to be seen not only as a tool for economic development, but also as an important means of engendering national identity. Educational policies changed to invent a nation out of a group of disparate peoples and cultures.

The role of the state and its impact on private life is another theme that recurs throughout this book. Singapore is, physically and mentally, a small society. The state, since its inception in 1965, is present in most areas of a Singaporean's daily life, be it encouraging population growth, institutionalising religious education, persuading graduates to marry, or keeping the country clean. Several chapters devote their attention to the role of the state in defining, describing and delimiting the social environment — whether in 'big' national policies in education, housing and transport, or in the realm of personal life, such as birth and marriage. While Erb examines how birth, formerly a private, familial matter, has become part of a public discourse, several chapters — Yung and Chan's on entertainment, Chua's on coffeeshops, and Erb's on childbirth — point to a trend where many facets of daily life which were once in the public arena have, with modernisation and increasing affluence, moved into the private, familial realm. While one may want to observe sociologically that the realm of everyday life is necessarily implicated within the realm of political and administrative practices — the public-private divide thus being a mere illusion, the shift of many activities from the public to the private realm has made it more difficult for public policies to have a direct, immediate impact. In a more critical vein, PuruShotam examines the issue of women in Singapore society, especially women's rights and the role of the state in delimiting these rights.

The discussion on how the architecture of homes in Singapore has changed exemplifies another theme of this book: Singapore is a nation with diverse cultures, each adapting to social change in their own way. Quite a few authors — Erb, Selina Chan, Kong and Tong, and Chua — highlight the diversity of cultures that make up Singapore society. Erb, for example, details the various birth taboos of the Chinese, Indians and Malays in Singapore, while Kong and Tong detail the historical development of the major religions in Singapore: Taoism, Buddhism, Christianity, Hinduism and Islam.

While religion is an expression of group solidarity and participation in religious rituals is about bonding social relations, Kong and Tong also expose breaches in inter-religious relations, such as in the 1851 Punggol riots and the inter-religious riots caused by the Maria Hertogh court case in 1950. Chua describes how various ethnic groups in Singapore — Chinese, Indians, Malays and Europeans — create different house types to adapt to the tropical environment. He argues that the architecture of the home reflects the ethnic and class composition of the population. In fact, examples of the hierarchical nature of Singapore society, with its clear class divisions, are articulated in several other chapters of this volume, including those on transportation, sports and education. Early Singapore society was very much fragmented, with its many ethnic enclaves and vernacular schools. These ethnic and class divisions are also starkly illuminated in small, mundane, everyday matters. For example, in the chapter on transportation, Waterson describes how Mr. Peet, the then junior reporter of *The Straits Times*, was told that he must not ride a bicycle to work; it simply would not do for a member of the European staff to be seen parking his bicycle alongside those of Chinese clerks and Indian printers. It would be 'beneath his dignity.' There were also clear class divisions within the local population, with the more well-to-do Straits Chinese forming their own clubs. Many of the chapters detail the social organisation of the various ethnic groups in Singapore. Early Singapore society can be characterised as having clear ethnic boundaries in neighborhoods, housing styles, transportation and ritual behaviour. Fragmentation in early Singapore was visible, whether in education or, as Pereira demonstrates in his chapter on sports, in ethnic sports clubs, such as the Ceylon Sports Club, the Chinese Swimming Club and the Sikh Cricket Club. Yet, while ethnic boundaries among the Chinese, Indians and Malays remained visible in most social occasions, they were temporarily forgotten in others. The reconstituting of existing boundaries and social space occurred in one particular public space, the coffeeshop, a 'melting pot' bringing together people of different ethnic and professional backgrounds in a perceived equality made possible by eating together around a table.

While each chapter provides a sense of diversity in Singapore society — how different ethnic groups and social classes lived their everyday lives — they also highlight the many similarities that can bond Singaporeans. Several chapters suggest that in Singapore, with so many cultures living in close proximity to one another, there have been signs of hybridisation of cultures in the markets, coffee shops, hawker centers, playing fields and at work. Selina Chan's chapter focuses on the Straits Chinese or the Peranakan. This new ethnic group, the result of intermarriages between Chinese and Malay, is a distinct people, incorporating and mixing the cultural attributes of the Chinese and the Malays. The Straits Chinese continue to practise Chinese ancestor worship, but also have many Malay customs. They have developed a new language which is primarily Malay, but incorporates numerous Chinese words. They follow Chinese patrilineal descent rules but also adopt Malay matrilocal principles. Their adoption of Malay costumes is not to denounce Chinese-ness but to downplay the significance of Malay costume as a representation of Malay identity. Other chapters also show evidence of acculturation or cultural fusion. For example, in Selina Chan's chapter on food, we witness the creation of many indigenous Singapore dishes, such as *mee goreng*, a fried noodle dish drawn from both Malay and Indian cultures; or *nasi goreng*, a Straits Chinese dish created by mixing Chinese and Malay food practices. In religion, Kong and Tong show how adherents of Islam, Christianity and Hinduism in Singapore have mixed their own beliefs and practices with local traditions, including the use of holy water to ward off evil spirits in the home, amulets engraved with images of Jesus, and Catholic masses that include Chinese New Year cakes and Mandarin oranges.

A social history of the everyday life of Singaporeans would be incomplete without an examination of how people relax, play and have fun. Yung and Chan trace in their chapter the history of recreation, entertainment and leisure among the Chinese in Singapore, from street operas (*wayang*) and roadside storytelling to amusement parks and, finally, to the advent of radio and television. By describing each of these forms of entertainment and tracing the historical transformation in entertainment space, Yung and Chan argue that leisure in early Singapore was more public than it is now, with greater emphasis on community solidarity. With the advent of radio and television, entertainment has become less communal, more individualistic and voluntary. Leisure moved from the streets to shops to homes to individual bedrooms —

from having been tied to communal, cultural and religious events to pure entertainment and its consumption as commodity for pleasure. In his examination of sports and sporting activities, Pereira demonstrates how 'play' can be used as a lens to understand ethnic, class and gender differences in early Singapore society. He suggests that sports such as cricket, horseracing, golf, soccer and rugby were once the purview of the educated colonial class. Clubs for Asians were formed only in the late 19th century, a reaction against discrimination by the European clubs which barred the entry of indigenous peoples and women. Also, sporting activities and clubs were divided along ethnic lines, with a certain degree of inter-ethnic competition and rivalry. With the formation of the Singapore state, sports became one of the ways of asserting national identity and expressing national pride. Singapore's sports history mirrors its social history.

It is not the aim of this book to romanticise the past. Rather, through combining photographs and text, we have attempted to recreate the look and feel of life in early Singapore society. We do not wish to reify the past but by drawing on the sociological imagination and the anthropological vision, to present it as a living culture, always mindful of its inherent contradictions and tensions.

1 Moulding a Nation: Education in Early Singapore

Maribeth Erb

Opposite: Raffles Institution (captured here in the 1960s) eventually became a top secondary school. If he had known, Sir Stamford would have been proud of it, but the institution's path was not what he had originally envisioned.

Below: An aerial view of the original Raffles Institution at its Bras Basah campus in 1863.

Sir Stamford Raffles had a vision for Singapore that was closely tied to his ideas about education. He envisioned a 'Singapore Institution' encompassing a number of colleges that would teach natural sciences and Western philosophy, as well as the cultures and languages of the major Asian populations in the region. This institution would provide education for the local population and Europeans interested in the East, and become a world centre of Asian studies (Doraisamy 1969:7–9; Bell 1972:189; Bloom 1986:349). The upper class would constitute its body of students, as mass education was not the norm in the early 19th century (Chelliah [1947] 1960:16; Bloom 1986:350). Raffles had few illusions about how much financial support the British government or the East Indian Company would give to his institution, so the wealthy students would have to bear most of the expenses of education themselves.

Singapore as Trading Station: 1819–1867

Raffles' vision was long in being realised, and it never was accomplished in exactly the way that he imagined. But if greater attention had been paid to the issue of edu-

cation in Singapore, and if early colonial administrators had held on to the spirit of Raffles' vision, the tensions and conflicts that emerged in later Singaporean history might have been avoided.

Before Raffles arrived in Singapore, the population of Singapore might have been about two hundred, consisting of a few families of *Orang Laut* (sea people), about a hundred Muslim Malay fishermen who had settled on the island in 1811 and a community of about 40 Chinese pepper and gambier cultivators (Bloom 1986:349). In all of these communities, children were taught what they needed to know for everyday community survival. Some, however, had more orientation than others towards ideas about learning and education originating from outside their immediate community. The *Orang Laut* were unlikely to have had any formal education at all. The Muslim Malays, on the other hand, had Koranic schools, where boys were sent to live with a renowned teacher; in exchange for lessons in Arabic and the Koran, they would help their teacher in his fields and orchards. Girls also received some Koranic lessons, but not as systematically as boys (Chelliah [1947] 1960:35). Although there are no reports on Chinese education prior to 1829, there were probably some writing schools, where boys were taught ideographic writing and the teachings of the Chinese sages. They were given enough training to help their fathers in their business accounts; for further education, they were sent to China. Girls were given no lessons at all (Chelliah [1947] 1960:35). Chinese parents did not think it was worthwhile to give daughters an education since they would be leaving the family as they marry, and their main tasks in their husband's family would be producing and raising children.

Upon declaring Singapore a free port, things changed rapidly. The population almost instantly increased. Many Chinese and Indian merchants, who had been living in Malacca, grabbed the opportunity to do business in this new British duty-free trading station (Bloodworth 1986:4). Besides businessmen, other Europeans were attracted to Singapore. The first missionaries from the London Missionary Society arrived on the heels of Raffles and shortly after, in 1822, established the first Western-style school where a variety of subjects, such as reading, writing and arithmetic, were taught. One year later, Raffles laid the foundation stone for his institute.

Since Raffles could not stay in Singapore, it was left to the new Resident Crawford (who succeeded the first Resident, Colonel Farquhar, Raffles' original appointee) to act on Raffles' vision of the development of education in Singapore. But the fate of Singapore was still too uncertain, as far as Crawford was concerned, to build such an elite educational institution. In any case, he thought Raffles' scheme far too grand;

A Chinese Free School in Amoy Street — funded by wealthy members of the Chinese community — was established in 1854.

Crawford preferred to confine educational concerns of the Colonial Government to the primary level (Chelliah [1947] 1960:19–20; Doraisamy 1969:10). So Raffles' 'Singapore Institution,' an unfinished building, became an 'eye-sore' and a 'shelter for thieves' for approximately 13 years (Singapore Press 1832, quoted in Chelliah [1947] 1960:40; Doraisamy 1969:10; Bloom 1986:351; and Bazell [1921] 1991:431).

As a possession of the East India Company and under the administration of the Governor of India, Singapore was meant to be a place to make money, not to spend it. Therefore, the prevailing administrative attitude towards any kind of public welfare was frugality (Bell 1972:198). As far as the colonial administration was concerned, schools served the purpose of training enough individuals to be minimally numerate and literate in English so they could take up low-level positions in the government or work in commercial firms (Bloom 1986:356). Hence, missionaries were encouraged in the ensuing years to continue their role in educational development, receiving small grants of aid from the Straits Settlement Government.

The missionaries opened various English and vernacular schools, and even paid considerable attention to female education for the first time. The first school for Chinese girls, St. Margaret's Girl's School, was opened by the London Missionary Society in 1842 (Doraisamy 1969:16). Raffles Girls' School was established in 1844 for children of poor Protestant parents, and the sisters of the Convent of the Holy

The Convent of the Holy Infant Jesus, on Victoria Street or North Bridge Road, 1907.

Infant Jesus opened a third girls' school in 1854 for mainly European and Eurasian pupils (Doraisamy 1969:22–23). Raffles' Singapore Institution was also resurrected, partly due to missionary efforts. Following the model of schools in Penang and Malacca, Reverend F.J. Darrak, the Anglican chaplain of Singapore, established a free school in Singapore in 1834. 'Free,' in this case, meant the institution was open to all ethnic and religious groups (Bell 1972:191, Bloom 1986:356). In 1837, the trustees of Raffles' Singapore Institution invited the Singapore Free School to use their vacant building; and in 1840, the latter took over the administration of the school (Bell 1972:356; Bloom 1986:191–192). Although it started out by offering multilingual classes in English, Cantonese, Teochew, Malay and Tamil — which was rather close to Raffles' vision — the lack of students or teachers forced them to abandon the other languages one by one. By the mid-19th century, the Singapore Free School, which had taken up residence in Raffles' Singapore Institution, had become a mediocre English medium primary school (Doraisamy 1969:22; Bloom 1986:356). In 1868, it was given the name of its founder, and came to be known as Raffles Institution.

Although both English and vernacular languages were deemed important, the

One of the missionary-sponsored schools in the early 1900s was the Church of Zenana Missionary School.

only vernacular language recognised by the Colonial Government was Malay. So even though the number of immigrants of these languages increased yearly, funding for Chinese or Tamil language education was not forthcoming. However, the Malays who received government attention did not find the government schools particularly appealing. Malay parents might have been afraid that their children would neglect their Koran classes (Bell 1972:202). But as one critical commentator suggests, this lack of interest in schooling was probably very sensible, given the poorly planned and badly organised institutions offered to them at the time (Bloom 1986:357). Even in the English schools, there was a tendency for parents to withdraw their children from school at an early age — as soon as they qualified for a job as a clerk — at about Standard III or IV.[1] In general, as the then Governor E. A. Blundell pointed out to the Directors of the East India Company, education was not popular, and that 'time and liberal policies' were necessary for it to catch on (Bell 1972:194). Despite this humanitarian approach the Colonial Government appeared to have, there was very little money given to develop education, and therefore very few schools for children to attend in contrast to the rapidly growing population.

Hence, the prevailing emphasis on the part of the Colonial Government was on English education. This had a number of side effects. First, a class of English-educated elite slowly emerged. Second, development of education in various languages was in the sole care of the missionaries and respective communities. Although this allowed each ethnic or clan group to maintain control over the education of their own children, it also created communally- and ethnocentrically-oriented people, deepening the fragmentation among them.

Singapore as a Colony (1867–1942)

If one considers that Singapore was not an independent nation in the last century, thus lacking a cohesive national identity, it is possible to understand the development of this fragmentation and the unfortunate situations that developed in the 20th century. Most people who arrived in Singapore had no intention of staying; they saw it only as a place to increase their wealth. As the years passed, although more people settled in Singapore, their sense of belonging was still to the place of their roots and to others originating from the same homeland. Law and welfare were very much in the hands of these communities, and not something which the Colonial Government paid much attention to. The government cared so little about regulating immigration or immigrants that large numbers of immigrants, especially from various parts of

China, might have arrived in Singapore and left without being aware that the British Colonial Government existed. Because resident groups of clansmen and kin took care of them during their stay, the only government they knew was that of their own organisations and societies (Bell 1972:160–162).

It becomes possible to see, therefore, that British 'protection' was very contradictory. Although there was a belief that European colonialism was necessary for improving and civilising the lives of local people through education and religious proselytism, the real goal was exploitation of the human and natural resources of the colonised territory. Educating the natives becomes problematic for the coloniser. If one educates them to be good citizens, then they will indeed want the full rights of citizenship. If one educates them to be open-minded and more aware of the rest of the world, then they will certainly realise that they and their countrymen are being exploited. The mishandling and imbalance inherent in these contradictions sowed the seeds of the end of European colonialism in the Straits Settlements and Malaya, and also resulted in widespread conflict in the later colonial and early post-colonial era.

After the demise of the British East India Company, the colonial office in London took over the control of Singapore and the other Straits Settlements in 1867. Singapore's increasing size and importance in the global trade network demanded more and better trained local personnel for the administration of government services; and the education system had to provide these personnel (Bloom 1986:357). The colonial office, after paying closer attention to education in Singapore, declared it to be in a backward state (Doraisamy 1969:24). Major changes were implemented. An Inspector of Schools and a Director of Education were appointed in 1872, and a more methodical system of grants-in-aid was set up (Bloom 1986:356). Though money had been granted in the past, this was much more systematic; the grants were awarded on the basis of results. Two branch schools, run and funded directly by the government, were opened in 1875. Raffles Institution became a secondary school, and the branch schools groomed their finest boys to enter Raffles Institution (Bell 1972:200). More of these branch schools were set up, but they were not very successful, perhaps because difficulty in gaining admission to Raffles Institution had frustrated the budding scholars' motivation to attend them (Bell 1972:201). Initially, boys from the various ethnic groups learned English through their mother tongues. Slowly the use of the vernacular languages was curtailed, and English was taught directly in all of these branch schools (Chelliah [1947] 1960:47).

Vernacular education became increasingly problematic in Singapore. In 1893, a

Moulding a Nation: Education in Early Singapore

commission was sent to look into the situation of vernacular schools. As a result, all Malay schools were closed on the grounds that they were not functioning properly. This drastically hindered what little development there was of Malay education in Singapore (Doraisamay 1969:26). Policies towards Malay education became increasingly absurd. In the early 20th century, Richard O. Winstedt, a Malay language scholar, was made Director of Education; but instead of improving Malay education, his policies added insult to injury. Winstedt harboured rather romantic ideas of the Malay as a 'noble savage' (Bloom 1986:368–369). He saw Malays as 'simple-minded folk, living happily off the land' and tailored Malay schools to fit this notion (Bloom 1986:368–369). What was taught to Malay children had nothing to do with the practical needs of urban life. Instead, they were taught fishing, gardening and basket-making, even up to the tertiary level. Another factor that made these schools unattractive for Malays was that children were taught only in the Malay language. They were not being prepared for secondary education, which was strictly in English (Bloom 1986:369). It was no wonder Malays had no desire to take advantage of this education even though it was free.

The Colonial Government paid little attention to Tamil education as well, since immigrants from South India were not considered the indigenous population of the Straits Settlements and Malaya. The establishment of Tamil schools was not consid-

This picture of Malay houses and Malay schoolboys was taken in 1905. Malay education was the only indigenous language stream supported by the colonial government. The schools, however, were badly managed, and children only attended them sporadically.

Boys learning basket-making at school in 1954.

A mission school for Tamil children that was established in 1873.

ered cost-effective because of the small number of Tamil speakers congregated in any one area (Bell 1972:203). It was for this reason that many Indian children had private tutors. If they had an opportunity to receive an English education, they would have taken advantage of it. Studying the Tamil language was considered very important by the South Indian community and pressure was exerted to make sure it was continued (Kannusamy 000081/022).

Despite the rapidly expanding Chinese population, the colonial administration almost totally ignored Chinese vernacular education. Scores of Chinese left China in the 19th century due to civil war, and many went to *Nanyang* (the 'South Seas'), which included Singapore. By the end of the 19th century, Chinese immigrants amounted to about 75 percent of a population fast approaching 200,000 (Bell 1972:174,175). More Chinese flooded to Southeast Asia in 1895, after Japan had defeated China in a conflict over Shandong territory and after the Manchu government had lifted restrictions on emigration.

Though they left China, they were not forgotten. The Chinese government hoped to maintain some control over emigrants through the systems of education set up overseas (Bell 1972:205; Doraisamy 1969:29). The political interest in education increased particularly during this time of reform in China. When this reform movement was put down by the Boxer Rebellion of 1899–1900, some of these reformers left China to continue their work overseas. One of them, Kang You-Wei, convinced wealthy merchants in Singapore to back his new system of education — a mixture of Confucianism and Western science — and to build new schools. Another reformer, Sun Yat-Sen, opened a branch of his revolutionary party, the Kuomintang, in Singapore in 1906. Over time, the Party's emotional and nationalist doctrines filtered into the Chinese schools (Bell 1972:217). Wealthy entrepreneurs, or *towkays*, many of whom had made their fortune in rubber, saw it as their moral duty to support education, even though they themselves might not have received very much education. Men like Tan Kah Kee, originating from a small fishing village in Fujian province, had had only a few years of formal education. Yet Tan became a great patron of education in both China and Singapore, founding the Amoy University in Fujian, schools in his home village and district and helping to establish five primary and secondary schools in Singapore (Ward *et al.* 1994: vii–viii). He was an inspiration to many others, including Tan Lark Sye, who came from the same district in China as Tan Kah Kee. Tan Lark Sye had received only three years of primary education. In addition to promoting education in his natal village, he was a great supporter of Chinese education in Singapore and later became the inspiration behind the founding of the controversial Nanyang University (Chew 1996:19; Sim 1950:2).

Tan Kah Kee with teachers and students on board RMS Carthage at the Singapore Harbour Board in 1949.

An integral part of the Chinese education system in overseas communities at that time was Chinese patriotism. This patriotism was so strong that in 1919, when World War I ended and the Allies refused to support China's claim to Shandong in opposition to Japan, the students in Singapore's Chinese schools rioted. It was only then that the colonial administration became aware of their grave mistake in ignoring Chinese education (Bell 1972:208). They resolved to take control.

In 1920, an Education Ordinance was passed by the Legislative Council requiring all private schools and teachers to register with the government. The Chinese population, suspicious of the Colonial Government, saw this as an attempt to take direct control of their schools and resisted. When grants-in-aid were offered to Chinese schools in 1923, in an attempt to sweeten the rod, very few took up the offer. One of the qualifying provisions for getting aid was that Chinese pupils be instructed in their mother tongue (that is, their own regional language) and not in *Guo-Yu* (Mandarin), the unifying language of the new Chinese educational system inspired by the reformers. Clearly the British administration wanted to curtail the potential that Mandarin had, both in unifying the Chinese in Singapore with one another and with the political movements in China. Most Chinese schools were eventually registered, but the aid for Chinese education, which was offered very late (in comparison with English and Malay education), was seen as a political interference (Bell 1972:210).

Education became an increasingly political issue from this time onwards. It was implicated in issues leading to the struggle for independence and the increasing sense of alienation that the different ethnic groups felt towards one another. Instead of seeing Malaya and the Straits Settlements as places that could be shaped into pluralistic homelands, the various ethnic groups kept their eyes fixed towards the homelands of their ancestors and their actions and ideas were very much shaped by happenings there. Nationalist movements in both China and India had a strong impact on those emigrants who had their roots in those countries. Political teachings were especially well-organised in the Chinese schools. After 1940, the Kuomintang disseminated their party principles through a system of education called 'party-transformed education' (Bell 1972:217). Under this system, students were sent to China to be trained as teachers and then back to Malayan schools to teach. On the other hand, Malays, who were firmly rooted in Malaya and Singapore, felt increasingly inferior to the immigrant populations. In 1926, Mohammed Eunos, a respected leader in the Malay community, formed a political party to spur Malay youths towards attainment of higher educational goals and more central roles in politics and administration (Bell 1972:218). Fragmentation along ethnic lines, therefore, became increasingly problematic. It was clear that only those who had been educated in English schools — which had overridden the ethnic and language divisions and integrated people of different cultural and linguistic backgrounds — could think of Singapore as a real, multicultural home destined to have a unique identity and future.

Meanwhile, the Colonial Government, despite its good intentions, continued to support a poorly-designed education policy. By showing preferential treatment to Malay education, which was not helping the Malays anyway, they enraged both Malays and non-Malays. As they tried to suppress Chinese-education, they further alienated not only the Chinese educated, but also the Anglicised Chinese who were proud of their roots and the traditional Chinese emphasis on education (Bloom 1986: 369–370).

The Road to Merdeka

Despite growing dissatisfaction with the British rule, there was no well-organised independence movement. Thus when the Japanese invaded Singapore, many people of all ethnicities and political leanings rallied to the British defence of Singapore. Even the Malayan Communist Party came to the aid of the British defence of Singapore (National Archives of Singapore 1985:20). The fall of Singapore to the Japanese saw systematic campaigns to eliminate those who had tried to defend the British colony and especially the Chinese who had been giving aid to support China's resistance to Japan for some time. Tan Kah Kee, who was then Chairman of the China Relief Fund, managed to escape Singapore during the war to hide on a Dutch island incognito (Sim 1994:1). Many others were not fortunate enough to escape the war with their lives. For those who were not brutally exterminated during the war, the Japanese Occupation was a time when the whole issue of education exposed its most naked political intent. The Japanese envisioned themselves as the liberators of the rest of Asia from European domination, and while this turned out to be in some sense historically the case, their liberation became another form of domination. Being part of the 'Greater East Asia Co-Prosperity Sphere' meant adopting Japanese culture. All traces of European cultural influence was to be eradicated. Singapore was re-named Syonan-to, 'Light of the South.' Residents of Syonan-to were expected to learn Japanese; and were exposed to a massive campaign of 'Japanisation,' that is, immersion in Japanese language and culture (National Archives of Singapore 1985:69–84).

During the Japanese Occupation (1939–1942), schools were an important part of the 'Japanisation' programme aimed at indoctrinating the people of Syonan-to with Japanese language and culture. Both adults and children were required to attend these lessons.

After the war, although the inhabitants of Singapore and Malaya rejoiced in their freedom from Japanese 'liberation,' they could no longer view the British Colonial Government in the same light as before the war. The new post-war British government perhaps realised this and started to take clear steps towards preparing their colonies in Asia and Africa for self-government. Improvement in education was considered one of the major ways to create a feeling of national unity upon which to

PAST TIMES: A SOCIAL HISTORY OF SINGAPORE

Lessons organised by the Social Welfare Department for under-privileged students, circa 1949.

build an independent nation-state. So free primary education was guaranteed for all between the ages of six and fourteen (Bloom 1986:364; Bell 1972:266). Unfortunately, infrastructure was inadequate and there were not enough schools or teachers. So when the population rushed to take up the government's offer, many were turned away. Schools were to be built, but not quickly enough.

Since the Colonial Government was unable to give adequate help, people were forced to take matters into their own hands. The education of Malay children, although seen always as a priority for the Colonial Government, was practically non-existent after the war. One inspiring story is that of Awang bin Osman. Though not a famous philanthropist like some of his Chinese counterparts, he almost single-handedly arranged for the building of a school for the children in Punggol, a village far too distant from the urban areas for the children to have taken advantage of any schools available there. Being a member of the Rural Committee, Bapak[2] Awang was aware of the conditions of the post-war Colonial Government: if a school was to be

In addition to schools, many créches such as the one shown here (in 1949) were set up to give children a more rounded education.

built, the community would have to raise funds and the amount would be matched by the government. Bapak Awang despaired of building a school, since the Punggol villagers were so poor and had no regular source of cash income. One day, however, he noticed a European man sitting under a tree near the village, drawing the rural scenery. After striking up a conversation, it turned out the man was from the Rotary Club and was willing to help Bapak Awang and his village raise funds to

28

build a school. Through protracted efforts Bapak Awang managed to build the school and for five years took care of the maintenance of the school building himself. (Awang Bin Osman 000319/16–18). This dedicated, self-sacrificing spirit says much for the post-war generation who held great hopes and aspirations for the improvement of their children's lives in Singapore.

The majority of Chinese parents also harboured great hopes that education would provide their children with better lives. Many wanted an English education for their children, as it seemed to meet the needs of a nation that desired to be industrialised and independent. However, for most of them, due to a lack of English school facilities, Chinese schools continued to be their main alternative (Bloom 1986:365). These schools, however, produced primarily China-oriented, not Singapore-oriented graduates. The first Chinese leader to champion bilingual education and a more Singapore-oriented system was Lee Kong Chian, also a rubber tycoon like Tan Kah Kee, but unlike some others, a highly-educated man (Chew 1996:24–26). His vision for education and Singapore was not as affected by the Chinese nationalist fervour of the post-war era that had inspired other men like Tan Kah Kee and Tan Lark Sye. Lee Kong Chian's multilingual and multicultural vision was more moderate and was far more in line with the original Rafflesian vision for education in Singapore — indeed what the British government had hoped for the colony. They had wanted to prepare Singaporeans to be oriented towards their own country and the Malayan world (Bell 1972:250–254).

A social welfare village school — handicraft work for the boys in 1949.

After the Communist Revolution of 1949, those educated in Chinese schools in Singapore were faced with difficulties if they wanted to pursue further education. In the past they could have gone to China, but to do so after the revolution meant a high risk of not being able to return to Singapore, either because the Chinese authorities would not let them leave or because the Singapore authorities would not let them return. So a number of wealthy Chinese merchants, headed by Tan Lark Sye, started to plan the opening of a Chinese university in Singapore, what they saw as the next logical step for Chinese education for *Nanyang* residents (Bell 1972:422–423). On the other hand, this university, meant to be solely in the Chinese language, exacerbated the already existing problem of a language stream education that was not easily available for all Singapore residents, and oriented those educated within it not towards a Malayanised world-view, but towards a Chinese one. It was seen to a large extent by those who were English-educated to be an impediment to the progress of developing a Singaporean identity. Indeed Chinese education at that time was, increasingly, becoming a rallying point for not only anticolonial feelings, but also highly inflammatory communist and Chinese chauvinist sentiments.

In 1954, when the Colonial Government demanded registration of all males between 18–20 years of age for National Service, it became the excuse for the beginning of a series of riots over the next decade that Chinese school students participated in, at the instigation of both the communist and anticolonial movements (Bloodworth 1986:62–68; 116–151; Bell 1972: 534–555). The initial sentiments were anticolonial and pro-self-government, and the rioting was very much in the interest of all the residents of Singapore. Indeed these first riots may have had some influence, perhaps, in nudging Singapore along the road to independence, because in 1955 Singapore was granted the first stage in a series of moves towards self-government.

Students of the Nanyang University—the first Chinese language university in Southeast Asia—opened its doors in 1956.

But increasingly the riots of students in the Chinese middle schools, and later in Nanyang University itself, were in defense of what they saw as attacks against Chinese education itself, and became counterproductive towards the aims of an integrated, unified Singaporean nation. It became clear that the future of Singapore was to be moulded by those who desired to see Singapore ethnically unified, who thought of Singapore as multicultural, and who saw a strong component of English education as a way of achieving this aim. The University of Singapore, established in 1962, was headed by one of those men, Lee Kong Chian, who became the Vice-Chancellor of the university.

Conclusion

Is education a means to gain freedom, or a system of political manipulation? Does it open one's mind, or narrow one's view of the world? It can be seen, in interpreting the development of education in early Singapore, that education is a bit of both. Raffles' vision of both vernacular and English education has been, to a large extent, realised, but only after a rather tumultuous one and a half century. Problems may exist in the continuation of education and language policies created during the years of Singapore's struggle for independence, and the unity which these policies have forged may possibly be challenged and torn apart again (PuruShotam 1989). For better or worse, educational policies will continue to mould the minds of Singaporeans; and to effectively create a nation out of this group of people, these policies will always have to be delicately negotiated.

Acknowledgements

Many thanks to Ms. Elizabeth Chan, Principal of Punggol Primary School, who generously supplied information about the first schools in Punggol village. Thanks also to my research assistants Haniah Abdul Hamid and Chan Hooi Ching for their invaluable help.

Endnotes

1. Equivalent to present-day Primary 5 or 6 respectively.
2. Bapak is a Malay term for 'father.' It is used as a term of address and as the equivalent of 'Mr.'

2 Silent Witnesses: The 'Woman' in the Photograph

Nirmala PuruShotam

Opposite: Women were willing to take the risks of detention to make their voices heard in Singapore of the 1950s. This photograph captures a central problem: is this a woman who willingly went to jail, or is this a woman who served the administration that was ready to haul women too for detention?

One of my favourite things is a black, iron box, with the word 'Singer,' for the Singer Sewing Company, embossed on the lid. The box used to smell of the oil used on the sewing machine, to keep it running smoothly. And inside the box was a colourful world of thimble, threads, buttons, little stainless steel implements — that looked like silver to a child's eye — that would be called out when the machine broke down. I remember being with my mother as she sewed, and the treat of being asked if I wanted to help turn the machine. 'Slowly, not so fast' she would gently admonish; she intent on sewing. I intent on seeing how fast I could make it go. I think of the cloths — the colours, the feels, their transformation into dresses, shirts, pajamas — made to our specifications. Made also to fit us so that we were comfortable with our bodies, unlike the clothes we buy today, which make us read our bodies as wrong, as having to be tailored to fit the clothes.

I roam places, searching, in the museum, at the archives, looking through prose and poem, for the black box. But it is not there. I think of all the other silences that this represents. The voices that were spoken; the non-verbal texts by which women perform and do 'woman.'

> **Wom-an** (woom'en), n., pl. **wom-en** (wim'in), adj — n 1. an adult female person, as distinguished from girl or man. 2. a wife. 3. a female lover or sweetheart. 4. a female servant or attendant. 5. woman collectively; womankind 6. the nature, characteristics, or feelings often attributed to women; womanliness. -adj. 7. *a woman plumber*. [bef. 900; ME *womman, winman*, OE. *wifman* = *wif* female + *man* human being. See WIFE, MAN].
>
> Random House Webster's College Dictionary, 1995, p. 1500.

History is about the creation of times and spaces via which select voices are amplified; indeed, some peoples can speak and others must be silent, or even silenced. History is replete with silences: the words that women may have spoken when the men went to war, or went out to work, or to strike at work. If men had a dream, women did too; but history seldom records it. The dictionary rendition of woman, as I shall show, encapsulates these silences. It limits who a woman is, where to find her most of the time, and what to see and record when you find her; it gives us an 'objective' definition of the word, omitting the experiences without which it is not possible to understand the meaningfulness of the category 'woman.'

Still it is the year 2002. So, I look for 'woman' on the Merriam-Webster Online. It tells me that there are 8 entries found — 'woman,' 'fancy woman,' 'little woman,' 'other woman,' 'strange woman,' 'woman of letters,' 'woman of the streets,' 'woman suffrage.' The 'main entry' is

> Main Entry: **wom•an**
> Pronunciation: 'wu-m&n, esp Southern 'wO- or 'w&-
> Function: *noun*
> Inflected Form(s): *plural* /**women**/'wi -m&n/
> Etymology: Middle English, from Old English , *wīfman*, from *wīf* woman, wife + *man* human being, man
> Date: before 12th century
> **1 a** : an adult female person **b** : a woman belonging to a particular category (as by birth, residence, membership, or occupation) — usually used in combination <council*woman*>
> **2** : **WOMANKIND**
> **3** : distinctively feminine nature : **WOMANLINESS**
> **4** : a female servant or personal attendant
> **5** : **a** *chiefly dialect* : **WIFE** **b** : **MISTRESS** **c** : **GIRLFRIEND** 2
> - **woman** *adjective*
> - **wom•an•less** /-l & s/ *adjective*

The breaches feminisms have ensured are not clarified in this rendition either. But there *are* breaches — odd moments that stand out because women could speak in spaces normally reserved for men, in a language that made sense to man-the-gendered; odder moments when women made spaces for themselves also in languages that were admitted to be sensible even to man-the-gendered.

These uncommon social spaces for women in Singapore are particularly intriguing in terms of the period that is recognised as the '50s. The 'black box' of this time is that embossed by the printed words found in what we refer to today as the 'Women's Charter.' But even here, there are now more silent spaces and silenced voices. How do we relocate the lost voices?

The photograph collection in the National Heritage Board, in this respect, ostensibly holds out a promise. Here, there should be some material evidence that can help provide insights into the late '50s and early '60s. Common sense ascertains that 'straight' photographs capture a reality: some person, some event, and so forth, took place — the photograph provides 'evidential force' (Barthes 1981).

This is clearly seen in the recent subject of interest in 'old photos' of Singapore.[1] Indeed, this very book in which this article resides rests on an interest about re-searching for the past via the materiality of images that are to be found in old photographs. But photographs are texts that emit signs: the signs they emit are shaped by the space and time in which the photograph is located. In this respect, the historical weight of the photograph is not located in the past that it is supposed to tell us about. Rather the photo is located out of that past, such that

> Its literalness, … its deceptive simplicity, its obtuse *thereness* … its ordinariness belies [how it] … always [reflects] a specific … aesthetic, polemical, political [and/or] ideological point of view … that exists within a … body of … wider histories …
>
> (Clarke 1997:24 and 29, author's italics).

Thus the central question in my chapter is as follows: How is the photograph of the 1950s to be made to tell a story that will un-silence marginalised (women's) voices?

Women, the Late '50s, the Early '60s, and 'the' History of Singapore

The late '50s and early '60s have become a period that is generating great interest today. There has been more than a spate of writings about this time, including the visual reproduction of these times as 'turbulent' and 'poverty-ridden.' This was a time of racial riots, and underdevelopment; this is the time that records what a long way the people of Singapore have come. Yet this was the time of political nationalism, within which the first and — I would state boldly — the politically most astute and principled movements for women are located.

The 'imagined community' (Anderson 1983) that was to constitute the new nation of Singapore — first as a state in the Federation of Malaysia, and later, as an independent republic — was constituted by a variety of contesting imaginations about the future. Of primary consideration here, there were clearly (also retrospectively) core patriarchal tenets. This point shall be taken up a bit later. Suffice to say, at this point, that by the early '60s, the supremacy of the patriarchal was reiterated, and the ghost of the feminist positions are barely discernible in the presently available Women's Charter, first passed in 1961.

Both the Charter and the subsequent political economy that was instituted are, in contemporary times, usually used as proof that women in Singapore have come a long way. Accordingly, the common sense history of Singapore is that women had it bad then, and they have it good now. Located within this condensed history of women having come a long way is a similarly common sense awareness that the changes women enjoy are the gifts granted them by a male polity, that therefore has seen to their interests.

As is in the contradictory character of social knowledge in addition to the paucities of life then, the late '50s and early '60s are also perceived with nostalgia and sentimentality. This was the period that was not yet modern; and hence a space in which the tradition was relatively unchallenged. One of the most crucial icons of the untouched tradition of this time is 'The Family' (see PuruShotam, work in progress). In contemporary Singapore, there is a fairly recurrent reference to the threat to the family that both modernity generally and modern (or, worse still, post-modern) women pose to the family. Modernity, further, is signed by the opportunities women have, today, to do waged work. The threat, of course, is the threat of changing forms of familial relationships, including the avoidance of marriage altogether, or the avoidance of marriage and child-bearing. By implication, women desired marriage and children in the past, and this desire kept the family intact. Further, traditionally women did not work, and hence, once again, they could concentrate fully on the work of the family, that was primarily women's work.

The first question, as a subset to my larger question — which is, to reiterate, how is the photograph of the 1950s to be made to speak the silent and the silenced — is how do the photographs of the late '50s and early '60s bear out these versions of the story? Following this, what other stories can one discern from these same photographs? Additionally, are there photographs that posit alternate narratives other than the ones in which women were merely cultural victims at these times? All these questions, of course, are interrelated, and hence will be answered together as well as separately in the next sections.

Framing Women's Vulnerabilities

The story as one in which women are mostly victims of time and space can be easily found and re-told via the photograph collection in the National Heritage Board. Thus, we can find among the photograph collection here reminders of how a mother of two children had to beg on the streets for their living, simply by reading a taken-for-

Silent Witnesses: The "Woman" in the Photograph

granted association that sees begging as disempowerment (rather than, for example, a weapon of the weak, certainly; but a weapon nevertheless).

This poverty that the picture can be made to claim, however, is borne out by their vulnerability in an economic structure that did not provide enough jobs, for everyone. Indeed, it was a context that established the meaning-fulness of man as the breadwinner. Waged work for women was scarce: Occupations are importantly gendered activities. Correspondingly, in the '50s, the range of work for women was even more limited than it is today.

Thus, at that time, the major sectors of work were to be found in 'services,' 'commerce,' 'manufacturing and agriculture,' 'forestry, hunting and fishing' insofar as most of the 'economically active persons' of this time were located here (1957 Census: 202, Table 84) . More specifically, the largest percentage of 'economically active' women (49.5%) were employed in 'services' followed by employment in 'agriculture, forestry, hunting and fishing' (16.0%); manufacturing (14.2%); and 'commerce' (14.0%).

The extent of the domination of the public arena of work by men, at this time, is, perhaps, best underscored by the statistics that indicate that of all those employed in the area of services, recognised as a female dominant area of work today, 73.4% were male. Thus, in Singapore today, the teaching profession is associated with women, while the 'office environment' is largely feminised — in contrast to these photographs of a teachers' group picture, taken in January 1958, on the first day of the school year; and this photograph of an office, dated in the 1950s.

A mother and her young children begging on the street, 1959.

Bottom Left: This picture of a group of teachers was taken in Singapore, 1958.

Bottom Right: A typical office in the 1950s.

Additionally, in contemporary Singapore, and, indeed, the world over, most manufacturing jobs today are perceived as requiring female labour — because it requires, what is socially perceived as feminine characteristics, such as patience, the ability to do repetitive work nimbly, and so forth. In contrast to this, the 1957 census report of Singapore clearly indicates that males at that time dominated even this sector. Thus, 81.5% of all those located in the domain of 'manufacturing,' in the 1957 census, were men (Department of Statistics 1957).

The economically active population was defined in relation to persons aged 10 years and over. Of these, 53.4% were males, and 46.4% were females. Of the total males aged 10 years and over, 76.6% were described as 'economically active.' In contrast, only 19.2% of the total female population aged 10 years and over were described similarly.

Crèche on Banda Street, 1961.

Most of the women in the category of the economically active, viz., 74.5%, were 'home houseworkers.' The bulk of them, 73.7%, were married. On the one hand, one can state unequivocally that most of these economically inactive women were engaged in unpaid family oriented work. But more pertinently, just as men brought in the wages that enabled the women to make the *kaya* (coconut and egg based 'jam') to spread on the bread he earned; the men could enjoy the comforts of home and the family, because of the work of cooking, cleaning and et cetera that the women of the home, particularly as his mother or wife, put in. Waged work could of course enable one to buy bread and *kaya* at the coffee shop or the hawker stall. In this respect, this choice enabled by earning a wage underscores the women's — as against the man's — dependent position in marriage and the family.

Correspondingly, the husband's goodwill to remain committed to the marriage ensured a marked vulnerability in women' lives. This was compounded by the fact that at this time, wealth, status and prestige as 'man' was importantly tied to the institution of 'Chinese polygamy,' as it came to be understood.[2]

Some women, of course, did find gainful employment, part or full time. But a woman who goes out of the house to seek employment has to find some way by which the housework, childcare, and care of the aged and the sick is also accomplished. This crèche in Banda Street, one of only six, run by the Department of Social Welfare in

Silent Witnesses: The "Woman" in the Photograph

1961, for 'mothers who are working,' provides a glimpse into the scarcity of resources that could enable women to consider gainful employment outside the home. It is no wonder then, as noted above, that the bulk of women in Singapore in the '50s who did not engage in gainful employment were married women.

It must be noted that unpaid tasks that women did for the family ran the gamut and included laundry, home doctoring (including the making of herbal and other medicines), waste disposal, pest and vermin control, textile and decorative crafts. Some women made *kaya*, pickled vegetables and fruits, reared chickens and pigs, grew vegetables, and so forth. Unpaid tasks kept such and other women inside the home, and also took them out for the specific tasks: these women at the 'Singapore Consumer Association's cheap fish stall,' set along Orchard Road, were caught by a photographer as they haggled for a price in keeping with their budgets. Shopping for ingredients was and is one of the myriad parts of preparing the home cooked meal. As is also still prevalent today, women also had to negotiate with gods and spirits, for the mundane needs of the living and of those in the hereafter.

Certainly, then as now, not all women were engaged with doing the housework and childcare and care of the aged sick. However, for the bulk of the population of females, housework involved daily labour.

Singapore Consumer Association's fish stall at Orchard Road, 1953.

Worship is still part and parcel of the multitude of tasks undertaken by women. This photograph of worshippers at a temple was taken in 1957.

39

PAST TIMES: A SOCIAL HISTORY OF SINGAPORE

Above: One could guess that this woman, coiffured and lip-sticked, who stepped out of the polished limousine that she rode in April 1955, was probably involved in housework—if at all—as a managing supervisor of servants.

Below: The structural differences between the *attap* houses (*left*, dated 1950) and this Straits Chinese home (*right*, circa 1950) also dictated a difference in how the housework was performed.

The housework of the homeworker then was not as standardised as it is today. First, the basic infrastructures for making a home have been considerably changed with the spread of Housing and Development Board flats, with such minimal conveniences as flush toilets and running water. Second, there has been a proliferation of a middle-class way of life, and keeping with it a new consumerism that has changed the face of being wife and mother or keeping a home (see PuruShotam 1998).

In contrast to this, home and hence housework in the '50s and '60s involved more variable demands: standards of cleanliness, the concern with beautifying the home, etc., must clearly have varied. *Attap* houses as shown in these photographed circa 1950 in Aljunied Road, set amidst coconut trees and banana plants, with structures that separated the kitchen from the main house, constituted a way of work that is no longer experienced by women today. The interior of this home of a clearly well-to-do Straits Chinese household hints at the tasks 'hidden' in this picture that would be perhaps more widespread today: flowers in the vase, diaphanous curtains, and the polished table indicate a sensibility to housework as the production of a 'lifestyle,' which has become the catchphrase of housework in contemporary Singapore.

Household amenities were widely different, and hence indicate widely different experiences. At one time the toilet, for instance, was the bucket system. People lined up on back streets to defecate into buckets; while others did it upstairs often in the kitchen area. The bucket would be collected, sometimes sloppily, leaving even more work for the women of the household in its wake.[3]

In contrast to this, the Singapore Improvement Trust flats, built in 1960, provided

40

flush toilets and running water, which dramatically altered housework for women who shifted into them at this time. But if one preferred to move into the Commonwealth Drive flats from the Chinatowns of the 1950s, another may have hesitated to move in from the *kampung* house to such flats. Life in a *kampung* house may not have been idyllic, but housework there included much that was done with other women; it was not as isolated as it is today (see Chapter 5).

Similarly, household appliances that we take for granted today were not available. In the past, laundry day involved a list of tasks that included steps that are unheard of today. Thus, soiled clothes were collected and separated into whites and coloureds then as now. But such tasks as soaking them in 'blue' (a chemical that would make whites whiter) and boiling certain kinds of clothes — particularly when there was an illness of epidemic proportions, an actual washing process in which each individual piece of clothing had to be rubbed across a wooden washboard which could leave the knuckles, at the least, red and raw — are unheard of today. Thereafter the same hands would wring the clothes out, and hang them out to dry. After drying, in some cases at least, there would be preparation for and the actual ironing of the clothes. This was a time when not all homes were equipped with electricity or water. Many women would no doubt have desired the electric iron of that time: not lightweight, without steamer and certainly not cordless, but still a much-improved version of the charcoal iron:

> the first step was to prepare the charcoal. It had to be chipped down from larger blocks to small pieces. These had then to be heated up to a red-hot state in charcoal stoves. [The charcoal irons were equipped with a compartment into which] the hot charcoal pieces were transferred. The sole-plate [of the hot iron has to be [constantly] cleaned … by [running] the iron … [along] … a [strip] of waxed cloth or [a] banana leaf … [T]he charcoal [in the iron had to be] occasionally fan[ned] … [Sometimes] ashes accumulated … [flew] out through the side of the iron [and] … must be quickly wipe[d] off … the clothes [it thus soiled] with a small wet towel …
>
> (Lau 1992:25–27)

It is telling that such work is not recorded: the camera appears to have turned a blind eye to women when they actually are in the process of making the house a home, for instance. Indeed, most women would not stand before a camera to be caught doing such work.

An entrant in the Great World Talentime, 1955.

Alternatively, when women go before the camera to pose, they perform for the photographer, who often arranges them in a way that attends to what it is that makes a woman photograph-able. The texts, in these instances, are not hers to construct. The pose she does is the display that he finds attractive and meaningful; and it is a display of passivity and docility. Conventions as to how 'woman' is constructed before a camera of course vary, from photographer to photographer, from context to context. Simultaneously, apart from these differences, the woman before a camera attends to seen-but-unnoticed ideas about posing, with respect to certain conventions of that moment when she is photographed. Looking backwards in time, these moments can elicit laughter because the pretence is clearer then than when the women in question were 'making eyes' at the camera.

Thus, here an entrant in the 'Great World Talentime' of June 1955 has maintained a pose which has drawn laughter from people I showed it to, who recognise that she was attempting a sophistication that, in today's body language, is gauche. The woman's body was obviously carefully arranged to convey a certain meaning of 'woman' — notice the long hair swept to one side and held almost gingerly by bangled hands, and the attempted coy show of legs. The body appeared to be propped up, or at least held with some difficulty. The face was clearly well made up. And the smile carefully constructed not to show too many teeth. Some women, I should note, still recall how they used to be instructed not to laugh or smile too widely in the '50s, as it was not 'nice' to do so.

Thus the photograph-able woman — that is, a woman who presents herself in a way that makes her worthy of being photographed — defines what is recorded and hence available as material evidence about what women were. But the material evidence that is there is really also evidence of what had to be silenced, or what was not normally to be made visible. As wife and mother, women appeared before the camera in well-framed ways: they are not there to do the work they normally would be doing in relation to ascribed roles, but merely stand or sit, usually without any evidence that underlines that she is, first and foremost, a productive worker.

In the rare capture of a woman with her children in the next picture, taken in a clearly poor home, there is still some degree of posing. The children are still, as she is: it is a familiar place, and yet unfamiliar. For the women is in effect 'doing nothing.'

The very same photograph reveals a list of questions that need to be asked. This

Silent Witnesses: The "Woman" in the Photograph

woman had children and a husband to look after. What did she have to do for their upkeep day after day? Who cooked for them and washed up after them? Who bought the clothes that they were wearing for the picture? Indeed, who dressed them up, and prepped them for the photographer? And were the clothes actually bought, and not sewn? How many meals did she prepare per day for them? Where did she do her marketing? How did she get there? Did she walk, or perhaps take a rickshaw? Did she have the help of her all her children, or only her daughter? Was she able to afford paid help of some sort? Or, given the black dress she was wearing, and the sense of sadness that the photograph also conveys, was this woman a widow? If so, how with all this work did she cope with the added burden of finding the money, as a single earner, which bringing up a family entailed?

Indeed, the '50s and early '60s were a time of a way of life that included disasters such as floods and fires, in which lives were lost as well. The next two images capture the loss not only of the physical structure that made up 'home.' If we take care to 'read' what is in the picture, albeit hidden from the eye of the camera, we would be

Although effectively doing 'nothing' in this picture, circa 1950, this woman's labour can be extrapolated from all that is captured—from the setting of her home to the clothes on her children, and even from her children themselves.

43

PAST TIMES: A SOCIAL HISTORY OF SINGAPORE

able to begin to 'see' an organization of a way of life that involved largely the work of women. What was lost in the rubble had to be replaced by the labour of women? Behind the photograph of this woman (below), who is hauling away a sarong-full of what is left of a home, after the disastrous Bukit Ho Swee fire, one can imagine the long, long record of the toil that disasters entailed for women particularly. These could have included the care and comfort of those injured, the search in the rubble for what could be saved and the subsequent work to restore it to usable condition, the work to replace what could not be saved, the work of shifting to alternative accommodations and making a new home for the family, and so forth.

These images (taken in 1959) have captured the devastation of the fire at Bukit Ho Swee: In this field of silence (*top*) lies the material and psychological scares that would make its demands on the women who ran the homes and who had to keep the family going (*bottom*).

Seen in the light of a perspective that privileges the story of change and progress for women, the photographs provide proof that we have come a long way. But the same photographs also raise questions about this story. Thus, a singularly significant fiction in this narration is that in the late '50s and '60s women did not work; during the late '60s and seventies, tremendous opportunities for work were given to women as 'gifts' of the government, and hence their improved life opportunities and conditions.

While, I must quickly stress, I am not doubting the tremendous significance of

Silent Witnesses: The "Woman" in the Photograph

Flooding was common in the fifties and sixties, before the advent of the drainage system that now exists in Singapore. It ensured work in the house that is barely remembered today; work that is recalled in a small way, which shows two women sweeping out the flood waters of December 1954.

waged work as a means to empowerment, I am questioning the simplification of the story as it is read this way. For it underscores the irrelevance of what was the actually lived experiences of real women of that time. It did not, for instance, retort that women were (and are) indeed economically active even as 'just' housewives. The resultant fiction did not, further, stress that family work was an imperative aspect of life and had to be given due consideration in political and economic discussions. It did not therefore talk of what men did not do by way of contribution to the work that constituted family work.

This prepared women for work in the public realm in two important ways: one, as lower paid workers, generally, who were being given the opportunity to work, instead of 'doing nothing' by simply remaining home; two, as workers with 'natural' aptitudes which enabled them to do what they did at home, including the 'natural' aptitude to be bored, and hence suitable for particular types of labour that one would not expect a man to want to do.[4]

This has perpetuated the myth of housework as not work, and hence the invisibility that today's working woman — even with all the new technology, and indeed, because of the new technology — works at least two shifts, in two separate domains, of the workplace and the home, of what really is one single economy.

Clearly there is an eye behind the eye of the camera that snaps the shots; and then there is the gaze that can read the picture as is, and hence via hegemonic lenses. But, just as the questions the same photographs enable us to clarify ; the gaze can subvert the dominant, and direct re-search elsewhere.

Civil Society in the Late '50s: Silent and Silenced Witnesses

Civil society was alive and kicking in the Singapore of the late '50s. But this space and time has been erased, considerably, by a reference to this era as a time and space fraught with the problem of 'communist insurgency.' Indeed, in my attempts and also my students' attempts to speak of women's experiences in this time, we found we were up against the fear of speaking about the politics of the past, especially if one was engaged in it as 'Chinese educated' activists. In no small part is this because the activities of such people, which were once importantly and inclusively nationalistic in orientation, is today condensed as constituting both communist and communalist orientations — disseminated in social memory texts as invoking social disorder and lawlessness, from which the nation has thankfully escaped from.

Within both the general nationalism of the time, and the communist faces of it, was the struggle by and about women's rights. The 'older generation' of women — whom general social knowledge assumes were less modern, less feminist, and so less than us in some crucial ways — were actually leaders towards a way of thinking and being that challenged patriarchy fundamentally. There is, in this silenced history, a contemporary significance that, if brought back to the fore, has within it an inspiration and spirit that is truly civil society.

Civil society is generally mistaken to exist merely because there exists non-governmental voices, that have added their voices to issues once debated only by political parties and the government. This major character of contemporary civil society is well condensed in two kinds of statements that abound. First, it is a position that *appeals* to the government and party to expand space and time for civil society, failing hence to understand that space and time for civil society is the legitimate due of the citizen. That is, citizenship is about ownership of the nation. In this respect, it fails to differentiate between nation and government; and fails to grasp the point that legitimacy resides in the fact of citizenship.

Second, contemporary civil society is largely conscious of the very real existence of institutions and laws that can be invoked to finally detain citizens without trial, viz., with respect to the Internal Security Act. Obviously, the work of civil society would be to focus on the repeal of such acts that limit its evolution. However, such acts, instead, are more often than not used to claim the necessity to self-censor debates, or take 'stupid' risks and say what needs to be said. At the same time, any non-governmental statement has within it the possibility of distinction, and hence status and prestige. In this way, civil society activism can become attractive in itself and of itself, without the corresponding boldness of initiatives that it should demand. It can, consequently, cater to the fact of civil society's existence, without the fact of citizenship empowerment. There is here that quality of 'mock aggressiveness and mock desperation,' 'a ritual show,' in the end, 'of deference to authority'; even 'completely dependence on authority' (Naipaul 1979:30). Correspondingly, the key style of civil society communication can be reduced to making complaints to select government and bureaucratic authorities. This is best illustrated by citizen's letters to the forum pages of local newspapers, in which administrative clarification is often sought — and given — with little radical change of questioned rules, regulations and such.

In stark contrast to this, civil society at the dawn of the nation appears to be highly cognizant that the absence of nation is precisely the absence of the right to demand, not as a vassal of a feudal lord; nor as a colonised 'other' of the coloniser patron but as a citizen and hence as an equal participant. Governance in a nation, then, is not about vassalage or patronage, but, precisely, of representation. Representation, in turn, requires un-silencing; of dismantling the habitus of deference to authority and claiming, in its stead, the authority of the body politic to speak up on and shape governance.

It is imperative to understand that the present state of civil society, in this respect, is importantly rooted in a commonly dispersed idea of history, and the history of Singapore particularly. The demand for the equalisation of rights, and hence the challenge to authority by class, gender and race ascriptions, is pictured in relation to chaos: the very visuals of the turbulence of this time have been used to, at the least, hint at the chaos when authority is not treated with deference but defiance.

Evidence for this is importantly located in the almost complete absence of a reading of the '50s as a time of civil society in action, rather than only a period of communist insurgency. Accordingly, histories of Singapore are almost always devoid of any reference to women's participation, women's perspectives and women's demands for rights that challenged the normalcy of patriarchal authority. It is acknowledged that in recent years, some recognition is surfacing. But there is herein especial focus on one Ms. Chan Choy Siong, who was, also, a stalwart member of the People's Action Party. Educated in the highly politicised Mandarin school system of the time, Chan was one of nine candidates — described today as 'an unprecedented number,' even for today — who campaigned in the elections to the Legislative Assembly in 1959

(Wong and Leong 993:287). Most importantly, Chan is credited with a very strongly worded manifesto for gender egalitarianism, as I will show below.

While granting that Ms. Chan's contributions were very important, and that she should be recognised as an individual in her own right, I strongly contend that a political culture which focuses intently on some key players tends to create singular heroes and idols. As I shall argue below, Ms. Chan was not a champion of woman. She was much more than that: hers was more of a voice that *represented* women out there on the streets, women who were saying that they were standing up and should be counted; that they would exercise their vote with respect to those who would speak up for them. Ms. Chan spoke out to amplify demands made by a civil society of women: if they had not been there, one could ask, would Ms. Chan have surfaced as prominently as history can now attest?

Correspondingly, the women of the '50s can already be divided into two groups, minimally; those embedded in the private world of the family, and those with greater access into the public realm. The latter in turn comprised, at the least, the working class women and the middle to upper classes of women.

Working class women engaged in a series of occupations that ranged from agricultural jobs to labour intensive production work. The middle to upper classes of women who worked in the public sphere included particularly professionals, and wives of rich men with many servants and hence time to do voluntary welfare work. Professional work for women was limited by their gender. Generally the most significant areas of such work for women in the '50s were in the fields of teaching, nursing and library work. But education and hence worldviews were further defined by the cultural make up. One of the most important aspects of one's perspectives depended on whether one was 'English educated' or 'Mandarin educated.' While both educational backgrounds were provided for in a colonial milieu, and hence incorporated colonial attitudes and morals that were not questioned, the English educated were more influenced by received colonial knowledge. One reason for this, for instance, is that colonialists, including missionaries, established and ran English medium schools. In contrast, Mandarin medium schools were established and run by local communities (see Chapter 1). Women from such schools, including — to reiterate — Chan Choy Siong, drew their perspectives on the world, including on other women, via the dominant discourses which were vibrantly reformist and revolutionary in spirit, as their teachers and textbooks came from mainland China of that time.[5]

Silent Witnesses: The "Woman" in the Photograph

Above Left: Elderly women turned out in full force at the polling stations to cast their votes in 1961.

Above Right: Women employees of C.K. Tang on strike outside the store in 1960.

The photographic record, as I shall show below, of this presence of a civil society of women for women is a sufficiently straightforward visual record that certifies that female empowerment did happen, in a style and manner that has never been seen since. Accordingly, it becomes apparent enough that the Charter was no mere gift of a male polity to a passively suffering female populace. Women, the photographs record, were directly engaged in active politics. They turned out in full force at the polls, whatever their ages, to exercise the right to vote, as this photograph of 'old Chinese women, outside polling station,' taken in April 1961, shows.

Despite the aforementioned scarcity of waged work for women, workers were not afraid of making their demands clear. For instance, on August 24, 1960, women employees at the C.K. Tang departmental store huddled beneath oil paper umbrellas, presumably shielding themselves against the sun, went on strike. Their claims are summarised in a poster that reads 'Our Boss wants to see our strengths to settle our legitimate claims.' More of these striking women surfaced outside the same store with yet another strongly worded placard: 'For bonus our boss gives us handshake instead of money.' Strikers at the Robinson's Departmental Store almost a year later, in September 1961, hung out a list of 'Employer's Ten Commandments,' such as '1. I am Thy Master and Thou Shalt Obey Me,' and '2. Thou Shalt Not Join Any Union.' Clearly, these women were aware of the risks they were taking in making their demands known; they were willing to be herded into riot police vans to be taken away, if necessary.

Thus, Chan Choy Siong and the other women who stood for elections then could well be seen as drawing sustenance from a collective dream. They were not necessarily leading women into the future but wooing them to vote for self and party in the forthcoming elections, with a promise that they could be the ones to ensure the

49

Above Left: Robinson's employees put up a boldly worded banner, condemning their employer during the 1961 strike.

Above Right: The employees were eventually rounded up by the police.

realization of a sex/gender equal society.

Before the end of the '50s — when civil society would be increasingly tamed, and finally so quiescent that its arrival in the 1980s would be seen, noticed and (imagined itself to be) constantly open to surveillance — what became thereafter a party and government that had openly described its desire to protect patriarchy, had within it a spokesperson who was not just pro-women, but pro-feminist. Indeed, her strongly worded statement was part of the Party manifesto pertinent to wooing the electorate of women in the then soon to be held elections of 1959. That is, Chan was needed to speak a stand, because that stand had the value of attracting votes from a large enough number of women who had clarified and would continue to do so, that they did not like the lives they led, and wanted to see change; that they would exercise their votes in accordance to political parties that recognised their concerns. Chan's speech, published subsequently in *The Tasks Ahead: P.A.P.'s Five Year Plan, 1959–1964* (People's Action Party 1959) was part of a larger discourse that could not be ignored:

> In an unfair society women are handicapped because of political, economic and religious factors. *They are confronted with obstacles wherever they go.*
>
> In a semi-feudal and semi-colonial society, ... they are slaves of husband and children ... [Because] of lack of employment opportunities and lack of adequate education ... many young girls are forced to become prostitutes. Others provide cheap labour for exploiting employers, inevitably part of a colonial regime. As always in these circumstances, the poor suffer more than others.
>
> Chief Minister Lim Yew Hock's government did nothing to change these

conditions ... When the People's Action Party comes into power immediate steps will be take to raise the status of women (to) where it should be ...

(People's Action Party 1959: 17–18; my emphasis)

The promised steps included the passing of regulations that were revolutionary for that time, and which today, one could argue are not revolutionary enough. But they also include programmes for change that would be considered revolutionary even today, (viz., those quoted in italics). Thus from the same manifesto above (People's Action Party, 1959) ring these words, which Chan pronounced:

We will encourage women to take an active part in politics. We will help them organize a unified women's movement to fight for women's rights.
We will encourage women to play their proper part in Government administration.
We will open up new avenues of employment for women.
We will insist that the welfare of widows and orphans must be the responsibility of the Government.
We will insist that married women be given an opportunity to live a full life, including the right to work on level terms with others. Under the law maternity leave and allowances will be compulsory.
The PAP Government will establish more crèches to look after children while mothers are at work.
We will encourage factories employing large numbers of women to provide crèches on factory sites.
The present marriage laws which permit polygamy will be amended ...

(P.A.P. 1959: 17–18; my emphasis).

Privileged Social Memories

Yes, Chan Choy Siong said and meant those words, but while one could even say most of them got passed, the more revolutionary spirit of her text — the more revolutionary spirit of the time — were largely ignored by the time the related Women's Charter was first passed in 1961. With the passing of that moment, to reiterate, came a history that silenced the Charter. With that too, the history of a feminist constituency — a *movement* involving 'ordinary' women, rather than specific idolised individuals — that can, arguably, be used to create a living tradition for and by women and women's

This photograph, circa 1920, approximates the nostalgic impression of 'The Family'.

group in contemporary Singapore, has been largely obscured. The photographs record that the nation exists in relation to the lived experiences of those who speak up. The photographs also provide the means to silence this very past.

Thus, the final Charter took up the case mostly of marriage and the family. Its core revolutionary feature was the abolishment of the institution of secondary wives, misrecognised and hence socially realised as (Chinese) polygamy. The critique of and demand for the end of polygamy was an emblem of a position against oppressive practices women suffered from within the institution of the patriarchal family. The symbolic load of the end of this institution was that the real problems of women had mostly come to an end too; *the* solution to women's patriarchal oppression was located in the erasure of polygamy, and its replacement by the legalization of monogamous patriarchal marriages, which was achieved via the passing of the Charter in 1961. In one stroke the patriarchal family was significantly re-instituted, re-placed; indeed, re-invigorated. The form may have changed, but the substance was, in effect, promised the future that it has become.

It is here where we find that the photograph has been used to remind us not of the fight for rights as much as the romance of 'The Family'; not of the pain and suffering that motivated the women's movement of the late 1950s and early 1960s, which saw some focal concern with the ill-treatment of women via this same institution. Instead the photographs available erase such depictions. In its place we

Silent Witnesses: The "Woman" in the Photograph

have available material that encourages nostalgia and sentimentality about 'The Family' as it has been in 'our' past. This is well illustrated in photographs that are easily recognised as 'The Family,' that are found also in the ubiquitous and hence easily accessible family albums.

Despite the divergent faces, settings, dress, and other accessories that constitute the bodies, their contexts, and hence the individual families, there is a certain and powerful unitary quality that signals the power and prestige of being ensconced within a middle class family. The women in the photographs are clearly — and fortunately — someone's daughter, sister, or wife. We do not read 'secondary wife' for instance, in such depictions; unless we intentionally bring it into the picture.

Clearly, there are in these diverse photographs that 'image that the group seeks to give of itself as a group. What is photographed and what is perceived by the photograph is not, properly speaking, individuals in their capacity of individuals, but social roles' (Bourdieu 1966:24).

There is here an heirloom of the domestic, and, therefrom, the manufacture of emblems of the domestic (1966:28). Additionally, the photographs signify the wealth that being within a family provides one with. In some cases, the wealth includes the bodies of other women, the *amahs* (domestic helpers) that stand behind the work women must do — even if it is reduced to monitoring other women to do it for them — to accomplish 'The Family.'

Such photographs make available a powerful narrative that is the silencing foil against the single most important issue of the late 1950s. Family and family life motivated women to speak up, and formed one of the crucial bases for both political promise and political action.

In sharp contrast to this, one of the political elites' recurrent motifs of the heritage of Singaporean society today is that of 'The Family,' which takes us back to life in early Singapore too. That is, the same 'Family' that was critiqued and changed is frontally presentable as a living tradition that is nevertheless lost. 'The Family' in old photographs then, will in most instances be read within the present dominant discourse: it is (potentially) the material that acts as a reminder of a loss; a reminder that we are living in alienated times — as against the alienating experiences the 'Family' actually was

'Wealth' in the family also includes the bodies of those who work for its members, as embodied by the *amahs* in the background of this portrait, circa 1920.

for numerous, if not most, women. That is, there is the possibility here 'a trace or index of self that was once there ... the sensation that it represents a [lost] truth' (Blessing 1997:53). 'In short,' as Barthes writes, 'the referent adheres' (1981:6). In this case the referent is not of the 'family' as it was lived and experienced, read and critiqued by the women's movement of the late 1950s and early 1960s — but to reiterate, the 'Family' that we can be called upon to ache for.

Who is to Speak for the Woman in the Photograph?

The 'woman' in the photograph lays bare a possible living tradition. But this living tradition arises from the breath of text that gives the photograph its life, at any given moment. Given the issue of 'women's rights' in the late '50s, one would expect to uncover a veritable wealth of evidences that make for a living tradition about the 'liberated' woman of that time; or at least about the political woman of that time. Does one not?

The answer to this in turn highlights the language that photography is. The lenses behind cameras captured 'woman' in a myriad of forms. Some of these forms reduce the women of these times, simply by the selective recording which privileged the photographer's viewpoint over the photographed. Some of these forms present a story that can provide for a living tradition — a sense of who we were then and how far we have come. But what is that living tradition to be? Will it give us a social memory that sees in the present an improvement for women that was possible because it was gifted to women, as against fought and demanded by them? Will it make us think nostalgically how wonderful it is to be a *tai tai*, and hence how wonderful it was when women's lives were completely embedded in the 'Family' of yore? Or is it to be a lesson in the politics and meanings of civil society?

That is, a photograph appears to speak for itself. But this appearance can be deceiving. As with all texts, a photograph is read — to read is to make sense of words or pictures. To make sense is to do the work of selecting an interpretation, as I myself have done in this chapter. It is common, in doing this work of interpretation, to assume that a photo speaks in and of itself. So we look at a picture and think "family", and assume that, for instance, the man and the woman in that 'family' picture are husband and wife. But, for example, if we know about the context in which the photograph was taken, we are then faced with questions such as is this a man and his first wife, or a man and his fourth wife, or a 'mere' mistress? To further this example, when we look at a photograph which we interpret as that of a family, we see an institution that is 'normal' and hence moral and good. But we have no idea if this representation of the 'normal' and 'good' family is made up of people who abuse their spouses and/or their children.

My point is that in returning to our past through photographs, we need to be aware that each frame that we are presented with has a life outside of the picture per se that we are given to view. Photographs should not be used to tell a story as if life is experienced neatly and singularly. The lives we want to understand constitute a multiplicity of experiences. Yet we often take the line of least resistance and read the photograph in relation to what we already know. In doing so we once again repeat 'the fact,' rather than think differently and learn something new about our pasts and hence our present selves. The feminist perspective should not replace the dominant perspective. But the dominant perspective must give up its privilege and provide equal space to other readings. In this way we begin to do justice to the multiplicities of experiences that constitute the lives we want to understand. It does also mean, as I have tried to show, that we are forced to ask questions rather than provide ready made answers. Questions, I hope my chapter has made clear, are the best place to begin to search for the intersections of the personal and the social, through which we come to a deeper, more sophisticated understanding of who we are and why we are that.

Endnotes

1. One of the crucial moments for such popular interest arose from my own work, with Sharon Siddique, on a study of Indian community space in Singapore (Siddique and PuruShotam 1982). In this work, I pored through and re-photographed old photographs and other depictions, such as architectural drawings, of that space in Singapore that is popularly referred to as 'Little India.' There has since been a proliferation of attention to old photographs and architectural drawings in precisely the same manner that Siddique and I had approached such material: as evidence of what Singapore once was.
2. 'Chinese polygamy' was largely a British perspective on an institution that was more complex than the term implied. This in turn affected contestations and n-egotiations that also affected women's power within Chinese marriages in Singapore at the time. These issues are examined in Nirmala PuruShotam (work in progress).
3. There are few studies that gave insight into living conditions in Singapore at the time, leaving alone some vivid detail. See Barrington Kaye (1960) and Goh Keng Swee (1956) for two interesting publications concerning poverty in Singapore at the time.
4. Maria Miles aptly terms it the 'houswifization' thesis.
5. The details of the schooling system and their implications for the class, race and gender structures in Singapore then and today can be found in PuruShotam, 2000.

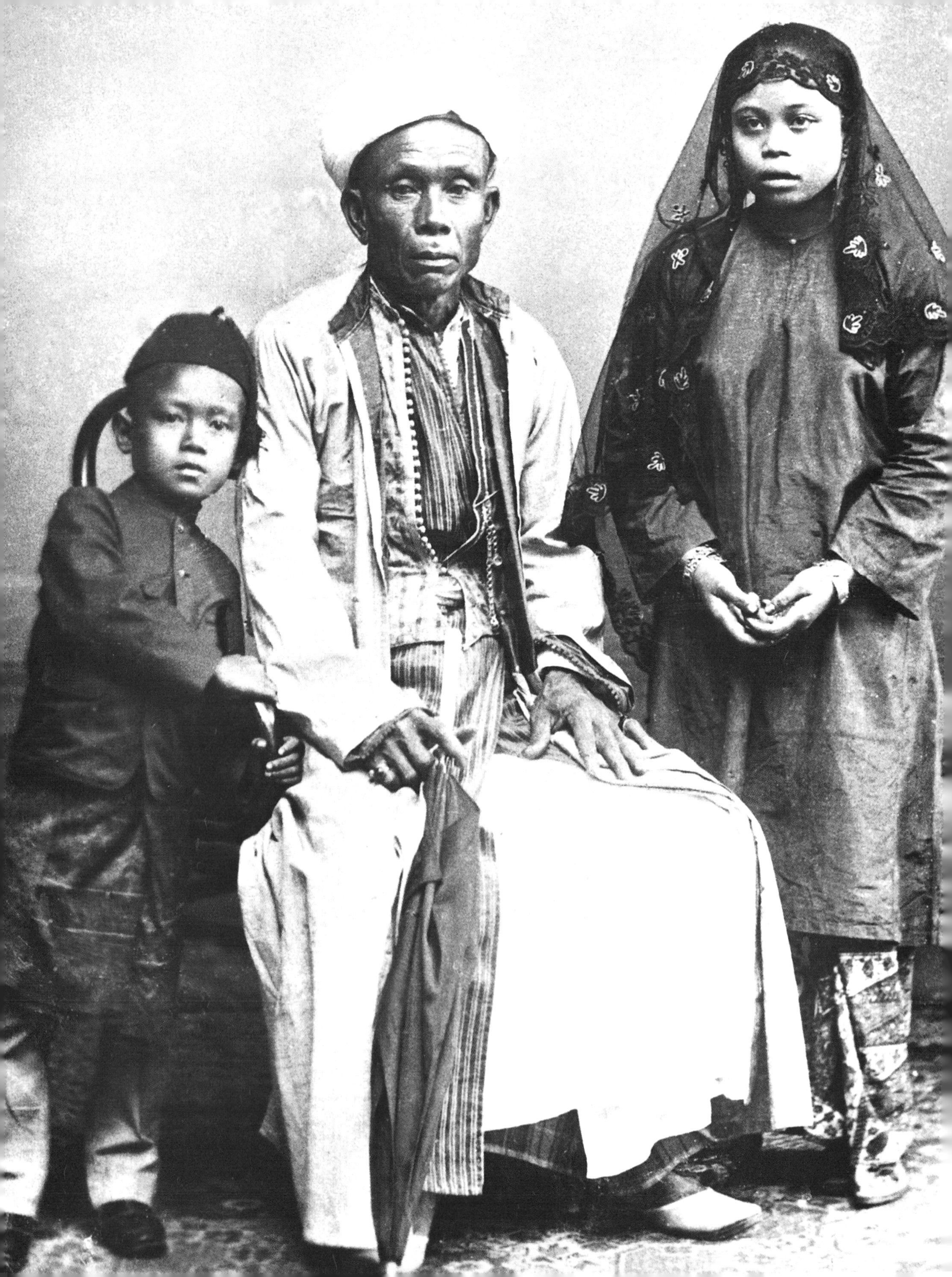

3 From Dispersed to Localised[1]: Family in Singapore 1819-1965[2]

Selina Ching Chan

Opposite: A Javanese family, circa 1900.

This chapter discusses the transformation of the family structure in Singapore by examining the changing marriage patterns. Owing to the migrant background of Singapore, the family structure at the beginning of the 19th century was a dispersed one. The term 'dispersed family' is used here to describe one in which members are scattered in different places or countries. This chapter considers how the dispersed family was later reunited, becoming a 'localised' one in which members stay in the same place.

Singapore as a Migrant Society

When Raffles landed in Singapore in 1819, there were about 150 people living on the island (Djamour 1965:3). Only 30 of them were Chinese, while the majority

A Straits Chinese family, circa 1920.

were Malay. Singapore was an important trading port in the Straits of Malacca and many migrants from Europe, the Malay Archipelago, India and China were drawn to this land.[3]

During each season of the 1830s, as many as 2,000 Chinese coolies from the southeastern coast of China were transported to the Straits (Djamour 1965:3). By 1836, the number of Chinese outnumbered the Malays. The Chinese made up 45.9% of the population while the Malays constituted 41.7% (Saw 1974:93). By the end of the 19th century, more than 70% of the total population was Chinese; and they continued to outnumber the combined total of Indians, Malays, Europeans and Eurasians even in 1947 (Freedman 1961:25). The Chinese migrants were mainly able-bodied males who were poor peasants in southeastern China. Some were free emigrants while others were contract coolies, refugees and exiles.

The Indian migrants arrived in Singapore in the 1830s (Sandhu 1970: 23).[4] Some worked in sugar, spice and coconut plantations while others took up jobs as administrators and clerks. The majority of the Indians were Tamils, Punjabis, Bengalis, Gujeratis and Singhalese made up the rest of the 'Indian' population. Together, they constituted 7 to 12 percent of the entire population of Singapore from 1819 to 1965 (Saw 1974:93).

This highly stylised portrait of an Indian family was taken in the 1890s.

Dispersed Family in the 19th and the early 20th century

The majority of the migrants in the 19th century were male bachelors who came to Singapore through their kin's or neighbour's introductions. Despite being away from their hometowns, the ties between these migrants and their families remained strong. Letters were frequently exchanged; for the illiterate migrants, professional letter writers were often engaged to write these letters. Photographs were occasionally enclosed. The following photograph shows a young Chinese man, Mr. Chia Yoon Chong, who had his photograph taken in a studio in 1939.[5] This was the first photograph he took at the age of 18 after coming from Guangdong to work in Singapore for a year. He earned his living as a roast pork seller in Chinatown through the help of his brother-in-law who was a pork dealer. In the photograph, he had deliberately put on his best clothes and jewellery. He wore a silver belt together with a quality shirt and pants, and there were three buttons made of solid gold on the shirt. The photograph was meant to show off the wealth he had acquired in Singapore; and the intended audience were those who lived in his hometown. It reveals how the ties between members of the dispersed family were maintained and reinforced.

A studio portrait of Mr Chia Yoon Chong, taken in 1939. This became a memorable picture for the Chia family; Mr Chia passed away in 1975, and the three buttons on this shirt that he wore were equally divided among his three sons.

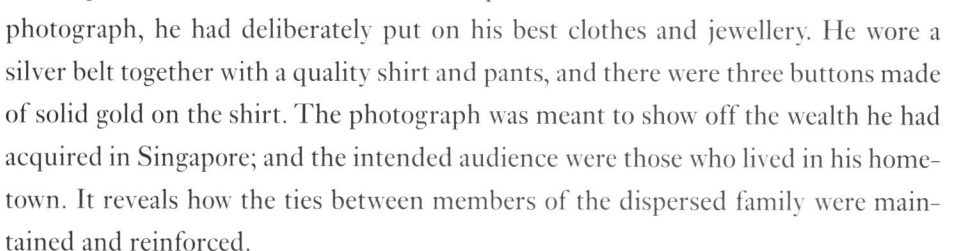

Not only did the migrants of different ethnic groups send their photographs back to their hometowns, they also sent remittances home. In the 1940s and 1950s, one particular migrant revealed in an interview that he sent around $90 annually to relatives in the hometown before the Chinese New Year (Sng 000517/026). Others gave money to relatives when they returned to China for visits. Not only did the spouse, parents and children receive money, relatives such as uncles or aunts were also given remittances. According to Chinese custom, the father, mother and siblings are one's closest relations while aunts and uncles are distant relatives. Those who are closer have stronger ties with the migrants, and should obtain more financial support from him or her.

The practices of remittances and regular visits to hometowns continued until the first-generation immigrants passed away. The ties between migrants and their relatives in the hometown were so strong that these migrants did not treat Singapore as a place for permanent settlement. Their aim was to work hard and become rich so that they could honour and venerate their ancestors and relatives in their home countries. This explains why many of them returned to China after retirement. For those who stayed, they still preferred to be buried in their hometown after they passed away.

By comparison, the ties between second-generation migrants and their home countries were relatively weak. They made regular trips to cities in their home countries instead of returning to their parents' hometown because they were unwilling to bear the inconvenience of travelling in the suburbs (Freedman 1957:75).

Marriage in the 19th century

The marriage pattern also revealed the close ties between the first-generation migrants and their hometown. Many of these migrants, from different ethnic groups, returned to their home villages for marriage. However, there was another factor influencing their marriage decisions: the unbalanced male-female ratio in the Straits. In 1836, the male-female ratio among the Indians was 8.5:1, and 14.6:1 among the Chinese (Wong 1975:20; Siddique and PuruShotom 1982:44). Female migration among the Chinese only began in 1853 and it was only from 1931 to 1937 that a large number of women started arriving and searching for work (Png 1969:102). The sex ratio became more balanced in 1950, but for the Indians, it still tipped over at 2:1. Given the highly disproportionate male-female ratio among migrants in the early 20th century, sexual crimes, prostitution and marital infidelity were rampant (Wong 1975:20).

A newly wed Chinese couple decked out in Western-style wedding costumes, presumably in the early 1910s.

The unbalanced male-female ratio among migrants explains the common practice of making special voyages to their hometown to find a marriage partner. Marriages in those days mainly occurred between people from the same dialect group. Romantic love was hardly observed as arranged marriages were the norm.

Sometimes, these marriages were arranged long before the individuals came to Singapore; some were formed by relatives who helped the male migrants seek potential brides in their hometown; others even asked friends who were visiting their hometown to find potential brides for them. Most of the time, the migrants consummated the marriage during their visits back home. The brides would occasionally follow the grooms to Singapore after the wedding. In most instances, the brides were left behind in the hometown. Marriage in those days did not mean that a man and a woman had to live together. The husband-wife relationship, couplehood and conjugality were never emphasised in the traditional Chinese society and the family life of these bachelors stretched beyond national and geographic boundaries. In fact, a Chinese woman's position in her husband's family was marginal. It would become established only after she had given birth to a son to carry on her husband's family descent. Hence, it was common for the brides to move to Singapore only after the first baby son was born.

Marriages between Chinese and local Malays were not uncommon in the beginning of the 19th century. They often sent their children back to China to be educated (Png 1969:102). An association—Kheng Tek Whay—was founded by these Straits Chinese merchants in 1831 (Yao 1987:215). Intermarriages between members of the association were encouraged. Marriage within the Straits Chinese community (or endogamy) was practised to prevent the entry of outsiders; and young Straits Chinese women were discouraged from marrying native Malays (Png 1969:102).

The Straits Chinese continued to practise Chinese customs such as ancestor worship. They identified themselves as Chinese though they also followed many Malay customs. One of the most significant was their adoption of Malay costumes—not to denounce their Chinese-ness but to downplay the significance of Malay costumes as a representative of the Malay identity (Yao 1987:219).[6] Although the Straits Chinese continued to practise certain Chinese customs, such as the patrilineal descent ideol-

A Straits Chinese family in the 1920s.

ogy, the Malay culture had also influenced them to the extent that a husband was allowed to live with his wife's parents, especially when the bride's family had no agnate, or male relatives on the father's side. In such marriages, the Straits Chinese son-in-law not only changed his surname to that of his wife, but also allowed his children to bear that surname. He would move in to live with his wife's family. This was very different from the Chinese son-in-law who would not change his surname although his sons' surname followed that of his wife. There was thus a selective synthesis of both Malay and Chinese cultures.

Marriages between the migrants and the locals also existed. For instance, the Eurasians were products of marriages between Europeans and Asians. These Europeans had, as a result of the colonial background of the Straits, been in the area for a long time. They were mainly from England, Holland and Portugal. European missionaries, many of whom were bachelors, also came around the same time. The rest were married but had their wives in their home countries. The single Portuguese and, to some extent, the Dutch, were encouraged to marry locals (Malays, Chinese and Indians) in order to have a better control over them (Braga-Blake 1992). Sometimes, illegitimate children were also borne to the mistresses whom the Europeans kept. These children were often subjects of discrimination and were sometimes neglected after the father left the Straits (Braga-Blake 1992:12).

A family of Eurasians, circa 1910.

In general, marriages were arranged by parents and were events designed to suit the preferences of the couple's families rather than their own. Romantic love did exist but was extremely rare among all ethnic groups. For the Indians and the Chinese, a marriage signified the transfer of a woman from her father to her husband. Indian girls were encouraged to be married right after puberty, and most Indian women married between the ages of 15 and 19 at the beginning of the century (Chang 1979:23). Caste endogamy was a general regulation for the Hindu.

Malay girls usually married between the ages of 16 and 19 while boys waited until they were between 19 and 23 years' old (Djamour 1965:77). Most of the Malays married within their own ethnic community through arranged marriages. Intermarriages between Malay, Chinese or Indians existed, but were less common than intermarriages between the Muslim Indians and Muslim Malays. Marriages that were territorially endogamous (that is, marrying someone who lived in close proximity) were also preferable. In fact, there was considerable reluctance to marry a person whose home was outside Singapore. This was because the parents disliked daughters to be far away from their natal families. It was also the norm for people to marry those from similar social backgrounds. Marriages between cousins were also not uncommon, especially among the Malays (Djamour 1965:71).

A traditional Malay wedding in the 1960s.

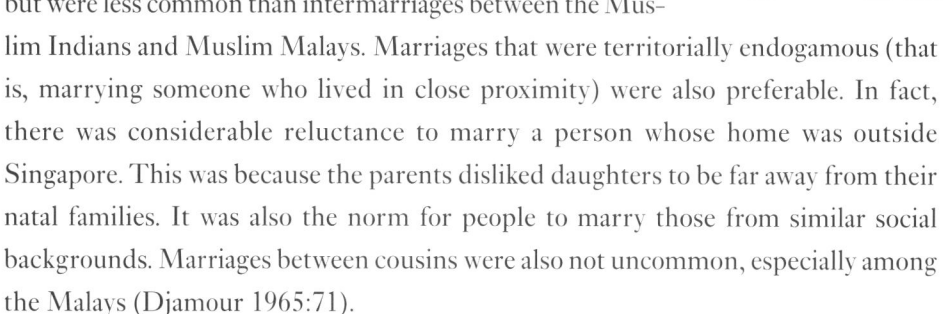

For the Chinese, the purpose of marriage was mainly to continue the patrilineal descent line, that is, to have sons to carry on the family name. Before the 1940s, as birth control was still unknown, some families from the low and middle classes had to give their daughters away. In some cases, a daughter would be 'pawned' to another family for several years so that her parents could get a loan (Lim 1997:13).

Polygamy was widespread among different ethnic groups. The Chinese, especially the rich, commonly practised it. The position of the secondary wife in Singapore was not the same as that of the concubine in mainland China. The secondary wife was not necessarily from a lower social class. On the contrary, she might be more educated than the first wife and usually had some working experience before marriage (Wong 1975: 18). Not only was she a wife, she was also a business partner. The secondary wife in mainland China was usually inferior in position to the first wife.

Among the Indians, the Hindus could practise polygamy if the first wives were not able to bear children. A Muslim man could have up to four wives, provided that he treated them equally. However, in reality, polygamy was not widely accepted among

Many Chinese families held weddings at their clan associations. This portrait from the 1920s may include clan members, aside from the couple's immediate family.

the Muslims, even in the 1940s. Polygamy for non-Muslim marriages was abolished in 1961 after the implementation of the Women's Charter. The minimum age for marriage is 18 (with consent of parents or guardians) and 21 (without parental consent). The Women's Charter granted both men and women equal rights to property ownership as well as to divorce. For Muslim marriages, they are governed by the Syariah Court since 1958 (Wong 1975:27).

A Detachment from Home Countries: The Marriage Pattern during the 20th century

The pattern of seeking brides from China became less popular when World War II broke out. This was due to two reasons. Firstly, it was impossible to make trips to China during wartime. Secondly, the female population in the local migrant community had grown significantly, thus reducing the need to seek brides from overseas. As the number of migrant women rose continuously in the 20th century, it had also become popular to find brides from the migrant communities in Singapore. Many of the couples got to know each other through school, relatives and friends.

Among the Chinese, voluntary organisations were grouped according to common surname (clansmen association) and hometown. These organisations, numbering about 250 in the 1950s, provided important network sources for potential brides and grooms (Freedman 1957:93). They were formed by migrants of Cantonese, Hokkien, Teochew, Hainan, Hinhua and Hakka origins on the basis of kinship ties or common hometown.

Freedman estimated that there were about 28,000 males in these clan associations and one in seven males belonged to an association (1957:93). Marriages within the same dialect group were encouraged while inter-dialect marriages were generally frowned upon. Clan exogamy, which is marriage outside of one's surname group, was a precept.

It was common in the 1930s for a middle-class Chinese girl to prepare her trousseau for marriage at 15 years' old. Age, talent and virtue were the main criteria in evaluating ladies for marriage, while profession and place of work were important factors in selecting husbands. The matchmaker played an important role in the introduction of the two parties. She would accompany a relative of the groom to pay a visit to the girl's home. The girl's mother would discreetly ask the girl to serve drinks and the guest would 'examine' the girl. There were certain general requirements: the girl 'should not have big mouths, big ears or moles around their eyes or noses . . . [and] when they walked, they should not waddle like a duck' (Lim 1997:32). After this preliminary examination, a date between the potential couple would be arranged. The first date often took place at coffee shops in the presence of the matchmaker. Coffee shops in Great World or New World amusement parks were popular venues for these matchmaking sessions. Close relatives would be present when the couple met. Dating would subsequently be conducted with the company of the bride's relative. Romantic love would develop thereafter, with courtship normally lasting from half a year to one year.

Not only did members in the associations play an important role in introducing and matching potential grooms and brides, but the premises of the associations were also often used to hold marriage ceremonies. Witnesses would be asked to go to the clansmen association to handle the marriage ceremonies. Relatives, clansmen and friends were all invited to witness the marriage. A photographer would also be invited to take the wedding pictures at the clansman association. Apart from the associations, weddings were sometimes also conducted at the Chinese Consulate, or in churches.

As for wedding banquets, they were commonly held at their *kampungs*. Relatives, neighbours and close friends were mobilised to prepare for the banquets. Since the late 1950s, however, with the increase in living standards, it has become popular to hold wedding banquets in restaurants. The Chinese had their banquets mostly at the restaurants in Chinatown. Wedding pictures would be taken on the wedding day at the studio, after the groom had fetched the bride from her parents' house. Occasionally, the relatives, bridesmaid and the best man would also have their pictures taken at the studio.

The Changing Family Structure: From the Nuclear to the Extended Family

Not only did marriage patterns change over the decades, but the family structure had also been transformed. The nuclear family was gradually giving way to the extended one. This was particularly true among the people living in the rural area. One interview revealed that it was conventional to construct further partitions within the house so that sons could continue to live at home after marriage. Besides the fact that living together was mutually beneficial, the cost of moving out and building another house was also prohibitively high (Tan 000616/007).

In the urban and suburban areas, it was common to observe families composed of two married couples from two different generations living together with their un-

A Chinese wedding picture taken in the studio, circa 1920.

married children (Freedman 1957:39). However, the size of the urban household was small when compared to the rural one due to scarcity of space.

Sons were more favoured among the Chinese and were given priority in receiving education. Poor Chinese families might even be willing to give away their girls just to keep their sons. Unlike the Chinese, the Malays adored children from both sexes. During the war when many of the Chinese gave away their daughters, the Malays were the ones who kindly adopted them.

Conclusion

The examination of family photographs has contributed to our understanding of the transformation of marriage patterns and family structure in the last two centuries. In the 19th and early 20th century, the nuclear family, with brides from hometowns, was the norm. This was significantly different from the usual practice in China, especially along the southeastern coast, where extended families were the norm. Extended families emerged in Singapore only at a later stage when local brides were more sought after than those in the hometowns. Following the emergence of the extended family, the ties between the migrants and their home countries also weakened. A process of localisation is observed from the growing cultural attachment to the local community as opposed to the migrants' home countries.

Acknowledgements

Special thanks go to Chia Tuck Fatt for providing the photograph of Chia Yooon Chong.

Endnotes

1. The term 'localized lineage' was used by Freedman to refer to a lineage with members staying at the same village (1957:17). This chapter uses the term 'localized' to denote a family with members staying at the same place.
2. Photographs shown here were analysed to further understand the family structure in the past. They were mostly posed pictures taken in studios, where the photographer usually determined the posture and position of the customers. The popularity of studios in those days can be attributed to the fact that few individuals owned cameras then; thus, taking pictures was a special and 'costly' event. Since most of these are studio photographs, they therefore reflect only the normative aspect of family life. However, an attempt to overcome this limitation is made by conducting interviews with some of the persons in the pictures.
3. Malacca was already a very important trading port on the Southeast China coast since the 17th century (Yao 1987:213).
4. They were very different from the early Indian migrants who came before 1819 and were mainly traders.
5. The following information was provided by Chia's daughter-in-law.
6. Straits Chinese today assert the uniqueness of their own ethnic identity by calling themselves the Peranakan (Clammer 1980).

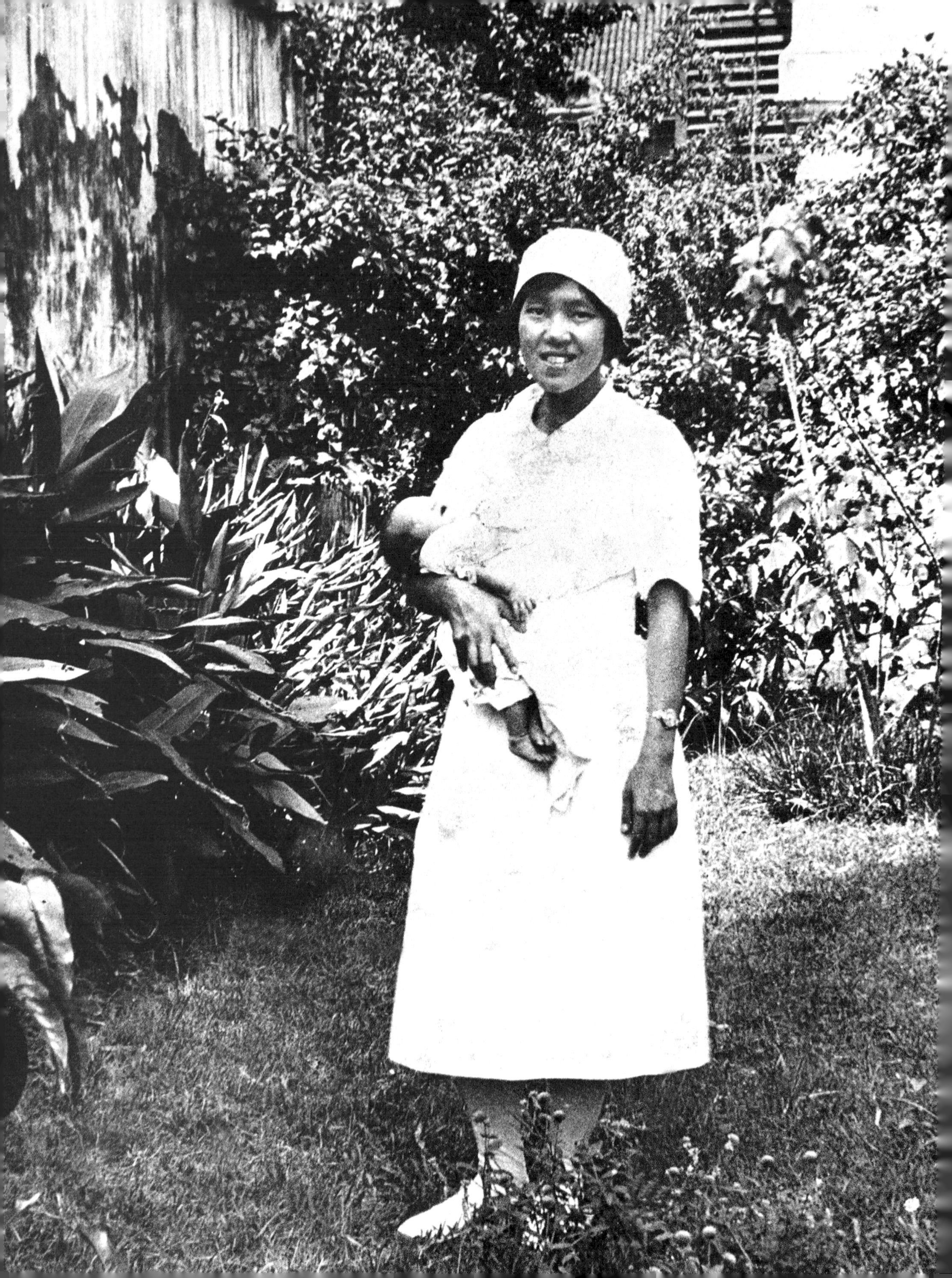

4 Coming into Being: Birth and a Nation's Growth

Maribeth Erb

Opposite: Madam Elsie Kiong, a health inspector in the 1920s and 1930s.

Reproduction is almost always socially controlled. Only recently have women started rebelling against this control and demanded the right to choose. It is not that women in all cultures at all times have had no control over reproduction; it is just that no one has thought about it, or spoken about it before as a 'right'. Control over reproduction, pregnancy and childbirth in the past, however, was not generally a matter of much concern to the state. Instead, this control was exercised by families, villages, clans, or some kind of pseudo-kinship or residential group that had a personal relationship with the women (and men) who were responsible for producing the vital continuing link into the future. In fact, the duty of women and their husbands might have been to not only produce offspring to ensure the family line, but also to produce as many of them as possible. This particular cultural ideal has played a very prominent role in Singapore's past. As such, the state increasingly felt the need to intervene, showing not only a concern with people as individuals, but as a population. Because of this, a certain amount of reproductive control passed out of the hands of people within the context of personal, intimate relationships and into the hands of the government. The development of birth trends and how it came to be almost synonymous with population planning is very much wrapped up with the history of Singapore and its growth as an independent nation-state.

Birth and Culture

Long before the medical profession showed concern for childbirth and treated it as a special discipline, women had had their own ideas about what they needed to do to safeguard the growing foetus in their womb and to facilitate their births. This was true as well for the ancestors of present-day Singaporeans. Many of their precautions lived on as sometimes vaguely understood beliefs as to what must be done to ensure the safety of both mother and child. Even in the present day, we can see the continuation of certain customary practices that still hold meaning for many modern Singaporeans. The beliefs of the various cultural groups in Singapore had, and still have, some striking similarities, which may reflect their long interaction and mutual influence over the centuries.

One common fear during pregnancies in the past was that a mother or a father might perform certain actions that would have an adverse impact on the unborn child. In Malay this is called *tertekan*. The belief is that during the first four months of pregnancy, the foetus in the mother's womb is still undergoing formation, thus it is vulnerable to the actions of the parents, to whom it is inextricably linked as a product of their union. The foetus is very much in a 'betwixt and between' state—yet to be fully formed, alive, or what one might consider a social creature—and therefore is in a kind of transitional state (Haniah 1992:21–22). There were a number of precautions that Malay parents took so as not to affect their unborn child. They could not go fishing, for if their fishhook tore the mouth of the fish, the child would be born with a cleft lip. Chopping off the legs or pincers of a crab was believed to cause deformity of the child's limbs, and if the father were to use a hammer, the child would be born deaf (Haniah 1992:22–23). Nailing or tying pieces of wood together was believed to result in deformities of the ears and lips. Also, in general, looking at ugly people could have an impact on the images in a pregnant woman's mind and cause the child to be born ugly; so she must only look at pleasant things (Mohamed Hassan 1967:16–17). There were other taboos that could affect a pregnant woman. For instance, if she sat in doorways, it was believed her birth canal would be obstructed during birth. Her husband must also not carry a towel around his neck when going for a bath, lest the umbilical cord be wrapped around the baby's neck at birth (Mohamed Hassan 1967:16–17).

The Chinese held similar ideas. *Tai Shen*, the 'placenta god' that animates the foetus' soul, is thought to be moving around rather precariously for about the first four months of pregnancy, after which the soul would be more firmly attached to the body. Before this period, it was considered dangerous to move the furniture in the house for fear the pregnant woman would suffer a miscarriage. Also, no one should patch a hole in the wall, hammer a nail, paint, cut, saw or sew in the sight of the pregnant woman for fear these actions would result in deformities to the unborn child (Lim 1994:16–17). In addition, needlework and shutting doors or windows could cause blindness in the child. Loud noise would cause deafness, while tying things may cause deformity in the hands or legs or the umbilical cord to be entangled around the infant's neck. If any of these things had to be done by a pregnant woman, or someone in the room with her, then the placenta god would be asked to leave the room. The name *Tai Shen* [胎神] would be written on a piece of red paper and pasted outside the room, after which it would then be safe to move the furniture and perform other prohibited acts (Ng 1994:69–71).

Another similarity among all the cultural groups, an idea also commonly found elsewhere as well, is that a mother's cravings for special foods must be satisfied or it will be detrimental to her baby. As the foetus is not yet exposed to the socialising influence of its parents, it is considered a creature with whimsical desires that can manipulate others with its appetite (Hainah 1992:22). Perhaps this was again associated with the baby's transitional state, and the idea of the baby as already a 'person', but not yet a 'social' person. Some studies done in other cultures suggest, however, that it is perhaps actually the woman who is doing the manipulating; cravings may be a way that women, usually dominated by others, can manoeuvre others to do as they wish during this most vulnerable time. Thus women may crave foods that are normally expensive or rare, thus forcing others to allow them to satisfy their desire for luxury foods. Conversely, pregnant women may be repulsed by foods that they normally would have to prepare and serve to others, as a way of getting out of doing these activities (Valsiner 1989:117–162; Lim 1994:11–12).

In general, among cultural groups in early Singapore, the types of food consumed during a pregnancy were considered very important. The Chinese, in particular, had very strong feelings about this, associating diet with the balance of *yin* and *yang*, which is cold and hot, respectively. If too many 'cooling' foods were consumed by the pregnant mother, this would result in 'wind' for the foetus and lead to colic, coughs, colds and asthma later in the child's life (Lim 1994:15–16). In the case of 'hot' foods, consuming ginger may cause the child to have eye problems, or even cause a miscarriage since it is believed to expel air from the body (Ng 1994:78–79).

All the different cultural groups in early Singapore considered the seventh or eighth month to be an important time for the developing foetus. Apparently, the foe-

Tonics prepared with ginseng are a popular choice among expectant Chinese mothers. This photograph of a Chinese woman preparing to cook some ginseng was taken in 1984.

tus was thought to have been fully formed as a human being by this time (Hainah 1992:25). The mother is certainly more aware of the movements of the foetus, and that the time of delivery is fast approaching. This might be the reason that ritual activities performed to promote easy childbirth and to predict the sex of the child were commonly carried out at this time. An expectant Malay woman would traditionally engage a midwife while in the seventh month of pregnancy, by bringing the latter a tray on which was placed all of the ingredients to chew betel nut, a mild narcotic. These ingredients included lime powder, an areca nut and betel leaf (Mohamed Hassan 1967:21).[1] After a midwife had been engaged, the parents-to-be would hold a special ceremony called *lenggang perut* (to rock the abdomen). The midwife would spread out seven sarongs of different colours, and the pregnant woman would lie over them. The midwife would then massage the pregnant woman's abdomen with oil, and taking a peeled coconut, she would roll it slowly down the woman's abdomen, seven times. On the seventh roll the midwife would let the coconut fall down and roll onto the floor. When it stopped rolling the midwife would check its position: if the 'eyes' of the coconut point upwards, then the child was thought to be a boy; if downward, then a girl. The midwife would then lift up the sarongs, cradling the pregnant woman gently within them and rocking her body to the left and right once or twice. It was believed that this rocking would ensure a safe and easy delivery (Haniah 1992: 22–26).

Around the seventh month, Indian Hindus would also perform a ceremony to influence the birth and to divine about the delivery. At the seventh month of pregnancy, a woman would return to her own parents' home, and all of her married relatives were asked to attend. The woman would sit on the floor with banana leaves placed all around her. Nine different kinds of food and three kinds of rice were placed on the leaves, but no meat dishes were allowed. The ceremony must be performed at dawn and with the pregnant woman facing the morning sun, since the early part of the day symbolises the blooming of life. Married female relatives of the pregnant woman would place red or other coloured bangles on her arms, as a source of protection. She would then put bananas in her *sari* and distribute them to the children present. Three packets of rice would be presented to her, one of them sweetened. If she chose the sweet one, this signified that she was carrying a boy. Then she would break open a coconut, revealing the flesh within. If any of it was rotten it was believed to forecast a difficult delivery (Raja 00800/013).

Among the Chinese, around the eighth month, a pregnant woman's family would send gifts to her and her baby, including accessories for the baby and foods such as ginseng, bird's nest, and red dates (Ng 1994:89). The gender of the first guest to step into the house at this time, about one month before the birth, was thought to be an omen as to the sex of the child. Other ways that the child's sex was predicted were through observing the kinds of foods the pregnant woman enjoyed eating. If she had a preference for sour foods, then it was believed to be a boy; if she enjoyed hot foods, then a girl was expected (Ng 1994:92–93).

In preparation for childbirth, the Malay family of the past would hang bunches of a leaf called *mengkuang* (screw-pine) under the part of the house where the delivery was to take place and where the mother would lay during her confinement period (Mohamed Hassan 1967:28). To pick the best place, a medicine man would drop an axe head onto the ground. Where the axe fell upright was thought to be an auspicious place. The medicine man would then surround the area with thorns, bees' nests, ray's tails, bitter herbs and other sharp and bitter things to keep away evil spirits. They would also stick nails in the windows with sharp ends sticking out. People would burn rubbish and the skins of onions because it was believed that evil spirits stayed away from bad smells. One evil spirit associated with childbirth was the *penanggalan*[2]. The Malays believed that the *penanggalan*, a head with entrails and no body, would come to suck the blood of newborn infants. (Mohamed Hassan 1967:25–29).

After birth came the initial period of 'socialisation'. The baby and mother were still considered to be in a transitional state after birth. The baby may be visible as a physical person and separate from its mother, but it is not yet a 'social' person until the family and the community formally recognised it. This is often only done after a period of confinement, in which mother and child would stay in the house, segregated from the rest of the community. Naming of the baby occurred at this time. The confinement period was also almost universally associated with all kinds of precautions, indicating a concern with the precarious state of health of the mother and child during this transitional period.

One of the precautions taken after birth often had to do with the placenta. All ethnic groups believed that it should be carefully and respectfully buried. A common belief in the Malay world was that the placenta was the sibling of the new born, and had died to give the baby life (Haniah 1992:30). When hospital births became more prevalent, the proper way to dispose of the placenta, as deemed by the Malays, became a problem. One Malay family of the past related how they were certain that the sickly state of their second child was due to the fact that they had allowed the hospital authorities to dispose of the placenta instead of arranging for the disposal themselves

(Mohamed Hassan 1967:30–31). Malay families also felt that the retention of the umbilical cord was important, since it was very effective as medicine if the baby later developed a stomachache (Mohamed Hassan 1967:37).

Part of the 'socialisation' process of the Malay baby had to do with 'opening' its mouth. Once the baby was cleansed after birth, its mouth was 'opened', by a relative that the parents admired, in hopes that the child would develop that person's characteristics. This relative would take a gold ring, dip it into sugar or honey water and put it in the child's mouth until he or she started to suck at it (Mohamed Hassan 1967:30).

The Malay mother would observe a period of confinement for 48 days after the birth, a period called *pantang*. She could not leave the house or even the bed for seven days, and had to abstain from certain kinds of foods considered to be *bisa* (poisonous) and 'cold'. At the end of her *pantang*, she would bathe in lime juice and water, thought to be effective in both cleansing and dispelling bad influences (Mohamed Hassan 1967:41).

Indian women experienced a confinement period of 28 to 30 days. This was thought necessary because of the evil spirits roaming around outside the house after birth. On the third day after the delivery, the hair of the mother would be washed and then dried with a kind of smoke thought to kill off germs and keep away the evil spirits. The newborn baby was also dried with smoke. The new mother's diet had to include foods that were considered warming, such as spices and also food that would produce a lot of milk for the baby, such as shark and ray fish (Raja 00800/013).

The confinement period for the Chinese was also 30 days, during which time the mother was given special foods, such as boiled pigs' trotters cooked with ginger and vinegar, that were meant to return strength to her and rid her womb of 'air' (Tham 1985:52). After the confinement, the baby's head would be shaved, and food sent to all family members who have given presents to the family. This food included eggs, dyed red, which were symbolic of new life (Ng 1994:104; SFCC 1989:52). The family then thanked their ancestors and gods by burning incense, and asked for the ancestors to protect the child (SFCC 1989:89). After that, the mother and child may leave the house for the first time, going to the house of her parents. The maternal grandparents would rub ashes on the baby's temples, and put a dot of red on the baby's head for a safe journey home (Ng 1994:107). The baby's name was not given during the celebration; however, it was usually decided long before. For a Chinese baby, the name is often associated with a family poem. It might also, however, be linked to the time of the baby's birth, being a way to make up for which of the elements—gold, wood, water, fire or earth—that were missing at the moment when the child was born (SFCC 1989: 87).

Malays named their newborns seven days after birth. Before the naming, a special ceremony had to be performed. Several trays were prepared, one on which was placed some cups of yellow rice and special water (*air tepung tawar*), another on which a coconut—its contents discarded and pure water added—was placed. The coconut was decorated with silver flowers. Each guest would then sprinkle some of the rice and water on the forehead of the baby, and then snip off a bit of its hair and place the hair in the water in the coconut. After this, the baby was named. The baby's head was then shaved, and all its hair was placed in the coconut. Then the coconut would be buried, together with a young coconut palm to mark the burial spot and serve as a kind of memorial to the baby's birth (Mohamed Hassan 1967:38–40).

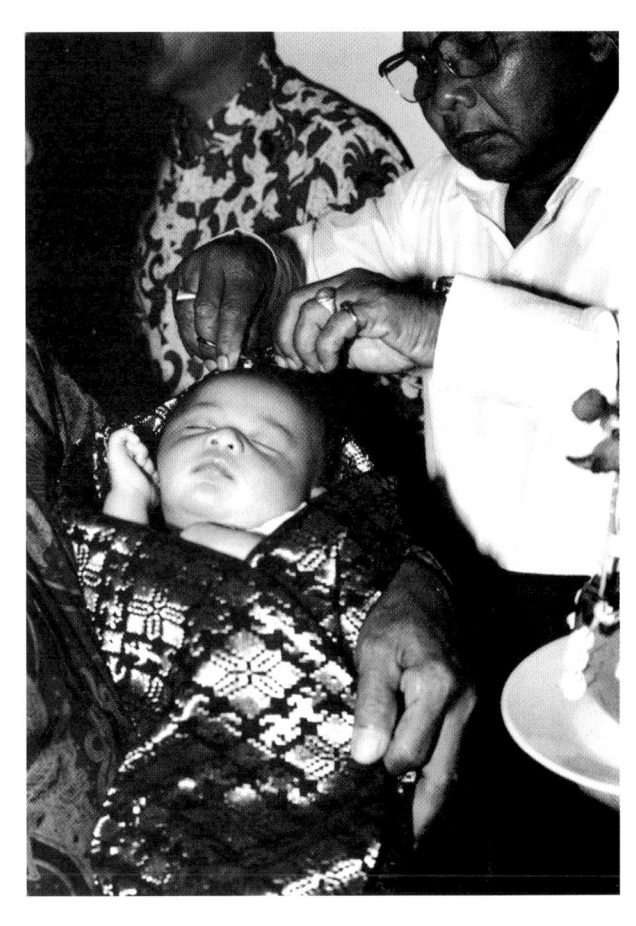

Cukur rambut or shaving the baby's hair a few days after birth, circa 1997.

Hindu Indians named the baby on the 16th, 28th or 30th day after birth, depending on whether the mother was still discharging blood on these days. The baby would only be named after the mother's bleeding had stopped. On the day of the naming ceremony, a chicken with one leg was cooked for the baby and the mother. Other foods, such as dried fish, chicken eggs, vegetables and rice, were also prepared. The food was served on banana leaves in front of the mother, who would sit facing the east, the direction of the rising sun. Before the meal, a mixture of flour and sugar was placed on an oval plate in front of the mother and the baby was rolled around in it. The child could then be given a name, depending upon the stars that were in ascension at the time of its birth. The mother would then be fed the food from the banana leaves. Afterwards some of the rice was rolled into balls by the mother and given to women who had not yet given birth (Mrs Raja 00800/013). Relatives would give the baby presents, often gold ornaments. For protection from evil, they would also give black threads, tied around the baby's waist, wrists and ankles, and black charcoal

The Hindu newborn baby undergoes the ritual of having charcoal painted over its eyes to protect it from evil spirits, circa 1985.

would be painted over its eyes. To bless the child, relatives would dab honey on the baby's forehead and milk in its mouth (personal communication, Vineeta Sinha)

We can see that, in the past, women and their families had their own way of attempting to ward off difficulties with pregnancy and childbirth. Various actions or rituals recognised the child as a person well before birth. Some attention was paid to predicting the sex of the child, and ensuring a safe delivery. There was also a considerable amount of concern over the safety and health of the mother and child during pregnancy and delivery and after birth. Before medical intervention, infant and maternal mortality rates were quite high, and one can see that these ritual and preventative actions addressed a need to ensure safety and health in the growing family.

Birth and the State

Despite the high infant and maternal mortality rates, it took the British colonial government some time before they saw childbirth as something that needed their attention. It was not until 1888 that the first maternity hospital was established, and as it will be seen below, it was founded in a flurry of embarrassment.

One of the earliest hospitals in Singapore was built in 1858 at a place where buffaloes had been previously penned. In Malay, the area was known as *kandang kerbau* or 'buffalo stall'. At that time, it was known as the General Hospital, and had two sections, one for Europeans and one for local people. In 1872, after an ordinance was passed to control contagious diseases, the female ward of the General Hospital was turned into a ward to treat venereal diseases in prostitutes. When a cholera epidemic broke out in 1873, patients were evacuated to the 'Sepoy Lines', which the authorities eventually decided was a more suitable place for the General Hospital.[3] Later in 1884, the Governor decided that the hospital at the *Kandang Kerbau* should be a hospital devoted to the treatment of licensed prostitutes suffering from all kinds of diseases, not only venereal (Lee 1990:599-600).

Meanwhile, in 1885, at the new General Hospital at the Sepoy Lines, a proposal was made to let nuns treat the sick. Some prominent members of the European community objected, and petitioned the Secretary of State for the Colonies. One of their arguments was that the nuns were prevented by the regulations of their order to assist in childbirth. Since it had been brought to his attention, the Secretary asked for further information about maternity hospitals and midwifery in Singapore, stating that normally maternity cases would be nursed separately from other cases in a hospital. This put the authorities in Singapore into a flurry for, in fact, there were no maternity facilities at all! In the previous five years, only two midwifery cases had appeared at the General Hospital. The Secretary of State was assured that steps would be taken immediately to initiate government maternity services (Lee 1990:600).

So in 1888, a building at the junction of Victoria Street and Stamford Canal became the first maternity hospital for women in Singapore. Eight beds were available—four for European women and four for local women. In the first few years,

The first Maternity Hospital at Stamford Road and Victoria Street junction, circa 1900.

however, the hospital's existence was rather precarious; it opened and closed for various reasons, such as foul smelling mud being dredged up from the canal and lack of staff. Very few patients were admitted and none of them were truly 'local' until the end of 1890, when an Indian woman was admitted. Twelve more Indian women were admitted in 1891, along with 13 Europeans and four Eurasians. Despite the fact that Chinese were overwhelmingly in the majority, it was not until 1892 that the first Chinese patient admitted herself to the hospital. In 1894, two women opened up the first private practices in midwifery (Lee 1990:600).

Some Eurasian women attached themselves unofficially to the maternity hospital to learn midwifery, as suggestions to open a school for training midwives were rejected until 1910. In 1897, due to the appalling level of maternity and infant mortality, the Secretary of State for the Colonies suggested that local women be trained as midwives, but the Governor did not think it was possible (Lee 1990: 601). Slightly more than a decade later, they proved him wrong.

Patients to the hospital increased yearly, so in 1907, the Governor proposed that a new maternity hospital be built (Lee 1990:601–602). The Secretary of State approved, and in 1908 a new Maternity Block at the General Hospital at the Sepoy Lines was completed (Lee 1990:602). There was growing attention to the issue of infant mortality, and also talk that the government should make it compulsory for a competent midwife to be present at all births. Towards this end, the government

Potential licensed midwives undergoing training, circa 1958.

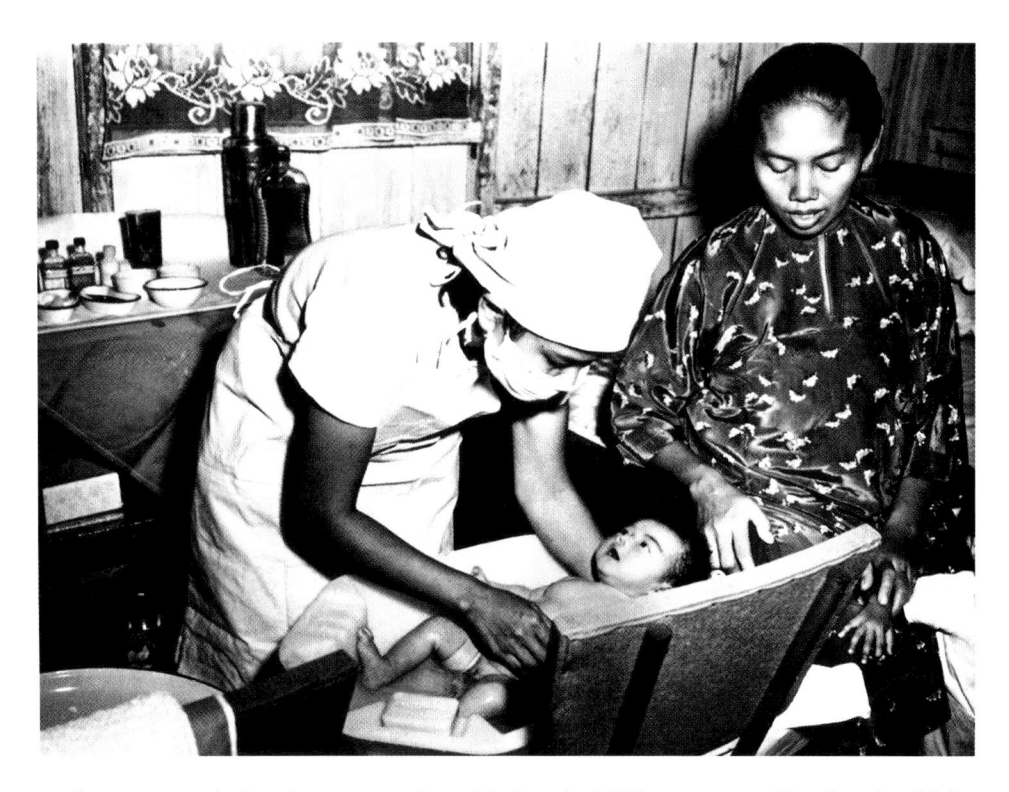

A midwife making a house visit, 1962.

took steps to train local women to be midwives in 1910, a course offered and paid for by the government. Four local women received certificates of competency in 1911 (Lee 1990:602–603).

At the same time, the Medical School in Singapore started classes and its first students graduated in 1910. However, their results in midwifery were very poor. Upon investigation, it turned out that they had not been allowed to practise freely in the Maternity Hospital to gain proficiency because of the fear that women would be too embarrassed and refuse to come to the hospital. The Medical School decided to open an outpatient maternity department to allow medical students to gain the practice they needed (Lee 1990:603). The government granted permission to use the old Maternity Hospital at Victoria Street, and so the External Midwifery Department was opened in 1913. The Medical School could not afford its upkeep, however, so the following year the government reopened the Victoria Street Hospital as a Free Maternity Hospital, absorbing the External Midwifery Department as part of its facilities. Pupil midwives were also trained at this hospital (Lee 1990:604).

In 1915, to lower the infant mortality rate, an ordinance was passed. It became illegal for unqualified women to practise as midwives. However, the law would only be enforced in areas where there was a sufficient number of trained midwives, which

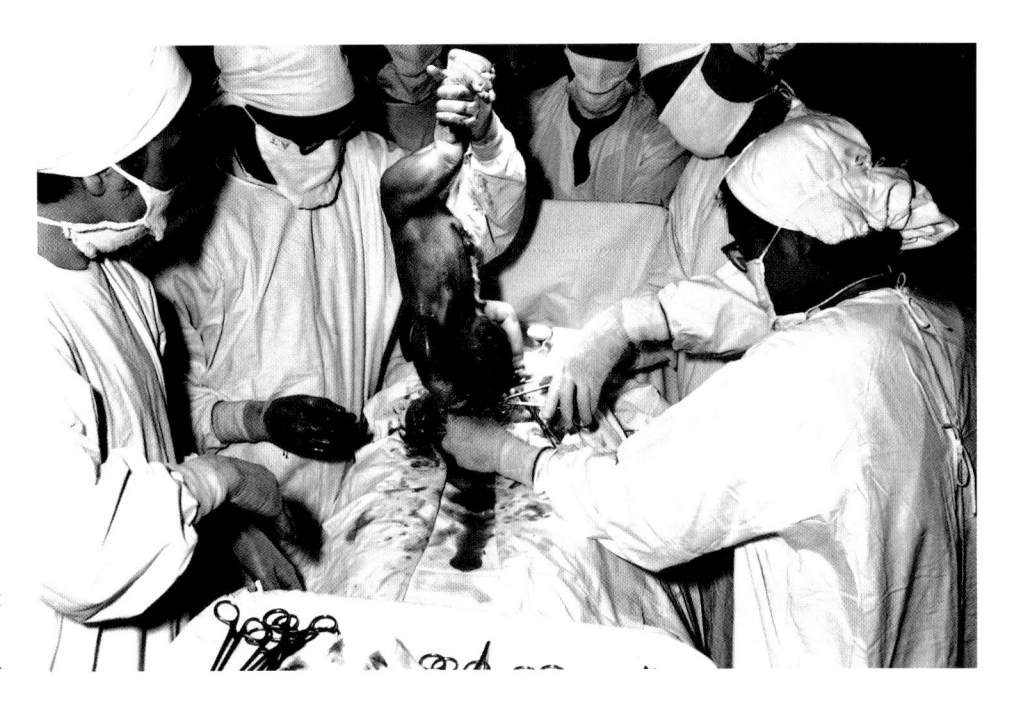

The birth of a baby at Kandang Kerbau Hospital in the 1960s.

meant only the municipality of Singapore and not the rural areas. It was necessary, therefore, to make provision for the training of midwives, and the re-training of those who had been practising without government certificates. The most numerous of these were Malay midwives (*bidan*) who were popular among all ethnic groups. In fact, it was Malay women who were the most reluctant to make use of the facilities of the maternity hospitals. And unfortunately, perhaps because of this, the infant mortality rate among the Malay population was the highest (Lee 1990:604). The Midwives' Ordinance Bill was enforced only in 1917, when provisions were made to discover, visit and assist the untrained midwives still practising in the colony (Lee 1990:605).

Provisions were also made to improve the teaching of midwifery at the Medical School, particularly after a poor evaluation in 1919. Dr. J.S. English became the first Professor of Midwifery and Gynaecology in 1922, and he reorganised the system of practical work in midwifery (Lee 1990:605–606). By 1923, the two hospitals with maternity services were so overwhelmed with cases that patients had to be sent away at times. Expansion plans had to be made. A proposal was made to convert the Kandang Kerbau Hospital—which, up to that point, had been used primarily for prostitutes and poor women—into a Free Maternity Hospital, and so renovation work began. In 1924, the hospital re-opened with 30 beds, almost double that of the previous building at Victoria Street (Lee 1990:606).

Although urban women were increasingly making use of the Maternity Hospitals, this was not the case for women in rural areas. In 1927, a health campaign commenced in the isolated, rural areas of Singapore (Simmons 1939). It was initiated by a Public Health Matron, Ida Simmons, who particularly directed her attention to maternity and child health-care. From her own account, it was a gruelling task, but over a ten-year period, the campaign was a tremendous success in providing care to *kampung* folk, and changing their attitudes towards health-care.

Some of the things that she found the rural people doing in those days would shock the educated, modern urbanite (see Simmons 1939: 1–2). In one case, she found a baby sucking milk from a tube half a yard long. When Ms. Simmons gave the mother an hygienic feeder with a short teat, she wanted to take the tube outfit away. The upset mother said that the bottle would be fine for the baby, 'but what would the pig do?' She had been giving milk to the baby and the pig from the same feeder! Simmons also found that immigrants from China had brought their ideas of appropriate care from the colder climates of the north. For example, it took some convincing to get the Chinese grandmothers to accept that fresh air and a daily bath were good for an infant, and that they didn't need six layers of padded coats!

Jalan Eunos Clinic at the Kampong Batak maternity and child welfare centre in 1952.

At the beginning of her work, the infant mortality rate was 263 per thousand in the first year of life, closer to 300 for Malays (Simmons 1939:1). Rural people were afraid to go to the Maternity and General Hospitals, if they even knew about them. The health-care campaigners set up travelling dispensaries on roadsides to administer to the sick, and visited new born babies in their homes. After a while, welfare centres were set up in old shophouses with a nurse and midwife in attendance at all times. At first few came, but after 10 years of work, 14 clinics were set up and people thronged to them daily to obtain help. Initially, people had been afraid to undress their infants and brought them to the Clinics unbathed, but over time, with the nurses' instruction in infant care, women would bring their babies washed and dressed in their Sunday best. With the determined efforts of the rural health campaigners, the infant mortality rate fell significantly to 86 per thousand in 1937 (Simmons 1939:3).

Meanwhile, the number of maternity cases in the municipal areas of Singapore made it necessary to enlarge the premises of the Kandang Kerbau Maternity Hospital. The hospital expanded in 1936. Even though immigration to Singapore had been restricted in 1931, the population of the island was growing at a rapid rate due to the large numbers of newborns. Birth control was already an important issue in the United Kingdom itself, and though overpopulation was becoming a fear in the colony, the government felt that the local people were not ready to accept the idea of birth control (Bungar 1991:45–46). It was during the post-war baby boom that this hesitation came to an end.

Obstetric patients at the Kandang Kerbau Hospital in 1958.

By 1947, 60 percent of the population had been born locally, and the post-war baby boom was in full swing (1991:47). From 1947 to 1951, the Kandang Kerbau Maternity Hospital increased their number of beds to 240, and the number of patients rose annually. There was also a concomitant decrease in the mortality rate among maternity cases. The local population was no longer afraid to step into the hospital, and the desire for antenatal and postnatal care increased as opposed to the pre-war period. To accommodate more patients, the average length of a hospital stay was decreased from 10-12 days to four days, and then in 1951, to three days per patient (Lee 1990:610).

In 1954, a domiciliary aftercare service was introduced to give care to patients living in the city area, who were permitted to be discharged 24 hours after birth, as long as their homes were found suitable for recuperation (1990:611).[4] Later in 1955, a domiciliary delivery service was started to ease the burden of the hospitals. Those patients who were attending the hospital clinic for antenatal care, were free to chose home delivery or hospital delivery, again as long as their homes were deemed appropriate. In 1956, this Service became part of the Teaching Unit for medical students, nurses and pupil midwives (1990:611).

In response to this post-war baby boom, the Singapore Family Planning Association (SFPA) was formed in 1949. In the same year, three clinics were opened to provide family planning services (Bungar 1991:47). Two new clinics appeared in the rural areas of Nee Soon and Bukit Panjang in early 1950 (Ebert 1959:122–123). Although the government had given them a grant to start off their work, much of the funding was from private donations and the voluntary services of nurses, doctors, clerks, attendants and interpreters (Lam 1959:22). The government continued to give support by increasing its aid over the years, and by 1959, family planning was recognised as an integral part of the national health programme (Bungar 1991:48). By 1965, due to the SFPA's inability to continue running their expanding services, they requested the Ministry of Health to take over the responsibility of family planning. The Ministry agreed, and in September that year, a white paper on family planning was published, with the goal of establishing a Family Planning and Population Board (Bungar 1991:48–49). Over the years, family planning and maternal and child care facilities had slowly merged with population planning.

The growth of a post-colonial nation-state meant the development of control over the population, and that included population planning. The figures on birth had continued to soar (incidentally, 1966 was a world record-breaking year for Kandang Kerbau)[5], and the aim of economic growth demanded that this be put in check. What had started as a rather accidental interest on the part of the colonial government in pregnancy and child-

The post-war baby boom can be seen from the cramped conditions of this Social Welfare Children's Crèche in 1949.

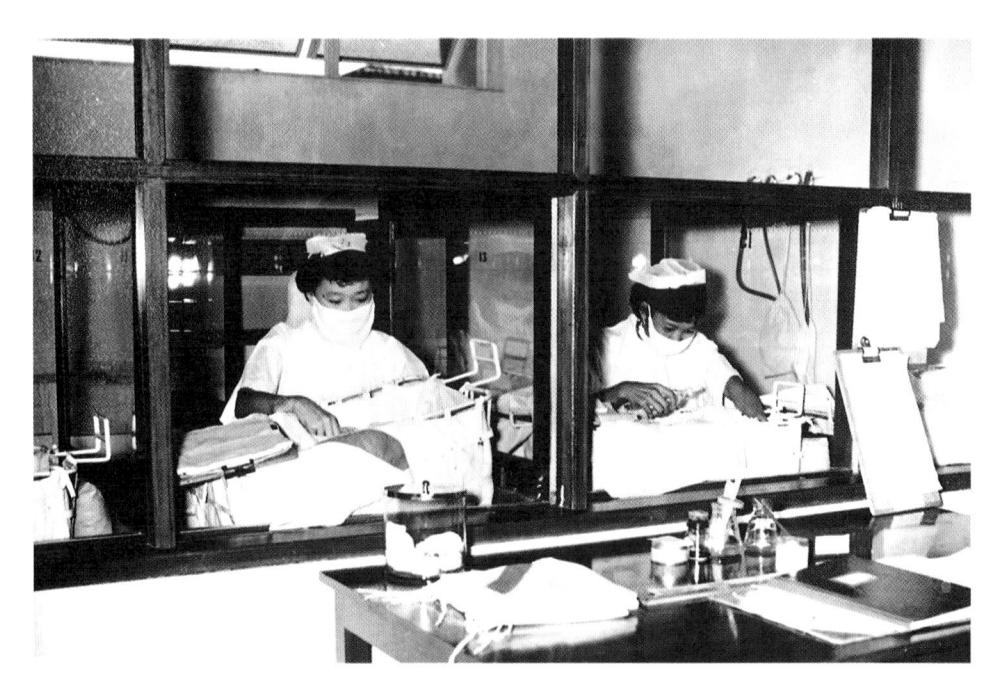

Nurses in the infants' ward in Kandang Kerbau Hospital in 1958.

birth in 1885 ended up as a very determined effort on the part of the post-colonial government to control birth and the bodies of women and their children.

Conclusion

Does one need to talk about rights in childbirth? In looking at the range of pregnancy and childbirth customs in early Singapore and the history of care for pregnant and delivering mothers, one is struck again with the eternal contradiction of 'freedom' versus 'control'. Is any social creature free? Clearly, customary rituals, institutions by social groups are an imposition on the individual and are part of a system of control over the persons of women and children. Also, and perhaps most importantly for the issue of childbirth, customary ideas and rituals may often not result in the most hygienic of conditions, as Ida Simmons found so graphically to be the case in early 20th century Singapore. The state, on the other hand, concerned with health and hygiene, strove to limit the individual's freedom to decide on these issues. When the monitoring of conditions of childbirth becomes instituted, however, it eventually merges with the wider issue of whether people should be free to have children that they can or cannot 'adequately' care for and therefore whether they should be free to make their own reproductive decisions. Are social creatures, therefore, ever free and do they have the right to choose?

Acknowledgements

Many thanks to the Department of Corporate Development in KK Women's and Children's Hospital (formally Kandang Kerbau Hospital) for their generous help in giving us access to many of the photographs used here, as well articles on the history of maternal care in Singapore. Vineeta Sinha of the Department of Sociology, National University of Singapore, was most helpful in information about early health care in Singapore and Hindu birth customs, and in searching out her own family photos. Huzaimah Hamzah generously lent me some of her family photos. Chan Hoi Ching also gave much assistance in the reading of Chinese texts. She has been of invaluable assistance, as was Haniah Abdul Hamid. My thanks to all of these people who generously gave their time.

Endnotes

1. Betel nut chewing is a very common practice in South and Southeast Asia, although it has largely disappeared from urban areas. It is a very important symbol of sociality. In many Southeast Asian cultures, betel nut chewing is a symbol of not only social intercourse. This is because once the betel leaf, areca nut and lime have been chewed, a person's spittle will turn bright red. This chemical reaction symbolises the processes of sexual reproduction and childbirth.
2. Spelt as 'penggalan' in Mohamed Hassan's text.
3. Lee uses the name 'Sepoy Lines', without any explanation as to where this was located. However, according to social scientists familiar with the history of what is known today as Little India, Sepoy Lines most likely would have been located there. Sepoy was the term used in India for native soldiers. Sepoy Lines most likely would have been the name of a row of houses, occupied by Indian labourers. Perhaps this row of houses had then been used to house the hospital.
4. The conditions for suitability were measured by hygiene and the number of people living in the house.
5. This information was given in the opening letter of the December 1996 hospital pamphlet called 'A Tribute to KK Hospital'. Here, the Medical Board Chairman Dr Lawrence Chan wrote: 'In 1966 KK Hospital delivered a record number of 39,835 babies and made it to the Guinness Book of Records for delivering the world's largest number of babies in a single maternity facility in a year'.

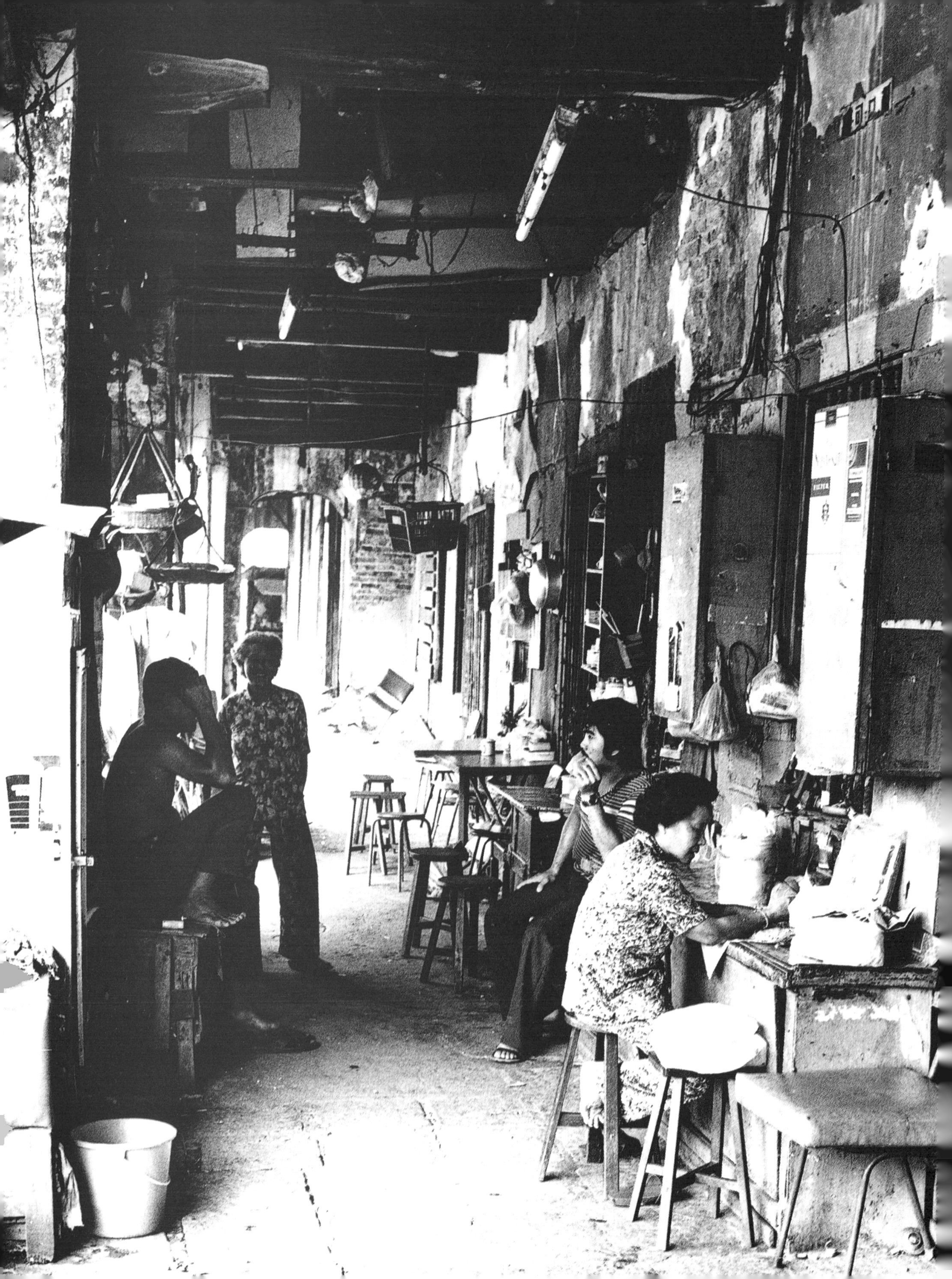

5 Erased Tropical Heritage: Residential Architecture and Environment

Chua Beng Huat

Opposite: Lounging on the *five-foot-way* of a pre-war housing in North Boat Quay, circa 1980.

The landscape of contemporary Singapore is an endless spread of high-rise buildings. Often, only the monumentality of these high-rise structures is seen, not their architectural subtleties. Furthermore, as one moves out of the business district into the public housing estates, where more than 85 percent of the population resides, the standardised high-rise blocks etch in the memory little else but homogeneity and monotony. In a brief three-and-a-half decades — less than one human generation — the entire physical environment of Singapore has been transformed. This change comes at the cost of obliterating much of the existing built-forms and the settlement patterns in order to make land available for the country's economic development and the improvement of the population's material life.

Prior to the ubiquitous use of steel, concrete and glass in high-rise structures, among the residential built-forms in Singapore were indigenous architecture with great flexibility which accommodated not only different household and economic activities but also different modes of community life. Four types of residential built-forms could be readily identified. They were the Malay house, the Chinese house found in rural areas or squatters in the urban fringe, the urban shophouse, and the bungalow of the privileged class of both colonial and subject populations.

The Malay House

The Malay house, with its distinctive feature of being built on stilts, was undoubtedly an indigenous architectural form of Southeast Asia. Similar stilt structures can still be found throughout Southeast Asia in Thailand, Laos, Myanmar and Cambodia. A common conception of stilts is that they were used to avoid flooding. This particular function of stilts is obvious if Malay houses were built above water along river banks or sea coasts. However, if this was the primary reason, the Chinese who lived side by side with the Malays would have adopted the system of stilts rather than

'Malay Houses', 1908.

build their houses squarely on the ground. Moreover, it should be noted that it was common to find the space below the raised floor boxed in by wooden curtain walls to secure more room for accommodation or storage. Also, being a well-shaded and cool place, it was a space for women to do some of the routine household chores and for children to play during the day. A more architecturally sensitive explanation for the stilts is that they served to ventilate the house, a serious concern in tropical Southeast Asia. They allowed low wind currents to pass through under the raised floor, thus cooling the house.

Indeed, the Malay house embodied a deep knowledge of the warm, humid equatorial conditions of Southeast Asia. To achieve climatic comfort, the Malay house had to be concerned with 'high temperatures, solar radiation, humidity and glare,' in addition to 'rain, floods and occasional strong winds,' especially during monsoons (Lim 1987:70). All these concerns were taken into consideration when building the house. The materials used were of low thermal capacity, radiating and retaining very little heat. Manufactured from local vegetation, they included *attap* (fronds of different palms) bamboo and wood. The high *attap* roof enabled quick water run-off on a rainy day and its wide overhangs provided the walls and interior of the house with shade from the sun. The walls were generously perforated with openings, providing cross ventilation to cool the house. Direct sunlight was minimised by the intricately-carved lattice on the walls, that allowed reflected light to illuminate the interior while keeping it cool.

The organisation of a Malay house depended very much on the wealth of the owner. A modest house would have two basic components, the *rumah ibu* or the main house, and the *dapur* or the kitchen at the back of the house. In more elaborate homes, a third component, located at the front of the house, would be found. This was the *serambi*, or the veranda. The three components might be housed under a single structure or in separate structures linked by short covered walkways. The *serambi* and *dapur* constituted two separate entrances to the house. The front entrance was generally used by men and the back by women. The arrangement thus helped to maintain the Islamic injunction against the co-presence of individuals of different gender who were not blood relatives.

A Malay village in Singapore, circa 1900.

The distribution patterns of Malay houses in a *kampung* followed a set of complex rules. A new house was built around the other existing houses rather than to accommodate traffic paths. Thus, the houses formed a cluster of free-standing structures, with as much distance from one another as possible without blocking the view from each house. This spatial and visual freedom in a *kampung* was further accentu-

A native Bungalow, circa 1900.

ated by the absence of fences around the houses, further reducing the distinction between private compound and public space.

These individual structures and the clustering of houses provided a set of public spaces within which the community life of the dwellers were routinely enacted. The open veranda at the front was the place where the men of the house met visitors, usually other male villagers. At the other end, the kitchen with its own entrance was a women's space for similar purposes. A substantial wooden platform would often be installed here, serving both as a bed space for children and a seat for the women during the day. The open spaces among the housing clusters facilitated these casual meetings as villagers went about their routines.

The Chinese *Attap* House

Migrant Chinese became the dominant population in Singapore in a brief few years after the establishment of a trading post for the East India Company in 1819 by Raffles. The first waves of immigrants tend to crowd into the urban areas designated for them by the town plan. However, by the mid-19th century, if not earlier, some had settled in rural areas, engaging in vegetable gardening and animal husbandry. They developed a housing structure using the same materials as the Malay house but injected features of the Chinese familial culture. In time, this was to become the dominant house-form for all Chinese who were not living in urban shophouses, as they were found not only in rural areas but also in squatter areas at the urban fringes.

Photographs of the early Chinese rural houses showed that *attap* was used not only for high roofs with wide overhangs, as in the Malay house, but also for the walls.

A farmer's *attap* house in the early 1900s.

The houses stood on the ground rather than on stilts. In contrast to the Malay house which emphasised depth and a narrow frontage, the Chinese house was laid out as a continuous single structure with very wide frontage but no more than two rooms deep. Houses generally faced and lined the road or the pedestrian path. An open veranda with low wooden fencing would run the entire length of this frontage. The fence clearly demarcated the private and public spaces. The owner of the house would occupy the centre of the structure and rental tenant families would live towards both ends.

The wide frontage was essential to the Chinese conception of the geometric arrangement of the home. Ideally, a Chinese house should have a symmetrical floor plan. The main entrance would be centrally placed in the wide façade and would lead directly and immediately into the ancestral hall. Facing the door would be the altar, upon which the household gods, represented either by paintings or wooden sculptures, would be placed. Photographs or tablets (or both) of ancestors would be placed to the left of the deities. Other rooms would surround the three sides of the hall, giving an overall impression of symmetry.

A view of the living room in an *attap* house along Henderson Road, circa 1950.

This ideal layout applied to all Chinese buildings. According to Kohl, who has traced the development of Chinese architecture in Malaysia and Singapore: 'satisfied with their fitness of purpose, serviceability and aesthetics, the Chinese have not altered their architectural forms since the Tang dynasty. One consequence was that the 'plan of the house and of a temple may be identical and the use of buildings may change from temple to home or school quite easily' (Kohl 1984:21). This flexibility was very evident in the Singaporean Chinese village. For example, the walls of the wide front could be removed to form a shop front, or the internal light partitions rearranged to become a community centre. Most Chinese in rural or squatter areas would have liked their house to approximate the ideal model if financial circumstances of the family allowed for it.

Only a minority of the *attap* houses in a Chinese village could in reality achieve such a configuration. The majority of the village population lived on rented residential premises, which tended to consist of only one sitting room with one or, at most, two bedrooms and a small kitchen; the kitchen could be found either in front, at the rear or even

Top: Light partitions of the Chinese village might be arranged to form a communal area, as seen here in this 1973 picture taken in Surin Avenue.

Above: Businesses such as provision shops (photographed here in the 1960s) were a common feature of the Chinese village.

to the side of the other rooms. Most of these premises were part of a larger structure built for the purpose of renting and thus subdivided to accommodate several tenants. The structures had low ceilings, very poor lighting and ventilation and often no windows in some of the rooms. The main, if not the only, source of light and ventilation would be the main door. Hence it was common to find an oil lamp lit within the home throughout the day. These less than desirable rental premises are mostly erased in the contemporary nostalgia for the *kampung* (Chua 1995).

In contrast to the Malay *kampung*, one's impression of a Chinese village was that it was socially less open, with each household jealously and consciously marking the limits of their properties. In a typical village layout, houses formed a continuous façade along the relatively well-defined main roads and unpaved pedestrian tracks. More commercial activities were evident compared to the Malay *kampungs*, as shops selling groceries such as dried provisions and Chinese herbs were interspersed with homes along the main road of the village. Beyond the main road, a network of unpaved tracks spread out; each track would have, in turn, its own branches which were extremely narrow, often mere gaps between adjacent houses. One such track might run the length of several houses and end abruptly, or lead to an unkempt open clearing surrounded by houses facing the open space. The overall impression of the Chinese village relative to a Malay *kampung* would be higher density and more congestion.

With a more pronounced sense of privacy, the social spaces for men in the village tended to be away from homes. Popular social spaces for Chinese men included benches set up in front of the village shops where they could sit collectively, and village temple halls where there was a continual supply of Chinese tea. The premier social institution was the local coffeeshop, or the *kopitiam*.

Like the open hall, the *kopitiam* had a wide open shop-front, with tables and chairs spilling beyond the sheltered premises. In the days when unemployment was high, the *kopitiam* was seldom without several males of different ages, huddled in groups or scattered at different tables. Idle young boys would regularly sit alone at a table, unable to join in the adults' conversation, but being there was all that mattered since this idling was a rite of passage into the adult world. On the other hand, cultural practices dictated that women stayed close to home. Hence, their socialising patterns were no different from the Malay women in their *kampungs*.

The Urban Shophouse

Bricks were imported from Penang only a few years after the British trading post was established in Singapore. Consequently, brick houses prevailed in city districts that were designated to different immigrant communities. With the exception of houses for the European population, almost all other brick houses in these designated areas were terraced shophouses.

Judging from this picture, circa 1960, the coffeehouse of the past had a majority of male patrons.

The earliest shophouses were typically two-storey brick buildings with one or two windows on the second storey. They were relatively low and squat in proportion and devoid of ornamentation on the façade. Units of shophouses were built contiguously and collectively formed blocks of houses. After 1910, shophouses are separated by streets and also by back lanes (Ho and Lim 1992). The houses could be quite deep in dimension, belying the generally narrow frontage. Stylistically, they were highly standardised: continuous clay-tiled roofs and colonnaded *five-foot-ways*, with units separated by party walls. As a consequence of this arrangement, the only source of light for the intermediate units were from the openings — such as the high windows and main door — in the façade and the back doors. Such limited sources of light, accentuated by the depth of the house, made the interior rather dark. Consequently, in better appointed shophouses, airwells were constructed in the middle of the houses to provide both ventilation and light. The name 'shophouse' might have been derived from the very first usage of such buildings, but did not reflect the range of uses to which the houses were put.

The best illustrations of their early usage as shophouses could be drawn from Boat Quay, the west bank of the mouth of the Singapore River. Here shophouses were used as offices-cum-warehouses by Chinese commodity traders from early 19th century until 1977. At the height of the commodity trade, the river mouth was constantly grid-locked with bumboats. Bare-chested coolies could be seen, laden with heavy bags or bales of imported commodities on their backs, walking up gangplanks

Top: North Boat Quay in the 1970s.

Above: A warehouse along North Boat Quay in 1986.

which sank and heaved with the weight.

In 1977, a ten-year environment project to clean up the river was initiated. The Chinese bumboats, which were used to transport cargo from steamers to quayside warehouses, were relocated to anchorage points at the west coast. The displacement of bumboats from the Singapore River was aided by the introduction of containerisation in the transportation of goods, which eliminated the need to pack commodities in bags, thus eliminating the need for transhipment and storage. This led to the decline in the importance of all the quays and offices-cum-warehouses along the Singapore River.

Away from the riverside, shophouses were also used as shops-cum-residences. In spatial layout, the demands of shops and warehouses were not dissimilar; both essentially required an empty space with an open front, kept empty in the case of warehouses while organised by display counters in the case of shops. In the latter case, the ground floor was used as a shop and the upper floors as residence for the family. Colourful clothing, hung outside upper-floor windows to dry on bamboo sticks, must easily be among the most photographed pictures of Singapore's Chinatown. The Chinese involved in different petty trades — barbers, Chinese letter-writers and fortune tellers — who carried on their business on the colonnaded *five-foot-ways* and roadsides were also popular subjects for photography. There were no house-forms in Chinatown other than shophouses until the early 1970s, when the monumental People's Park complex was built.

As residential spaces, shophouses catered to the wealthiest and the poorest of the Chinese immigrant population in Singapore, often in fairly close proximity to each other. An illustrative case was that of Tanjong Pagar at the turn of the 19th century. At the time, Neil Road was occupied by some of the wealthier and more influential members of the Chinese community. Among them was Justice of Peace, Ng Sing Phang, a leader in the Cantonese community and member of the Chamber of Commerce and the Chinese Advisory Board. According to his son, Ng 'didn't feel that Purvis Street off Beach Road [a congested city centre at that time] was such a good place to bring us [the children] up. In order to have a more comfortable place to stay, he bought over the shophouse at 170 Neil Road which was at that time half-completed. At that time, Neil Road was considered a very good residential area' (Lim and Chua 1989:89).

Being part of the officially designated area for the Chinese, Tanjong Pagar was the place where government licensed clearing-houses for new arrivals from China were located. After the development of the New Harbour and the opening of the Suez Canal in the 1860s, the Chinese population expanded by four times between 1891 and 1931 (Chew 1989:21). Thus, several hundred meters away from Ng's house, one could find coolie houses which accommodated in cubicles single, poverty-stricken coal carriers who worked at the harbour, rickshaw pullers and other members of the lowest rung of the Chinese population. Some of them were opium addicts.

While clearing-houses were themselves temporary lodgings for new arrivals, other shophouses in the area were converted into permanent coolie-houses. These *coolie keng*, in Hokkien, were usually rented by floor spaces and bed spaces, such as 'bunks in passageways, tiered bed-lofts, sleeping shelves under or over staircases, sleeping arrangements in *five-foot-ways*, kitchens and backyards' (Chew 1989:28). Compared

This shophouse (photographed in 1909) was used as a residence, probably for a Chinese family judging from the characters on each side of the entrance.

Old coolies, now too weak to work, in a clearing-house at Pagoda Street, circa 1980.

to the number of arrivals, the number of houses erected was very limited, leading inevitably to overcrowding. The worst health and hygiene conditions were found on these premises. For example, there were high incidences of dysentery which could spread very quickly in the congested lodges.

The overcrowded conditions within the houses meant that many of the household activities unavoidably spilled onto the *five-foot-ways* and the streets. These, combined with the sights and smells of commercial activities including the ever-present food vendors created a very rich visual and sensual street scene. It was indeed a veritable image of the 'exotic' Orient to the European visitors (Savage 1992).

For most of Chinatown's residents, however, the overcrowding, poor public hygiene and absence of modern sanitary conveniences made Chinatown a place to escape from rather than savoured. The resettlement of the densely populated area started with the initiation of the national public housing programme at the beginning of the 1960s. By the time of the 1980 national population census, Chinatown had changed from being among the most densely populated areas in the country to among the most sparsely populated, making room for subsequent gentrification and recommercialisation.

Bottom Left: An old-style barber at 'five-footway', North Boat Quay, taken in 1986.

Bottom Right: Chinatown street scene, circa 1970.

Erased Tropical Heritage: Residential Architecture and Environment

The back streets of Chinatown, circa 1970.

The Bungalow[1]

The most impressive houses, in terms of proportion, were the bungalows built initially by members of the European community and later by rich Chinese and Arabs. With the exception of the earliest houses built before 1820, which used timber and other local materials, European bungalows were built with bricks imported from Penang and Malacca.

Bungalow as a house structure was brought to Singapore by the British colonial regime from India. The term 'bungalow' originated in Bengal and was a derivative of the native term *bungla* or *bungala* — a simple, single-storey mud-walled structure raised slightly off the ground on a hard core of broken bricks and rubble, and with a veranda that ran around the entire house. When transposed to Singapore, the timber floor was raised on timber posts or brick piers and the brick walls had arched openings to ventilate the underside of the raised floor, a style adopted from Malay houses. The height of the posts or piers and the walls might give the impression that the building was a two-storey rather than a single-storey building. Over time, the European residence evolved into either a two-storey building or a single-storey bungalow with features best described by an observer in the mid-1800s:

> Bungalows, a term often applied to any style of dwelling-house in the East, are…only of one storey, elevated some five or six feet from the ground upon arched masonry…The walls from the flooring to the roof are seldom less

than 15 feet high, which give a lofty ceiling to the apartments and the roof is covered with tiles. The most striking feature of these buildings, however, is the broad veranda which runs right round the house and about 8 to 10 feet in width, resting on the plinths of the pillars that, extending upwards in round columns with neatly moulded capitals, support the continuation of the roof which projects some 4 feet beyond the pillars, forming deep overhanging eaves. On the veranda, which is surrounded by a neat railing, all the doors of the bungalow open, and as these also serve the purpose of windows, they are pretty numerous; they are in two halves, opening down the centre like cottage doors at home [Britain], with the lower panels plain and the two upper ones fitted with venetian to open or close at pleasure. From the centre of the buildings in front, a portico projects some 25 or 30 feet, and generally about 25 feet broad, covering the carriage way and a broad flight of stone steps leading from the ground to the veranda.[2]

As residence of the colonial ruling class, the scale and location of these European bungalows reflected colonial English-White supremacy. In contrast to the small area, absence of air and light and overcrowded conditions in the urban shophouses and squatter attap dwellings, European bungalows were edifices of exclusivity to encode the superiority of its residents. As Edwards (1992:34) had written,

> Political dominance and high social status were symbolically encoded in size and the very architectural style of the house, namely Palladian and at a latter age, High Victorian. Of crucial symbolic value was the setting itself. Houses were generally set on high ground as much for visual and aesthetic reasons as for health considerations. Part of the aesthetic imagery was the picturesque manner in which the garden was arranged: flower beds with imported English species, sweeping areas of lawn, informal arrangement of trees and shrubs. The larger the garden, the wider and deeper it was, the greater the air of exclusivity or privacy and the greater the public impression.

Most of the 19th-century houses are no longer in existence. Contemporary Singaporeans will recognise the above descriptions as approximating those of the 'black-and-white' bungalows, which were built in the 1920s and can still be found in some areas. Although two-storey in height, they are in fact bungalows because the ground floor is open and contains only the staircase to the upper floor. All the important rooms — the drawing, the reception and the dinning rooms — were on the upper floor, or the main floor that is surrounded by a continuous veranda along the front and sides; individual verandas to bedrooms and the dining room are at the rear. The kitchen is located in an outhouse.

In contrast to the private European houses, the 'black-and-white' bungalows were built by the colonial government for its officers and may, for this reason, be saved from demolition. Whereas large privately-owned landed houses are constantly being demolished to make way for high-rise buildings which increase property value and maximise land usage, some 'black-and-white' bungalows remain in government holding and are rented to high-income individuals. In view of the increased awareness of the need to conserve local heritage, these remaining buildings may yet be saved.

George Mansfield 's bungalow at Labrador Park, built in 1881.

Conclusion

Historically, the four types of house structures examined above were found in geographically separate areas on the island, reflecting both the ethnic and class compositions of the population. A cross-sectional view of the relative positions of these house-forms and their communities on the eve of political independence and urban transformation might have looked like this: moving inland from the commercial-administrative area on the waterfront and veering right would be Orchard Road, then a quiet commercial area catering to the European community living in its vicinity. It was here that the European bungalows in their isolated splendour were found. Taking a more central direction from the waterfront would be the congested shophouses of Chinatown. At one of the edges of Chinatown is the General Hospital, itself flanked by the Tiong Bahru low-rise housing estate, built for low ranking non-White civil servants. This housing estate signalled the limit of the city, beyond that stood the Chinese squatters of Bukit Ho Swee. The class segregation internal to the Chinese community then were coterminous with geographical segregation: from poor Chinese in Chinatown to relatively well-off Chinese in Tiong Bahru to poor Chinese again in squatters of impermanent housing. The Malay *kampungs* were not to be found in the contiguous areas of the city but were located near both the east and the west coasts of the island.

Of the four types of houses examined, the Malay and Chinese houses suffered the worst fate in the face of rapid urbanisation. Built of indigenous materials, which were considered impermanent because of the need for periodic replacement, they were the first to be demolished in the wake of the national public housing programme. To avoid massive displacement of families, public housing estates were generally built on urban fringes and semi-rural areas in the early years of the programme. The Malay *kampungs* and the Chinese squatters found in these areas were consequently the first to be affected by resettlement. Perhaps the most dramatic icon of the resettlement process was the Chinese *attap* village of Bukit Ho Swee being razed to the ground in 1961. Within a short span of three years, one of the earliest public housing estates was erected on the site of the fire by the newly constituted public housing authority, the Housing and Development Board. No *attap* buildings now remain in modern Singapore.

Of the two remaining house types, a few 'black-and-white' bungalows remain and are likely to be conserved by the government. The shophouses, on the other hand, have greatly appreciated in value as a result of the government's initiative to conserve whole areas in which such structures predominate. In the historical ethnic areas of Chinatown, Little India and Kampong Glam, significant quantum of shophouses are being designated for conservation of the architectural heritage. They are being refurbished and put to new commercial uses. Gone are the old ways of living. These shophouses are resuscitated to life by the entertainment industry, some of them transformed into theme parks for locals and tourists. However, with the exception of the quayside units, their commercial success hangs in the balance.

Endnotes

1. The details for this section are drawn from Lee Kip Lin's excellently illustrated and documented book, *The Singapore House: 1819-1942*.
2. From John Cameron, *Our Tropical Possessions in Malayan India*, quoted in Lee Kip Lin (1988:38,42).

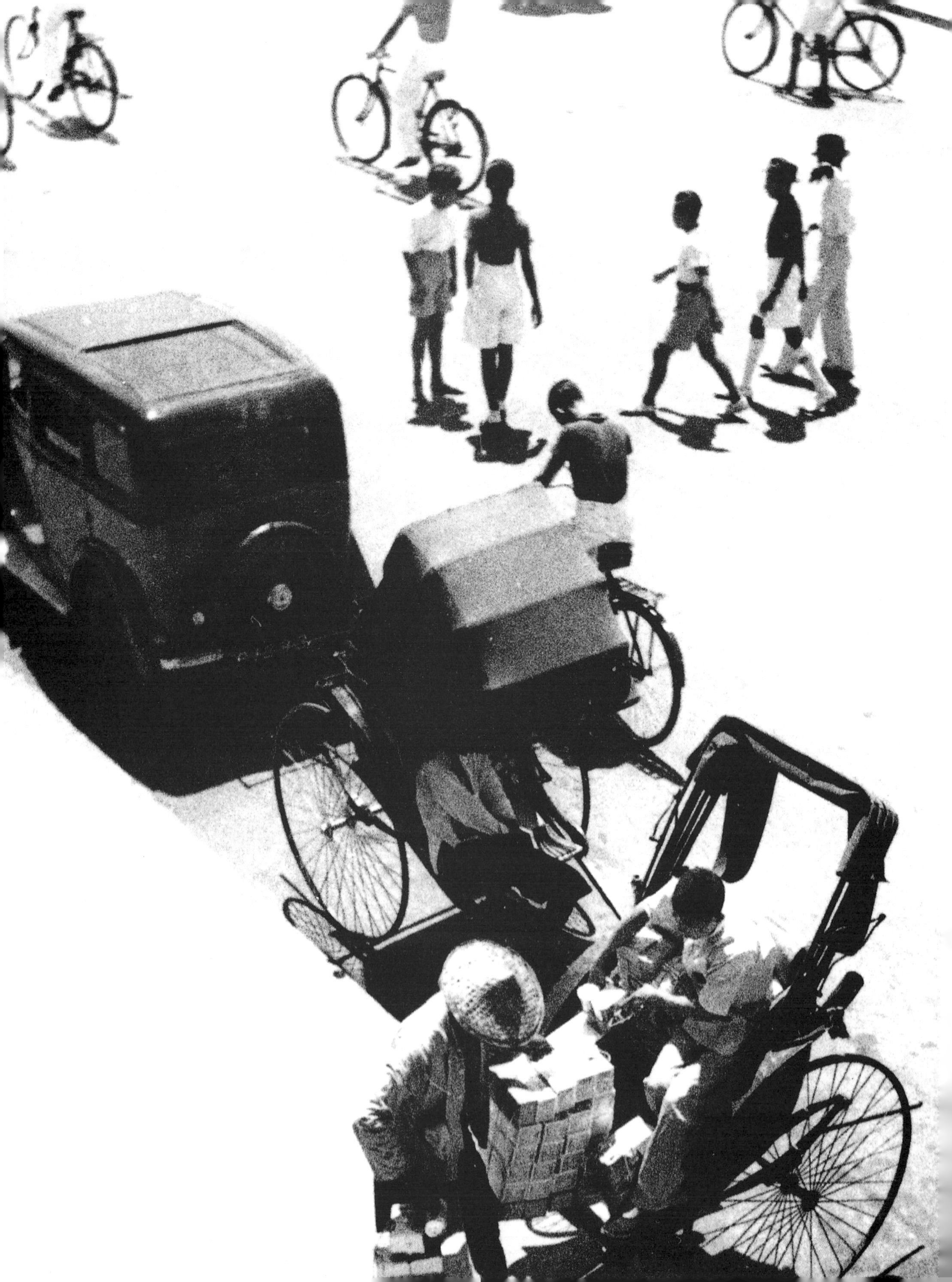

6 Gathering Speed: Transport and the Pace of Life

Roxana Waterson

Opposite: This view from a window, taken in 1945 just after the end of the Japanese Occupation, captured some of the last rickshaws still operating in Singapore by that time. Rickshaws were banned in 1947 on humanitarian grounds.

Singapore has always turned towards the sea, and until recently, it was by sea that travellers arrived here. Many early writers recall the beauty of their first sight of Singapore harbour, thronged with ships of all sizes, origins and varieties. In the words of a mid-19th century traveller, one could see 'every species of craft and floating machine invented since the days of Noah' (Yvan 1855:126). A newly arrived vessel would quickly be surrounded by a swarm of *sampans* bearing tropical fruits, corals, shells, monkeys or exotic birds while Malay boys in dugout canoes would dive for coins thrown by the passengers, or fetch up coral or seaweed from the bottom for a few cents.[1] The ceaseless activity of the harbour provided a foretaste of the vibrant bustle of the town: 'There is never a time when a ship is not sliding in from the ocean or going to the waves again. The rattle of anchor chains makes incessant music' (Collins 1923:31).

A Maritime City

In the 1820s, the first ships to arrive in large numbers at Raffles's new duty-free port were the junks from south China, which were to account for half of all trade during the 19th century. This fleet made the journey annually and stayed in the Singapore harbour from December to June. 'Throughout that period, boats filled with Chinese were continually passing to and fro among the shipping, giving the [sea] roads the appearance of a floating fair' (Earl [1837] 1971:365). On arrival, the decks would be crowded with immigrants who would be landed in large cargo boats, 50 or 60 persons at a time. Meanwhile, roofs would be erected over the decks of the junks, and the goods brought from China were laid out for sale. The second big trading fleet to call annually at Singapore were the Bugis *prahu*s from Sulawesi. They would come in September, laden with products collected from the islands all over eastern Indonesia, and stay till November. Their arrival was eagerly watched for by the firms along

Above: Bugis *pallari* being towed from the eastern anchorage to the Singapore harbour, circa 1870. Bugis trading vessels from South Sulawesi would arrive at Singapore in the hundreds between September and November, bringing produce from the islands of eastern Indonesia and returning home with the northeast monsoon.

the waterfront on Collyer Quay, each of which kept a telescope on the veranda. E. A. Brown, who came to Singapore in 1901, recalled in his book, *Indiscreet Memories*, 'a forest of sail appearing over the horizon away towards Rhio . . . until as far as the eye could see, there seemed to be nothing but masts and sails…I have seen as many as three hundred boats…and when they anchored off Tanjong Rhu and Clyde Terrace, the harbour presented a most animated appearance…Nowhere else in these eastern waters at that time was there such a centre of trade and activity' (1935:32).

The pace of sea travel seems unthinkably tedious in our age of jets. In the 1820s, if one sent a letter to England, to receive an answer within ten months was considered 'very punctual' (Makepeace *et al.* 1921:2:107). Steam was to change that. The Peninsular and Oriental Steam Navigation Company, founded in 1837, extended its operations to Singapore and Hong Kong in 1845. Its first mail service paddle steamer, the *Lady Mary Wood*, arrived here in August of that year after a voyage from London of only 41 days. With the opening of the Suez Canal in 1869, the length of the voyage from Europe was dramatically reduced, and the number of ships coming to Singapore greatly increased.

Although the pace of life in those days may strike us now as impossibly slow, it was

Right: The Straits Steamship 'Rasa,' 1933. The Straits Steamship Company, founded in 1890, had its offices at Raffles Quay on the corner of Telegraph Street, and provided a mail service to remote outposts up and down the Malay Peninsula.

not perceived that way at the time. On the contrary, it seemed to contemporaries that Singapore was always in a hurry, a place where 'the traveller and his kind are the only idlers' (Swettenham [1906] 1948:11). Looking back from the vantage point of the 1920s, Makepeace observed that the opening of the Canal and the development of steam navigation and telegraph had effected 'a complete revolution in Singapore trade and social life' by making it less remote from Europe. Previously, everyone in the European community knew one another and had developed their own local habits; afterwards, new social barriers were raised, 'coteries and cliques became the order of the day' and 'life here began to approximate more and more to English life, until today Singapore resembles nothing so much as an English provincial town where commerce is the principle interest' (Makepeace *et al.* 1921:516).

Early Conveyances

The person arriving by ship would reach the quay by means of one of the hundreds of lighter boats that plied the harbour, propelled by rowers standing up and facing the direction they were going, with their oars crossed in front of them.[2] After alighting, the newcomer might find that 'to the unaccustomed eye, the vehicles to be met with… are almost as strange as the boats in the harbour' (Swettenham [1906] 1948:10). The main form of public transport in the early days was the palankeen carriage or gharry, a box-shaped version of a hackney carriage, drawn by ponies brought from Java or Sumatra. These were built locally, sometimes lacking a driver's seat, and the practice was for the (usually Indian or Malay) syce or groom to run at the horse's head.[3] Before there was any effective street lighting, the syces would carry torches at night. For private use, four-wheeled open carriages and gigs, imported from India, were preferred. For a long time, the roads in Singapore were rather bad and public conveyances remained limited. In 1840, according to the journal kept in that year by Major James Low, a magistrate in the Straits Settlements Civil Service, the two major roads were those leading to Bukit Timah and Serangoon, with three others leading off into the country. Outlying areas were still heavily forested and presented a certain risk of attack by tigers. The canals or ditches bordering the roads, Low remarked, were also something of a hazard, thus 'some foresight and nerve are required in driving the generally badly broken-in ponies' (cited in Buckley [1902] 1984:363).

But the Europeans were undaunted. It was the fashion at that time to ride or drive in the cool of the afternoon, from around five to half past six, finishing with a few turns on the Esplanade. Horses were later imported from Australia and India and

Some Indian immigrants specialised in keeping cattle and selling dairy products; this buffalo-drawn milk cart was photographed in 1942.

The Singapore Fire Brigade, founded in 1888 and photographed here around 1890, was horse-drawn until 1912.

grand carriages continued to be used by the wealthy of all ethnic communities until they were displaced by motor cars in the 1920s. At the turn of the century, riding remained a popular sport with Europeans, who found the still unmetalled roads like Holland Road, Ayer Rajah Road and Buona Vista Road 'splendid places for a good gallop in the early morning' (Brown 1935:5).

For the transport of goods and all kinds of heavy work, buffaloes and oxen were widely used, as place names like 'Kreta Ayer' (water cart), 'Kandang Kerbau' (buffalo stall) and 'Buffalo Road,' remind us. Brought in from Malacca, Penang and India, they could be seen transporting goods from the wharves to the town; carrying water for street cleaning and household use; pulling conservancy carts for collection of refuse; hauling construction materials; levelling the grass on the Padang by pulling a large metal roller across it; and even for transporting passengers in the rural areas. Buffaloes could do more work than horses in the tropical climate, and thus continued to be used at the wharves in the 1920s. Horse-drawn coaches, however, were used in the earliest postal service, which started deliveries within the town from 1867; and around the turn of the century, large department stores like Robinson's and John Little's made their deliveries by horse and van

Train at Woodlands Station, 1910. Prior to 1923 when the causeway linking Singapore to the Malay Peninsula was completed, passengers would cross from Singapore to Johor by ferry boat.

to the Tanglin neighbourhood, where many of their European customers lived (Brown 1935:5). The first fire brigade was also horse-drawn, from 1888 until 1912.

The era of the train reached Singapore in 1903, with the opening of a line from Bukit Timah Station to Tank Road Station. Construction had been long considered but delayed due to a fall in trade revenues.[4] A few years later, a line was added from Tank Road to Pasir Panjang. There were stations at Woodlands (where one crossed to and from Johor by ferry boat), Bukit Panjang, Bukit Timah, Cluny Road and Newton. In 1918, the line was sold to the Federated Malay States Railway, and with the completion of the causeway between Woodlands and Johor in 1923, it became fully integrated with the main Malay rail system.

Class Distinctions in a Colonial Society

In the hierarchically divided society of colonial Singapore, transport provided a highly visible means of making statements about one's social status. For a long time, the majority of the populace remained pedestrian, since gharries were expensive and no other form of public transport was available. European ideas about the modes of transport most suitable for themselves shifted over time, evident in the history of the bicycle. The first pioneers were Mr T. S. Thomson and his friend, Mr Robert Jamie, a chemist at John Little's, who had ordered two three-wheelers from London after seeing one at the Great Exhibition in 1851. 'About 1866 or 1867, it was related in town one morning that Mr T. S. Thomson had gone on a sort of velocipede to the

First imported by the British as a novelty, the bicycle was soon adopted by local people who saw its practical advantages. This undated photograph of two Malays with their bicycles is to be found in sequence with some of the earliest photographs in the National Archives' collection, dating from the 1880s. The rather tight cut of the Norfolk jacket and knickerbockers (fashionable in England at that time, but given a looser cut in the 1890s to suit the needs of golfers), and the bicycle itself, which appears to be a 'Referee' Safety model, first manufactured around 1888 (illustrated in Sharp 1896:283), strongly suggest a date in the 1880s or early 1890s.

bungalow at Seletar, nine miles, and back again before breakfast'.[5] The British initially seemed to view cycling only as a sport. By 1901, however, a Cycling Club emerged and flourished for a while; its members going out on cycling picnics at weekends. Others were not slow to see the practical possibilities of the bicycle. Penny-farthings soon followed the tricycle and Makepeace *et al.* recalled that 'several Chinese blacksmiths used them to go to their work at Tanjong Pagar Docks from the town'(1921:511).[6]

Complaints in the newspaper about disorderly and congested traffic were frequent. By the 1880s, a member of the legislative council was adding a new protest against 'the noiseless but deadly bicycle.'[7] Once its novelty had worn off, it seems that Europeans began to find the bicycle beneath their dignity. When George Peet first came to Singapore as a junior reporter for the Straits Times in 1923, his seniors warned him off the idea of riding a bike to work; it would not do for a member of the European staff to be seen parking his bike alongside those of the Chinese clerks and Indian printers. By that time, an unspoken taboo had developed against the bicycle; the European Cycling Club was just a memory and the only non-Asian person who could afford the eccentricity of being seen on a bicycle was the Bishop.

Opinions also changed about the rickshaw. Singapore received its first consignment of rickshaws from Shanghai in 1880 but 'it was long before it was considered the proper thing for Europeans to ride in them' (Makepeace *et al.* 1921:523).[8] They were welcomed as a cheap, door-to-door form of transport by the rest of the population. Their introduction caused a strike by gharry-drivers the following year in 1881 but by 1910, the gharries had virtually died out in the face of this new competition and the rickshaw had become the main means of travel over short distances. Recalling the rickshaw strike of 1901, Brown wrote, '75 percent of the Europeans used rickshaws then to get back and forth to office, and for the Eurasians and other portions of the populace, they were almost the only means of transport' (1935:71). A few gharries survived into the 1920s, but by that time their use was only favoured by the ladies of very conservative Indian, Chinese or Malay families who would go out without being seen by pulling up the side shutters to close the windows (Peet 1985:78). Another volume of reminiscences from the 1920s mentioned that 'walking is almost taboo' and that 'if one has no car, one travels by rickshaw if no friend is able to lend a car' (Sidney 1926:19).

The British were divided about the rickshaw. It was technologically an improvement over the sedan chair, but the life of a rickshaw-puller was a tragically hard one.[9] The chief reason for this was that the pullers very rarely owned their own rickshaws but rented them from small businessmen or *towkays*, who usually originated from the same region or dialect group as the pullers. In the 20th century, the majority were Hengwah, Hockchia or Hokkien, though previously some owners were Cantonese. The owners profited far more than the pullers, and a series of strikes by rickshaw-

'Jinricksha Station, Singapore,' circa 1905. Rickshaw pulling, although a hazardous and exhausting occupation, was by the turn of the century providing an economic niche for thousands of unskilled immigrants from southern China, and was the main means of transport around the city for ordinary people.

'How would this do instead of electric cars in Glasgow?' reads the comment inscribed on this postcard of 1904. Pictures of this period record the enormous social distance that obtained between the rickshaw puller and his passengers, though habituation soon overcame the initial unease which Europeans often felt about this mode of transport.

pullers from 1887 to 1938, in which the authorities offered them little support, were not enough to change conditions significantly. By 1900, the demand for labour was high and *towkays* often employed boys as young as 12, who were too young to handle the physical demands of the job. The authorities tried to regulate the trade by making 'weakness' in a rickshaw coolie a chargeable offence, as was being 'ragged and dirty.' Much was made of the perceived moral danger of the rickshaw coolie as an opium addict — a hypocritical judgement in light of the extent to which Singapore's revenues during the 19th century depended on profits from opium. Many writers noted how their initial discomfort at riding in a rickshaw soon wore off as they began to take it for granted, and photographs of this period almost painfully record the exaggerated social distance that obtained between the heavily-dressed European passenger and her or his half-naked puller.

In 1913, the Straits Times mounted a press campaign against what it called 'the deadliest occupation in the East, the most degrading for human beings to pursue,' but these humanitarian concerns were countered by others, including representatives of the Chinese community, on the grounds that to ban them would deprive people of employment. In spite of its hardships, the job had become a niche for thousands of unskilled immigrants from South China, and most inhabitants of the city

Those who could afford it often kept their own rickshaw and hired a puller by the month. This photograph (taken 1919), and presented to the National Archives by Lionel H. Cutts, shows two boys in a rickshaw (which was doubtless used to ferry them to school) at their house in Gilstead Road.

relied on them for getting around. Some people even kept their own rickshaws. Reese observed that 'many residents own their own rickshaw and hire the man by the month' (1919:102).

Once motor traffic increased, the rickshaw-puller's job became more hazardous and accidents were common in spite of the skill with which they learned to handle the shafts. Sidney recorded that the rickshaw-pullers wore differently shaped hats according to their clan or dialect group and generally went barefoot and dressed only in shorts, with sometimes a short coat: 'As they dash past, collisions appear to be inevitable, but they manoeuvre their rickshaws with great care, and owing to the fact that the Chinese are so used to these vehicles, they will avoid a collision with almost miraculous ease. When a person is in the way, the puller calls out in a nasal high-pitched voice, and the person in the way, without looking round, seems to know what to do and there is no collision' (1926:27). The British authorities, however, increasingly wished for rickshaws to be removed from the roads in favour of motor traffic and so the number of rickshaws began to decline from 10,000 in 1923 to 4,000 by 1941. The last and longest strike of the rickshaw-pullers lasted for five weeks in October and November of 1938, when they demanded lower rates of hire from the owners, but during this period, there was a sharp increase in the number of bicycles registered, which suggests that the public were finding ways around their dependence on the rickshaw. The mass of the Chinese public failed to support the pullers; many were made destitute by the strike and had to accept Government offers of repatriation (Warren 1986:123). The end came during the Japanese Occupation, when

Trolleybuses at the junction of High Street and New Bridge Road, circa 1930. By this date, Singapore boasted 'the largest trolleybus system in the world'. Fares were set at 10 cents per mile for First Class and five cents for Second Class, but other local forms of transport such as rickshaws and 'mosquito buses' were always cheaper.

trishaws were introduced as a replacement. One risked humiliation then when travelling by rickshaw, since the Japanese were fond of stopping them, and, in an 'anti-imperial' gesture, obliging the passenger and puller to change places.

Trams and Trolleybuses

Another vehicle long vanished from the Singapore scene is the tram. The Singapore Tramways Company offered the first regular tram service from Tanjong Pagar Dock to Johnston's Pier in May 1886, with 14 steam tram engines. Lines were added down South and North Bridge Roads to Crawford Street, and along Serangoon Road to the Pauper Hospital at Lavender Street, and along Telok Belangah Road to Borneo Wharf. The trams' relatively high fares, however, could never compete with rickshaws and bullock-carts for cheapness and convenience, and the expenses of capital investment, as well as the import of fuel and machinery, and the need to satisfy shareholders caused the enterprise to fail after only three years. The tramway was bought over very cheaply at auction by the Tanjong Pagar Dock Co., and even this had to close by 1894. A decade later, when England was in a 'ferment of tramway construction,' an electric line on the same routes was opened, with extensions to Tank Road,

Paya Lebar and Geylang, but this too was to be a short-lived experiment, surviving only from 1905 to 1927. Fares were extraordinarily high compared to other available modes of transport, and even compared to fares in England at the time, especially given the fact that incomes in Singapore were much lower (York and Phillips 1996:15). Bullock-cart owners were quick to appreciate that they could get a smoother ride by going along the tracks, and carts with a gauge of one metre suddenly appeared, trundling along in front of infuriated tram drivers and refusing to get out of the way (York and Phillips 1996:12). There was violent action from rickshaw-pullers, too, who frequently obstructed the lines with stones or blocks of wood, but could rarely be caught. On their behalf, the Chinese Guilds also tried to organise a boycott (York and Phillips 1996:28). The trams, with 'their rattle and warning bell,' were so noisy that the residents of Orchard Road refused to have a tramway built on their street, so for a while in 1906, a double-decker motor omnibus plied up and down Orchard Road (Sidney 1926:37). This venture, however, expired when the owner ran out of spare parts. In 1926, Singapore Electric Tramways Ltd. became the Singapore Traction Company (STC), and switched to trolleybuses, rail-less but with an overhead cable. A white line was painted on the road to help the driver stay underneath the overhead wires. Trolleybuses continued to run until December 1962. The trolleybuses, too, faced

The seven-seater 'mosquito bus' was built on a large motor car chassis, and became a common feature of Singapore traffic from around 1930. They darted around at a high speed, picking up and setting down passengers all along their routes in fierce competition with the trolleybuses.

fierce competition — this time from the small motor buses (mostly Chinese owned) which by the 1930s had become known by the distinctive nickname of 'mosquito buses.'

This ingenious local development appeared soon after World War I, and by 1927, there were 456 of them in operation. They consisted of a seven-seater timber body, open at the rear and built on to an American large car chassis — the favourite being the Ford model T. According to York and Phillips, some former rickshaw men found a far preferable livelihood driving these buses, which undercut the trolleybuses by plying along their busy routes picking up passengers for a three-cent fare (1996:46). They dodged recklessly in and out of the traffic at high speeds, their relentlessly honking adding to the medley of noises on the street. They were also useful in outlying areas not reached by official public transport. These local enterprises, which were so cheap and convenient, gathered far more local support than the official British-run transport system. Although the Singapore Traction Company (STC) at that time had the largest trolleybus system in the world, it was difficult for them to compete with the mosquito buses because they could not put their motor buses on the same routes without depriving the trolleybuses of trade even further. The police were obliged to act firmly in the face of the number of accidents caused by mosquito buses. Licensing laws were tightened in 1933, restricting their numbers and the routes they could run. This led to the formation of 12 well-regulated Chinese bus companies, which soon moved on to larger buses, mainly serving outlying districts.[10] STC did its best to assuage public dissatisfaction with the removal of unlicensed mosquito buses, by expanding its services with the addition of 55 new motor buses. If the mosquito bus has vanished from the Singapore scene, its descendants — the Thai *tuk-tuks*, Indonesian *bemos* and Philippine *jeepneys* — remain a characteristic element of traffic in other Southeast Asian cities today.[11]

Perhaps the stormiest moment in the history of Singapore transport came in the 1950s, when bus workers were among the most politicised members of a population wherein the tide of anti-colonial feeling was by then reaching its height. In February 1955, the Singapore Bus Workers' Union (SBWU) was formed, its members including 250 workers from the Hock Lee Bus Company. Hock Lee retaliated by starting its own union. The company found 200 men who were redundant and paid them a retainer so that they could be used to run the buses 'in case of trouble.' By April, this led to picketing of the company garages in Alexandra Road and a prolonged strike which was supported by a wave of other strikes, extending to the docks. A remarkable feature of these events was the support offered to the strikers by radical high school students, who gave donations as well as entertaining those on the picket lines with dancing and the singing of inflammatory songs.[12] Clashes with the police culminated in a night of riot on May 12 which left four people dead (see Chapter 10). Settlement followed rapidly, but further strikes were called in August and September (this time including the employees of the British-owned Singapore Traction Company, who demanded higher wages even though they were still in the middle of a two-year wage agreement which had been made the previous year). In November, the SBWU brought all 12 remaining bus companies out on strike together, bringing public transport to a standstill (Clutterbuck 1973:108-11; York and Phillips 1996:93-105). One after-effect of the strike was the end to the Traction Company's monopoly on city routes. The Chinese bus companies settled with the workers more promptly (by December), and there was public pressure for these companies to be allowed to take over the Traction Company's services. This also led to the Hawkins Report of 1956 on public transport, which recommended the setting up of a single Licensing Authority for bus services as a way to increase efficiency.

The Automobile Arrives

Alongside the medley of public transport vehicles, with their chequered histories,

Bottom Left: Charles Burton Buckley, who became Singapore's first car owner in 1896, with his Benz automobile, nicknamed 'the coffee machine.'

Bottom Right: By 1911, the number of cars on the roads required the setting up of a new Traffic Police Department. This Sikh traffic policeman, with his distinctive rattan 'wings', was photographed at work in the 1930s.

the motor car began its inexorable rise to dominance. In 1896, Charles Burton Buckley, a well-known local figure and author of *An Anecdotal History of Old Times in Singapore*, became the first car owner in Singapore. His motor car, a 4.5 horsepower Benz Victoria which he nicknamed 'the coffee machine,' had to be started by putting a teaspoonful of petrol in the carburetor and lighting it with a match to warm it up, and then hand-turning a large flywheel at the rear. Its top speed was 18.6 mph and it had to be pushed uphill. Buckley's example was soon followed by Mrs. G. M. Dare, Singapore's first woman motorist, who took to the roads in the same year in her 12 hp Star. The Singapore Automobile Club was formed in 1907 and by 1908, it was noted that a total of 214 people had acquired licences to drive motor cars, motor-bicycles and steam-rollers. The arrival of the car, as well as trams and trolleybuses which required smooth surfaces to run on, was to propel a tenfold increase in the extent of paved roads over the next half century.[13] A special traffic police department was formed in 1911 in response to these changes.

By the mid-1920s, there were close to 5,000 vehicles on the streets and a writer commented, 'One is bound to be amazed when first seeing Singapore and the enormous amount of motor traffic in the city' (Sidney 1926:25). The differences of speed between vehicles were now extreme, making the roads in some ways more dangerous and no doubt spelling the ultimate end of the rickshaw as authorities became more and more keen to remove it from the traffic scene. The Japanese Occupation tempo-

Prominent and wealthy members of all ethnic communities were quick to acquire motor cars. This picture, taken in 1900, just four years after the introduction of the first automobile to Singapore, shows some leading members of the Chinese community — Lim Nee Soon, Lim Boon Keng, Teo Eng Hock, Tan Chor Lam, and others — in their automobiles.

Gathering Speed: Transport and the Pace of Life

Members of the Alkaff family pictured with their cars in front of one of their bungalows in the early 1920s.

rarily almost wiped out private car ownership, but this rose again rapidly in the postwar years. By the 1960s, there were 10,000 new cars on the road each year. Although the severe restraints maintained on car ownership in Singapore today have kept it almost the only Asian city not overwhelmed by traffic problems, it has still become dominated by the automobile; there are relatively few pedestrian areas and cyclists are an endangered species on the roads.

As horse-drawn carriages declined, the car became the prestige vehicle and mark of status for any who could afford it. An interesting photograph of 1900 shows several prominent members of the Chinese community — Lim Nee Soon, Lim Boon Keng, Teo Eng Hock, Tan Chor Lam and others — posing in three open-topped cars in front of a large bungalow house.[14] The Alkaffs, a prominent Arab family, were also early car owners. A picture dating from the early 1920s shows several members of the family with three cars in front of one of their houses.

The idea of the automobile as a symbol of individual success achieved its most extraordinary expression in the late 1920s and early 1930s in the vehicles belonging to Aw Boon Haw — who had built a hugely successful business around the famous Tiger Balm ointment with his brother Aw Boon Par. Boon Haw was a flamboyant figure, always seeking new ways to advertise his product. In 1927, he was driving a Buick limousine when he hit on the idea of converting his car into a tiger. He selected a German model and had it customised, with a large red tiger's head at the front complete with wire whiskers and high-wattage bulbs to light the eyes at night, and two klaxon horns made to sound something like a tiger's roar. The car made a suitably awe-inspiring impression on unsuspecting Malaysian villagers when he drove around the countryside in a motorcade on one of his promotion drives. A second tiger car, in 1932, was a black Humber painted with gold stripes and with an even stranger-sounding roar than the first (King 1992:151, 288–9).

Aw Boon Haw's second 'Tiger' car, commissioned in 1932 as an ingenious means of promoting his famous 'Tiger Balm' ointment.

The Era of Flight

Aviation brought another great transformation in Singapore's connection with the rest of the world. The very first demonstration flight to be attempted locally was made in a Bristol Box-Kite biplane by French aviator Joseph Christiaens on March 16, 1911 at the Farrer Park Race Course (Hutton 1981:15). Some years later, on December 4, 1919, Captain Ross Smith became the first pilot ever to land in Singapore,

Captain Ross Smith with his Vickers Vimy biplane, the first to land in Singapore, en route to Australia in his pioneering flight of 1919.

Gathering Speed: Transport and the Pace of Life

on his pioneer flight to Australia in a three-engined Vickers Vimy biplane. He landed on the Race Course at Farrer Park after a 22-day flight from England.[15] Ten years later, Singapore's first airport for military and international passenger services was opened at Seletar. A direct link with Europe was established in 1933 when Singapore was included on KLM's (the Dutch Royal Airline Co.'s) route from Amsterdam to Batavia. In the same year, British Imperial Airways established a regular air mail service from London to Singapore. With the opening of Kallang Airport in 1937, the declared aim was to make Singapore 'one of the largest and most important airports of the world.' The local Wearne's Air Service provided mostly a cargo and mail service at this date, its passenger service being at first unpopular. After World War II, plans were made to form a national Malayan Airways, which became operative from 1947. Following the turn of political events in 1963, it changed its name to Malaysian Airways. In 1965, Malaysia and Singapore, now separate entities, formed a joint enterprise called Malaysia-Singapore Airlines.[16] By the 1950s, Kallang had already become too small to accommodate larger planes, so in 1955 the new Paya Lebar civil airport was opened. But the growth in air transport was now so rapid that within two decades this too would be replaced by the airport at Changi, itself still expanding.

Kallang Airport, circa 1947, with a Dakota DC-3 plane of the newly formed Malayan Airways. Kallang was Singapore's first international airport, but soon became too small and was replaced by a new airport at Paya Lebar.

Conclusion

The pace of life in Singapore has quickened tremendously from those early years — when most of the inhabitants went about on foot and the city was a distant outpost, separated from the colonial metropolis by months of voyaging — to the city of today, from which one can travel overnight to Europe. Where once most of the population went about on foot and only the rich could ride, today's public transport is a lot more affordable as well as more efficient. Although control of the automobile remains a pressing problem, the development of increasingly sophisticated public transport systems at least offers some consolation to those who will never be able to afford a car. And the rickshaw outing has become only an expensive amusement for groups of Japanese tourists, seeking to relive the past.

Endnotes

1. See for instance the descriptions in Kossak (1873:65), Scidmore ([1899] 1922:106), Marvin (1878:78) and others, cited in Singh (1995).
2. Buckley, in his *Anecdotal History of Old Times in Singapore*, notes under the year 1836: 'The European vessels in those days always engaged Malay *sampans* to wait on the ship, to avoid making the European crews row backwards and forwards in the sun. The Malays learned to build very perfect boats, about 20 ft long and 4 ft in width, very unlike the tubs they had used before the Europeans came, and they were able to hold their own against European boats, which it was said never beat them. They had a crew of three to five men, and the charge was 60 cents a day. For $30 they would convey letters to Penang, nearly 400 miles' ([1902] 1984:311). *Sampan* races were a popular form of amusement in the early decades of the century.
3. 'Palankeen' and 'gharry' are both Anglo-Indian words derived from Hindi. John Cameron states that it was an Indian custom for the syce to run at the horse's head, adding, unfairly enough, that the Malays preferred to 'jump up behind' because they were 'incurably lazy' (cited in Makepeace *et al.* 1921:509).
4. Railways had opened in England from 1885.
5. Reported in the *Motor Car and Athletic Journal* of 1908, cited in Makepeace (1921:510).
6. He adds: 'Incidentally, the first motor scooter which the writer ever saw was being ridden past the gates of Government House some short time ago by a Chinese motor-mechanic' — further evidence that the Chinese in Singapore were quick to make use of new technologies.
7. Quoted in Backhouse (1972:105).
8. It cannot have been that long, however, for by 1890, an ordinance was being passed requiring rickshaws to be lined with black American cloth, instead of the cheap red cloth from Japan which stained the passenger's clothes if it got wet (Warren 1986:53). Presumably the effect of this on the white 'tutup' suits which were the customary office dress of European men was what prompted this regulation, rather than an undue concern about the wardrobes of the humbler portion of the population.
9. See Warren (1986) for a detailed history.
10. Their numbers were later reduced to four; they eventually amalgamated to form the Singapore Bus Services in 1973. The interested reader will find the history of Singapore buses recorded in exhaustive detail in York and Phillips (1996).

11. In Singapore itself, 'pirate' taxis became, after 1945, the next major form of unlicensed competition. In spite of attempts to round them up, there were still 6,800 unlicenced taxis operating in 1970, but the formation in that year of NTUC Comfort, a Transport Co-operative for licensed taxi drivers, coupled with the application, from 1971, of stricter penalties for unlicenced drivers, eventually eliminated them.

12. At this time, communist influence was strong in both these groups (as also among taxi and trishaw drivers, as well as factory and dock workers). The bus workers had a chance to repay the assistance later, when in the following year the students of two Chinese schools went on strike and occupied their school premises (see Chapter 10)

13. Backhouse states that whereas in 1821 there were a mere 15 miles of road in Singapore, by 1919 there were 119 miles; by 1970 the figure was 1,204 miles (1976:107).

14. Lim Nee Soon was a successful rubber planter, factory-owner, merchant and contractor, whose interest in the pineapple business led him to be known as the 'Pineapple King.' He held many public offices, was a Justice of Peace, sat on the committees of several schools including Raffles College, and made large donations to educational institutions, notably the Chinese High School (Song [1923] 1966:516). Lim Boon Keng had studied in Edinburgh and was deeply involved in educational and social reforms. He sat on the legislative council and was a member of the Chinese Chamber of Commerce, and was later awarded the O.B.E., in 1918 (Song [1923] 1966:236). Teo Eng Hock was Lim Nee Soon's uncle and a merchant and rubber planter and dealer.

15. This was not as easy as it sounds, since the Race Course, the only available landing place, was barely long enough for the purpose. Although the Straits Times on the following day reported the landing as 'splendid', Hutton reveals to us that it was in fact hair-raising. Sergeant Jim Bennett, one of Smith's three-man crew, had to climb out of the rear cockpit the moment the landing wheels made contact, and slide down the tail of the plane so that his weight would help to stop the aircraft before it went through the race course fence, a feat which he fortunately managed with skill (1981:19).

16. This arrangement was dissolved in 1972, with the launch of SIA (Singapore Airlines) and MAS (Malaysian Airline System).

CSC
Magnolia
CERTIFIED PURE
ICE CREAM
COLD STORAGE
CREAMERIES LTD
S
120

7 Consuming Food: Structuring Social Life and Creating Social Relationships

Selina Ching Chan

Opposite: A 'Magnolia' ice cream cart on one of its rounds.

The two Hock Chee Guan posters from the 1930s announce the stores' dried pork as a nutritious snack as well as a perfect gift.

Hock Chee Guan, which dated back to the 1930s, claimed to be one of the earliest stores to sell dried pork. It emphasised that its products were specially made by its own professionals and claimed that the dried pork could 'strengthen the body and increase metabolism.' Although this claim may not have any scientific backing, the association of 'expensive' or 'prestigious' foodstuffs with health-enhancing properties was not uncommon in those days. More interestingly, dried pork was also portrayed as a proper gift. As recalled by the shop owner, people mainly bought packs of dried pork as gifts for relatives and close friends before the Chinese Lunar New Year.

Food by itself has no social meaning. Any symbolic meanings that it has are from its association with people. These symbolic meanings, however, change from time to time. Examining the changing meaning of food will therefore contribute to our understanding of the social transformation that has taken place in Singapore over the past few decades.

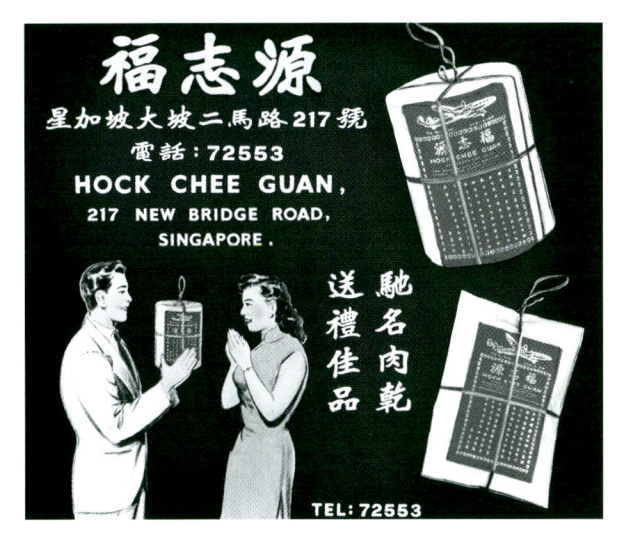

The meat stalls at the Beach Road market (shown here in the 1950s) were popular among the Muslim and non-Muslim communities alike.

The Structure of Social Life: 'Ordinary' and 'Extraordinary'

Before the 1950s, daily consumption of meat such as pork, mutton, beef or chicken was uncommon because meat was then relatively expensive. It was seen as a luxurious, precious and extraordinary food item, especially for the lower class, and only the middle and the upper classes ate it frequently. During festive periods, however, it was consumed by everyone in the gathering. For the Malays, mutton and beef were indispensable during Hari Raya. For the Chinese, chicken and pork were must-haves during the Lunar New Year. The wealthy Chinese particularly loved pork (Singh 1995:36).

(Chinese New Year, Hari Raya, Weddings, etc.)

Special days

Ordinary days		**Ordinary days**
(Vegetables and Fish)	(Meat)	(Vegetables and Fish)

Fig. 1[1]

The importance of meat in festivals was emphasised by an old Chinese lady whom I interviewed. She said: 'In the New Year, we have to have meat. In those days [1950s], life was not easy. My family was very poor and we had no money to buy pork. In one year, I had to borrow 30 cents from my neighbours to buy some pork for the New Year.' Some Chinese families who lived in *kampungs* reared pigs and chickens for sale. The poultry was served only during big festivals, such as the Lunar New Year.

The meat would, however, be consumed after they were offered to ancestors and gods. As for the eggs laid by the chickens, some of them were sold while the rest were consumed by the family. Occasionally, children would get eggs on their birthdays.

Weddings were another popular occasion when a large amount of meat was consumed. In particular, roast pig was of special significance in Cantonese marriages because they symbolised 'virginity.' In this way, it may be seen that meat was a necessity at festivals and distinguished a special feast from the ordinary meal.

Compared to meat, vegetables or fish were ordinary dishes. Vegetables had always been one of the main components of the staple diet and, as such, were considered ordinary food. Locally grown vegetables, such as tapioca, yams, beans, sweet potatoes, chillies, *kangkong*, and Chinese cabbage, were popular choices. In those days, tapioca and sweet potato leaves were common because they were grown extensively in *kampungs*.

Not only does the classification of food as being special or ordinary change over time, but the use of food as a dish or condiment also changes. Black beans (*doushi*) are one good example. People today mainly use black beans as a sauce to complement meat or fish. This is very different from when plain black beans were often used as a main dish to accompany rice or porridge.

Fish was considered an ordinary food since it was readily available in Singapore where fishing was an important activity. Being relatively cheap, it constituted a main component of the daily diet. My interview with a Malay who lived in the 1950s revealed that fish was

Fishermen at work in Katong in 1962.

A sugar cane seller, circa 1960.

A Sikh peddler selling goat's milk, circa 1950.

two to three times cheaper than meat in the 1950s. Even prawns and crabs were not that expensive. Fried fish with soya sauce or fish balls were also common dishes.

Interestingly, fish and seafood in general had become more expensive in the past decade; in contrast, meat is cheaper now. Fish has become a 'high-class' food for it is becoming more widely accepted as a healthy food. The middle and upper classes now tend to favour fish and seafood while the quantity of meat consumed has declined. This is very different from the past few decades when the middle and upper classes ate meat as a symbol of prosperity and the lower class ate mainly fish and vegetables because they could not afford meat. This transformation has come about due to two factors. Firstly, there has been an improvement in the standard of living; meat is no longer considered an expensive food. Secondly, the general public has become more health conscious as a result of education. Nevertheless, meat continues to be a necessity at festivals.

In the past, fruits and desserts were not considered a staple food. Of the people interviewed, many recalled that the fruits they consumed were not bought from the market but plucked from the fruit trees they had planted in their villages or *kampungs*. Locally grown fruits — bananas, durian, guava, mangosteen and papaya — were popular choices. Durian has always been one of the most favoured fruit. There was a Malay saying, 'One must eat durian even if one has to pawn one's *sarong* (the male Malay's costume).' Imported fruits such as apples and oranges were rare and were considered 'special.' Most people hardly ate these imported fruits.

Fruit juice was also uncommon. Drinking fresh fruit juice was considered a luxury. Fresh orange juice was certainly an expensive drink, meant only for the rich or the ill. Even sugarcane juice was not as common as it is today. Instead of drinking sugarcane juice, people would eat sugarcane. Drinking fresh milk was also a treat. It was usually sold by the Indian hawkers who rode on bicycles and delivered the milk to those who ordered it. It was mainly bought by the rich, particularly the Caucasian expatriates and those who were ill or aged.

Locally made bird's nest water was also considered a precious beverage, although the component of the drink was not bird's nest but seaweed jelly. I was told that hawkers selling bird's nest water always appeared whenever there was an opera. Many of the people I interviewed therefore associated bird's nest water with opera shows at the neighbourhood *kampungs*. In other words, it was the association of bird's nest water with operas that rendered the drink special in people's minds.

A mobile stall selling bird's nest water in 1957.

Soft drinks were called 'water from Holland' or *Holland shoo* by the Cantonese and *pop-shoo* by the Hokkiens because of the 'pop' sound from opening the bottle. F&N, Green Spot, Yeo's local drinks, Pepsi, Sarsi and Coca Cola were also popular. Soft drinks were expensive, costing about 10 cents per one-litre bottle in the late 1930s, and were not chilled when sold. Therefore, a store could at most sell a few bottles every night (Fong 000185/032). Such drinks were consumed mainly on special occasions and festivals. According to one family, they had to have orange-flavoured F&N soda during the Chinese New Year celebration. The red colour of the orange-flavoured F&N drinks was auspicious for the Chinese and thus marked the joyous occasion.

A typical teahouse where customers lounged and enjoyed their meals, circa 1950.

Food and Social Differentiation

Apart from the classification of food, the preparation of food is also worth noting. This process reflects the division of labour according to gender. Historically, it had been women who travelled to wet markets to buy food for the family. The job of buying and cooking food was a way of domesticating women. Markets mostly opened only in the mornings.[2] Things sold after 11 o'clock were considered stale. Housewives had to do their grocery shopping daily or every other day because the refrigerator was not common in those days. For those who owned a refrigerator, it was mainly used to store cold or leftover cooked food, not raw food. Families without a refrigerator would occasionally use those belonging to their neighbours. They might ask for ice or ask to store something there. One person I interviewed recalls, 'One day, my brothers and I were given a big piece of chocolate. We could not finish it and so we asked our neighbour who had a refrigerator to keep the chocolate for us. My brothers and I would only ask for our chocolate when we were really very keen to eat it. It was not nice if we bothered them too often.' The common practice of helping neighbours by allowing them to store food in their refrigerator reveals how mutual help among neighbours was part of communal life in the past.

Exchanging recipes with neighbours was another important aspect of communal life, especially for women who would prepare and cook meals for their families. During a family meal, gender inequality in the Chinese family could be observed in the way the members ate and behaved at the dining table. In some Chinese families, the men ate first and the women would eat the leftovers. This revealed a hierarchy between men and women.

Apart from eating at home, the manner in which people ate outside is also interesting. In the past, only men worked outside and consequently had more opportunities to dine at hawker places, especially during lunch when they could not possibly go home. Most of them ate alone. Eating out, although a daily routine, was not a time for social interaction with co-workers or friends. Since most women and children did not work outside, they seldom had a chance to eat out. We can thus see that the public-private dichotomy between men and women structured their chances of eating in the public (outside) and private (home) spheres.

The range of food in one's ethnic group is more apparent in home-cooked food than those sold in public eating places. Eating out with one's family was not a common event. Most of the people I interviewed told me they seldom ate out with their families. Eating out was in general only restricted to the middle or upper class. Some Chinese often associated their experiences of eating at Chinese restaurants with wedding banquets. In the 1960s, restaurants such as *Tai Thong* in Happy World, the *Diamond* and *Wing Choon Yuen* in Great World and *Tai Tong* and *New Peking Garden* in New World were popular locations (*Guide to Singapore and Spotlight on Malaya* 1960:75).

Besides restaurants, coffee houses could also be found. One of the earliest coffee houses called Top 10 was near Rediffusion in Li Yu Rong Building (Ong 01210/015). The furniture, curtains and decoration were made by Shanghainese. Western food such as steak and pork chop were served there. Ice cream shops, coffee lounges and snack bars of Western origin were mainly located in Raffles Place, High Street, North Bridge Road and Orchard Road (*A Tourist Guide to Singapore and Malaya* 1961:79). European food was also served in hotels such as Raffles Hotel. The Elizabethan Grill in Raffles Hotel served English, American and Continental cuisine with 16th century decoration and in the modern comfort of

Tah Sin Restaurant, circa 1950.

air conditioning (*Guide to Singapore and Spotlights on Malaya* 1965: 69). Raffles Bar and the Prince Bar next to the Raffles Place offered both European and Chinese cuisines.

In addition, the Islamic restaurant on North Bridge Road sold Indian curry (1960:77). Komala Villa in Serangoon was also a popular restaurant, mostly patronised by Indian bachelors. *Roti*, unleavened bread, spicy Indian chicken or mutton curries could be found in Jubilee Restaurant on North Bridge Road while vegetarian and Brahmin restaurants could be found on Market street. Javanese curries were found at Rendezvous Restaurant on Bras Basah Road (ibid.). *Nasi goreng*, a Straits Chinese food made of fried rice, shrimp, pork and eggs was also available. Since the Straits Chinese have Chinese and Malay ancestry, their cuisine is a hybrid of these two cultures.

Since eating out in a group (family or friends) was uncommon, the food that people consumed was mainly associated with the diner's culture. The older generation were reluctant to eat the food of other ethnic groups as they were less adventurous than people from the younger generation. One old Cantonese lady whom I interviewed even insisted that she would not eat anything other than Cantonese food. She said, 'Other foods are no good. They are not as tasty as Cantonese food.' Her insistence on the food of her ethnicity reflected the firm assertion of her ethnic identity. This is very different from the younger generation who are less conscious about their dialect group or ethnicity and would eat the food of other ethnic groups. Certain dishes would be identified with a particular ethnic group, for example, Hokkien *mee*, Malay *satay*, Hainanese chicken rice, and Indian *roti*. In other words, these cuisines had become distinctive representations of cultures.

Before the 1960s, street hawkers were a common sight. On different days of the week, hawkers would sell *satay*, bread, and Malay *kueh* in different *kampungs*. My sources recalled that customers staying on the second storey would put money in a basket and then use a rope to lower the basket from their window. The hawker would then put the bread and change in the basket and the customer would pull it up. *Satay* (pieces of grilled beef, chicken or mutton served with peanut sauce) was usually sold by Malay hawk-

An Indian Muslim man selling *roti*, circa 1900.

Food vendors along the Satay Club on Beach Road, 1952.

ers while bread (*roti*) was commonly sold by the Hainanese and Indians.

Among the street hawkers, some would push their mobile stalls and several small chairs to selected sites. Noodle hawkers would attract customers by making a 'tick tock' sound with a pair of bamboo sticks. Customers usually sat on the small chairs to eat the noodles. No table was provided; therefore, the customers had to hold the bowls in their hands.

Besides the mobile hawkers, there were also hawkers who were regularly stationed at certain places. They could be found in places such as Colombo Court, Bugis Street, Hokkien Street, Albert Street, Beach Road, People's Park and the Bedok sea front. Many of the street hawkers operated from six or seven o'clock in the evening to midnight. It was not surprising to discover 10 to 20 stalls selling different kinds of food in each of these places. Beach Road was famous for *satay*; therefore, the hawker centre there was called 'Satay Club.' Hokkien Street was famous for Hokkien *mee* (noodle).

If one compares the different ways of eating at various places, one will notice a significant difference in the ownership of space. Customers who buy *satay* or *kueh* from street peddlers would eat quickly and then walk away, or bring the food home to eat. For those who ate noodles or other such meals, the only space they had were the chairs provided by the hawkers. Eating at restaurants was better, since temporal ownership of the space around the whole table was possible. But eating at restaurants was costly and was considered an indulgence, while hawker food was the cheapest. The

Street food stalls in the 1930s seldom provided the luxury of seats or even tables; customers had to squat and eat in haste.

superiority of the venue was sometimes pegged against the amount of private space and time available for consumption.

Imagined Equality and Social Cohesion

While the ethnic boundaries between the Chinese, Malays and Indians remained on some occasions, they were temporarily forgotten in others. The process of reconstructing existing boundaries and social relationships is revealed clearly in the commensality pattern at one particular public space — the coffeeshop. As Chua recalled the coffeeshops or *kopitiams* in the 1950s,

> It was no more than a wide open shop front with a minimum of tools of the trade: an open-fire charcoal grill, upon which sat brass or stainless steel conical cylinders, open at the pointed end. Each cylinder had a handle, a spout and a cloth 'sock' containing coffee powder. Coffee-making was a simple process of pouring boiling water into the sock, draining the coffee into the cylinder and pouring the coffee into heavy ceramic cups for serving.
>
> (Chua 1997:158)

The coffeeshop had always been a popular place for men to gather. Both the poor and the rich went to coffeeshops and it was not uncommon to see the rich people carrying bird cages and drinking coffee while reading newspapers or chatting with one another. The coffeeshop was also a popular venue for matchmaking sessions.

As a location which brought together people of different ethnic and professional backgrounds, the coffeeshop was a place where it was common to see a table shared by several strangers. A perceived equality among people of different ethnic groups and classes was temporarily constructed by eating at a common table.

Besides eating, the coffeeshop was also a good place for collective idling and was part of the communal life in *kampungs* (Chua 1997:158). An important part of life in coffeeshops also included listening to serialised *kungfu* stories broadcast by Rediffusion, a cable radio network (Chua and Rajah 1996). It was an important place for the exchange of information before the arrival of television. The literate villagers would read aloud from the newspapers (Chua 1997:158). Story-telling and gambling were other activities that took place in coffeeshops (Chua 1997:159).

Coffee shops were mainly owned by the Hainanese. This was related to the fact that the Hainanese worked for the British during the colonial era and had learnt the technique of making coffee. The habit of drinking coffee was certainly learnt from the colonial masters and this makes the coffeeshop an imitation of the café. The coffeeshop, however, is very different from a Western-style café.

The way in which the coffee is prepared, served and consumed is unique. Coffee beans here were fried with butter. This was different from the practice in Western Europe or the States, where beans are roasted. A piece of butter was usually served with the coffee. People either added the butter to the coffee or ate it separately. It was believed that this method of drinking coffee would soothe the throat. The locals believed that coffee was a 'heaty' drink and butter a cooling food; when taken together, they would maintain the balance in the body. The coffee served here was mixed with condensed milk and sugar.

A Caucasian in a local coffee shop in 1957.

Besides selling drinks, the coffee shops also sold toast, biscuits, cakes and eggs. Eggs were half-boiled and served with soya sauce and pepper. Sometimes, raw eggs were stirred into hot drinks because this was believed to be nutritious. Plain toast cost 10 or 15 cents in the 1950s. Toast might also be served

Durian stall on Queen Street, 1962.

with butter or *kaya*, a bread spread made from coconut and eggs. These cost an additional 10 and 15 cents respectively. In addition, a special type of grilled toast was sold in Hainanese-owned coffeeshops. This was prepared by soaking bread in raw egg, with pepper and soya sauce added, and grilling it over a charcoal fire. Butter or *kaya* was spread on the toast when it was ready. *Qionghexing* in Killiney Road was famous for this type of toast.

Red bean paste biscuits ordered from Chinese confectionery shops such as *Nantangli* and *Meilibingjia* were also sold in coffee shops. Similar to coffeeshops, most of the confectioneries were owned by the Hainanese. *Dasanyuan* cake shop in Middle Road was famous for their egg sponge cake, walnut cake and bean paste roll soft cake (Fong 00185/032).

Concluding Remarks

No understanding of society is complete without the study of food. Food is a part of most important rituals and is often used to mark the significance of a wide range of cultural events and thus imparting a sense of cohesion to social events (Douglas 1984). The use of different kinds of food separates the 'ordinary' days from the 'extraordinary' ones. In the past, meat as a special food was a necessity in regular festivals and ritual celebrations while ordinary foods such as fish and seafood were consumed daily.

As a representation of one's culture and chosen lifestyle, the unique Singaporean food culture was best shown in the various ethnic foods offered at hawker stalls. On one hand, the hawker stalls revealed the homogenous consumption pattern of a community of mostly poor migrants. On the other hand, the local coffee shop reflected the heterogeneous nature of the multi-ethnic community. A cultural tolerance among people of different social and ethnic groups is observed by the fact that individuals, undisturbed by differences in class and ethnicity, shared a table. But these strangers ate different foods, thus still maintaining the social boundaries at some level. The coffeeshop is indeed a 'melting pot' where people of different classes and ethnic origins congregate.

Acknowledgments

I am grateful to Ananda Raja for his comments and advice. Thanks also go to Chiang Wai Fong, Yap Wee Cheng and Pang Chai Ping for gathering information on the topic.

Endnote

1. This framework is drawn form Van Gennep's analysis on rituals.
2. There were a lot of such markets around. Some of those old markets still exist today. Balestier Market was built in 1922; Song Ling Market around 1930; Holland Road Market in pre-war times; Upper Serangoon Road Market in 1938; Kallang Estate Market in the 1950s; Tiong Bahru Market in 1950; Serangoon Garden Market in 1957; and Membinar Barat Market in 1959. Commonwealth Avenue Market, Corporation Drive Market, Geylang Serai Market, Tanglin Halt Market, Beo Crescent Market and Commonwealth Crescent Market were built in the 1960s (Yap, personal communication).

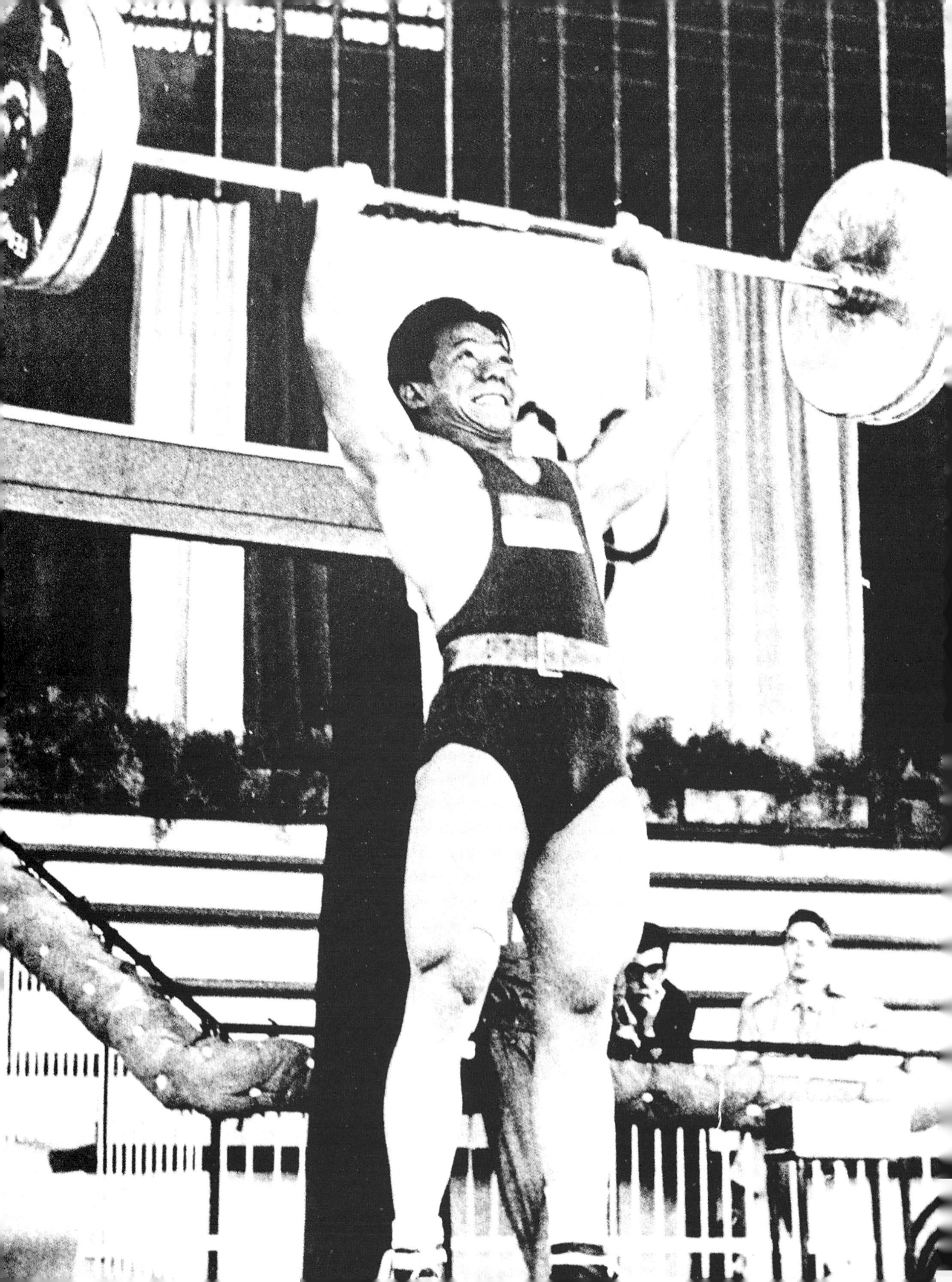

8 It's Us Against Them: Sports in Singapore

Alexius Pereira

Opposite: Tan Howe Liang at the Olympic Games in Rome, 1960. This winning lift won him the silver medal.

In recent years, sociologists and anthropologists have turned their attention to sports and its role in social life or culture. Some sociologists see sports as 'an arena of patterned behaviours, social structures and inter-institutional relationships' (Frey and Eitzen 1991: 503). Simply put, sports sociologists study the social organisation of teams and the impact of rules and inter-team competition. Sports anthropologists, on the other hand, focus on the relationship between sports and play[1] (a similar leisure activity), and the role of sports in the culture of a people, as well as how deeply it might affect participants and spectators, in a way almost similar to a religious manner.

In this chapter, the history of sports in Singapore from 1819 to 1965 is assessed using two sociological perspectives: the consensus and the conflict. The consensus perspective examines the social role of sporting competitions in early Singaporean life, especially their ability to confer identity and unify groups. This perspective has a view that social order is possible because people not only agree to the norms and rules of society, but also value them. This produces an implicit social contract amongst the participants. Concepts such as 'belonging' and 'social integration' are important aspects of the consensus perspective. In sports, this can be applied to the notion of a 'team,' which embodies many integrative factors. For instance, a team must have a unified goal and must work together to achieve it. There are also socio-psychological rewards, such as honour and prestige, when one is chosen to represent a team. This could also hold true for spectators who support a team. The consensus perspective, therefore, views sports as an activity that could bind a group together.

From a conflict perspective, sports is seen as a means of asserting power and maintaining control over certain individuals. This concept — which has its roots in the Marxist tradition of class struggle — would view sports, especially competitive sports, as being inherently divisive. Here, ownership of important resources such as property, capital (both social and economic)[2] and knowledge, are significant factors in society. Different individuals and groups in society have different levels of ownership of these resources. This separates the 'haves' from the 'have-nots,' and ultimately creates an unequal social relationship between the two groups. The 'have-nots' need to exchange their services (and loyalty) with those who 'have.' This often leads to dissatisfaction for both groups. The 'have-nots' would try to improve their position by working their way up to own enough resources while the 'haves' would be protective of their privileged position and would do everything in their power to maintain, if not strengthen it. Marxists believe that all societies are inherently in conflict. In the case of Singapore, the conflict perspective maintains that sports and sporting competitions are activities that divide people along various lines.

Mad Dogs and Englishmen

The earliest records of sporting activities in Singapore were from British sources. However, some traditional Malay sports had existed, even though they were not reported by the British. For instance, an important sporting event for the Malays was the sea-sports festival. Held over one day, the festival included *sampan* (small boat) races, *kolek* (small fishing boat) races, boat tug-of-war and several solo events, culminating in the Bugis yacht (small sailing crafts in the traditional Bugis design) race. The festival was a significant social and communal event. It brought the community closer together and forged a sense of solidarity and identity among the population.

It was the British who introduced the majority of the sports that have endured until today. Some of the sports that were common in everyday life before 1900 were horse racing, boat racing, cricket and golf. Other sports that are popular today — badminton, soccer (known as association football), rugby and hockey — were them-

Kolek racing, in the 1920s.

Members, all European, of the Singapore Cricket Club who took part in the lawn tennis competition, circa 1894.

selves not formalised until the early 20th century. 'Formalised' refers to the forming of a body of rules and institutions for the sports. For instance, football was only formalised with the establishment of the Football Association in London in 1863. The game was introduced to Singapore around 1889, and the Football Association of Singapore was subsequently formed in 1892.

To the British, sports was another alternative to leisure activities such as artistic events, musical soirées or literary performances. The conflict perspective highlights the fact that only certain classes in society, particularly the wealthy, would have leisure time. Between 1819 and 1867 (the opening of the Suez Canal), it was difficult to find anyone other than Europeans participating in sports in Singapore. This is not surprising, as the majority of the population at the time were labourers. The low participation rate was believed to be due to the physically demanding nature of menial labour. The assumption was that these labourers would not opt for a physical activity such as sports for their leisure. The more common (or at least more commonly reported) activities were gambling, opium-smoking and prostitution. Such activities were preferred because of their 'escapist' nature, and could have helped alleviate the labourers' hardship in Singapore. The phrase, 'Mad Dogs and Englishmen', originally referred to the leisurely middle class of English society, who could afford to play cricket in the sun while everyone else was toiling away. The imagery was further intensified in the tropics when playing any sport in the sun must have been indeed baffling to those who did not view sports as leisure.

The first sports club in Singapore was the Billiard Club (Makepeace *et al.* [1921] 1991: 320), formed in 1829, followed by the Sporting Club in 1843, which sponsored the annual Singapore Cup for horse racing. Other prominent sporting clubs formed before 1867 were the Singapore Cricket Club (1852) and the Tanglin Club (1865). While it might appear that people with similar interests would naturally come together to form a club in which to share their leisure interests, it was more than just the love of a particular sport which held certain clubs together. In the 19th century (and even for most part of the 20th), these clubs were exclusively European and male in membership. At first, it was believed that non-Europeans and women did not want to join these clubs; however, it became clear in the latter half of the 19th century that clubs were turning away Asian and Eurasian applicants as well as some women. Therefore, racism and gender discrimination rather than interest or ability lay at the roots of sports clubs.

The Pre-War Sports Boom

By 1914, the situation had changed significantly. Asians were reported to be keen participants in many of the sports once the sole domain of Europeans. For instance, Makepeace *et al.* wrote after the formation of the Football League in Singapore, '[the] native population took to the game very kindly, and established their own league games, Malay and Chinese, and the matches are generally pretty hard-fought games' (1921[1991] vol.1:334). By the late 1800s, 'natives' — here referring to Malays, Chi-

This 1923 photograph shows Chia Keng Tye, a wealthy Straits Chinese, and friends, decked out in tennis gear.

Chia Keng Tye's tennis court at his residence along Killiney Road in 1923.

nese, Indians and Eurasians — had become proficient at many sports, including cricket, tennis, football and hockey.

There are several reasons why Asians took to sports. Firstly, there was a significant increase in the number of Asians who were born and raised in Singapore. Secondly, many Asians had grown wealthier, particularly after the opening of the Suez Canal. Many had become petty traders or small business owners, thus having a higher disposable income and more leisure time. Many also attended European-styled schools, particularly the mission schools and the government schools, where sports was an important part of the curriculum. It was in these schools that many Asians were grounded in the fundamentals of formalised sports. By the turn of the century, a distinct leisure class of Asians interested in sports had emerged. Several wealthy Asians even had sporting facilities built in their residence, just like the Europeans. Chia Keng Tye, a Straits Chinese, had a fenced grass tennis court built in his home along Killiney Road.

Several clubs were formed by Asians for Asians. These included the Singapore Recreation Club (Eurasians), established in 1883, and the Straits Chinese Recreation Club, founded in 1885 (later renamed the Singapore Chinese Recreation Club). The Chinese Swimming Club, Indian Association, Sikh Cricket Club (today renamed Singapore Khalsa Association) and the Lanka Union (Ceylon Sports Club) were formed in the first half of the 20th century. From the consensus perspective, the establishment and flourishing of these clubs indicated a strong desire to identify

PAST TIMES: A SOCIAL HISTORY OF SINGAPORE

A picture of several members of the Singapore Chinese Recreation Club, taken outside their clubhouse at Hong Lim Green, circa 1919.

with one's own compatriots. Many of these clubs were also venues for social functions. Sports was once again simultaneously cohesive and divisive in an ethnically plural society. Each ethnic group had to form its own sports club because of the division between themselves and other ethnic groups. Examples of this would include the formation of separate Chinese and Malay football associations in Singapore. Even when there was contact between different ethnic sports clubs, the competition on the field was symbolic of inter-group struggle. For instance, it was known that there was a fierce sporting rivalry between the Singapore Cricket Club (European) and the Singapore Recreation Club (Eurasian). The 'rivalry' was intensified when many Eurasian members were unhappy that they were denied membership at the SCC on racial grounds, which at the time admitted only Europeans.

Another group which experienced discrimination in sports was women. After World War I, more women became interested in sports. Previously, only a few wealthy European women occasionally played tennis, usually at their own residences. They were frequently present as spectators at Horse Races at the Turf Club. There was, however, a marked change after 1920. Racket sports, particularly tennis and badminton, were popular with women. Although the spread of sports can be attributed to education for men in Singapore, it was unlikely that it did the same for women. Many

Nurses playing badminton at the Hospital Assistants Union Recreation Club, circa 1946.

of the convents and all-girl schools did not introduce sports into their curriculum before World War I, focusing instead on home economics and art. It was likely that this interest in sports was initially passed on from men to women — husbands to wives, brothers to sisters, and fathers to daughters.

By the 1920s, there was a growing number of locally born women. Coupled with the fact that Singapore was doing fairly well economically, many men and women were now able to enjoy leisure activities that were once the sole domain of the wealthy classes. But this did not mean that women were treated on an equal basis. While it was common for men to both play for fun and for competition, women were often not given opportunities to take part in organised competitions. Instead, their participation was entirely for private self-enjoyment. Before 1929, none of the sports clubs even allowed women to join as full members, let alone to take part in competitions. It was against this discrimination that the first all-women sports club was formed. The Girls Sports Club (GSC) was formed by a group of Eurasian women in 1929. Eurasian women were upset that they were not allowed membership into the Singapore Recreation Club, the Eurasian sports club. Setting up a clubhouse along Serangoon Road and using facilities of their husbands, members of the GSC began to excel in hockey, tennis, netball and athletics (Barth 1992:103). The desire to participate in competitive sports was probably the same for women of other ethnic groups. However, only Eurasian and European women, particularly members of the Young Women's Christian Association (YWCA), joined sports clubs during this time. After World War I, young girls were introduced to sports in primary and secondary school, and sports became an important aspect of education for both males and females. Once again, both the consensus and conflict perspectives could explain to the case of women's participation in sports in Singapore. While it might appear that women found solidarity among themselves in their sports clubs, it is also true that forming

Above Left: Girls Sports Club's hockey team in Kuala Lumpur, about to play against Selangor in 1940.

Above Right: The YWCA cricket team, circa 1940.

Above Left: This photograph shows non-playing captain Lim Chuan Geok leading the Malayan Thomas Cup team into Victoria Memorial Hall for the victory ceremony in 1949.

Above Right: A motorcade with the Cup celebrating the same victory in 1949.

their own sports clubs were the only option after being unfairly excluded by men in Singapore.

Team Singapore

Another interesting aspect is the history of teams that represented Singapore in sporting events. This section explores the idea that Singapore's social history mirrored the island's sporting history.

Before 1900, there were regular cricket, hockey and rugby contests between the three Straits Settlements; namely, Singapore, Malacca and Penang, or against the other Federated Malay States, including Selangor, Pahang and Johor. Most of these teams comprised Europeans even though they formed a small percentage of the overall population. For example, the Singaporean cricket team, which represented the colony against Hong Kong and Shanghai in Hong Kong in 1890, consisted of all expatriate Europeans who were members of the SCC (Makepeace *et. al.* 1921[1981]: 327).[3] After 1920, more Asians were included in many of these state teams. Due to the increasingly intense competition between Malayan states, the Europeans had no choice but to select the best talent available of any race to compete.

After World War II, there was a large increase in international sporting events. As a nation, Singapore was invited to participate in the Olympic, Commonwealth, Asian and Southeast Asian Games, as well as in specific individual sports tournaments such as badminton's Thomas Cup. Between 1948 and 1965, Singaporean sportsmen and sportswomen represented both Singapore and Malaya. Between 1948 and 1965, Singaporean sportsmen and sportswomen represented both Singapore and Malaya. This was because most people believed that Singapore, with its limited resources and land space, would ultimately remain part of Malaya. In the realm of sports, this led to many combined Singapore–Malaya teams.

The most famous example of this was the Thomas Cup team, which dominated international badminton between 1948 and 1956. The Cup, originally conceived as a badminton competition between countries in 1939, only took place in 1948 because it was disrupted by World War II. Players were pooled from all over Malaya, including Wong Peng Soon and Ong Poh Lim. Badminton had already gained a huge public following in Malaya, and immediately after the war, many Malayan badminton players took part in tournaments in Europe. During the first Thomas Cup competition, held in the first week of January 1948 in London, the team defeated the Danish team 8–1 in the finals. The team first returned to Singapore in May 1949 to a grand welcome. The subsequent defence of the Cup in 1952 was staged in Singapore where the Malayan team defeated the team from the United States 7–2. It was not only in the Thomas Cup that Singaporeans competed under the Malayan flag, but Singaporean athletes also competed at the 1956 Olympic Games in Melbourne.

Ong Poh Lim (left) and Wong Peng Soon as a doubles' team, circa 1940.

Participation and success in competitive sports were not always the case. Singapore participated as a nation-state in the 1948 Summer Olympics, which was held in

The Singapore contingent at the Opening Ceremony of the 1948 London Olympics.

PAST TIMES: A SOCIAL HISTORY OF SINGAPORE

Lloyd Valberg, representing Malaya in an event in Sydney around the 1950s.

London. Malaya's first entry in the Olympics was only in 1956. For the London Olympiad, Singapore sent only one contestant, high-jumper Lloyd Valberg and the chef-de-mission, Jocelyn de Souza, who was the founder and first president of the Singapore Olympic Council. More importantly, it was one of the first times that the Singapore flag was displayed at Wembley Stadium during the opening ceremony. Valberg, an officer in the Singapore Harbour Board Fire Brigade, was eventually placed an overall eighth. In 1960, Singapore's flag was raised in victory at the Olympiad in Rome, when weightlifter Tan Howe Liang won a silver medal. Singapore also participated as a separate nation in the First Asian Games in 1951 in New Delhi. The first gold medal for Singapore at the Asian Games was won by the water polo team at the Second Asian Games in Manila, the Philippines, in 1954. In the first South East Asian Peninsular (SEAP) Games, held in Bangkok, Thailand, in 1959, the Singapore national anthem, *Majulah Singapura*, was heard outside the island for the very first time. Tan Eng Yoon had won the gold medal in the 400 metres hurdles (see Seneviratne 1993).

The uncertainty of the sporting teams reflected the uncertainty in the political situation in both Singapore and Malaya at the time. The issues of nationhood and citizenship were problematic for both countries. The Singapore-Malaya merger of

Singapore's water polo team was presented with the gold medal at the second Asian Games held in Manila, the Philippines, in 1954.

Tan Eng Yoon (left with spectacles) competing in the 100 yards event, at a Malayan Amateur Athletic Association championship meet in 1955, held in Ipoh, Perak.

1963 had proved untenable; there were irreconcilible differences over the issue of ethnic policies, citizenship and economic development. By the time of the 1965 SEAP Games in Kuala Lumpur, Malaysia and Singapore were politically separated and the fallout from separation was also felt on the sports field. Two athletes encountered problems registering for the Games because their nationalities were changed as a result of the 1965 separation. These cases show how sports was directly affected by politics. But the sportsmen and women never did politicise their participation. From the newspaper reports of these major sporting events during this period (1945–1965), all the athletes were pleased to represent their countries, be it Singapore or Malaya.

Period	Society	Population	Sports
1819–1867	Frontier town Singapore	European expatriates Coolie immigrants	Dominated by Europeans, Asians uninterested
1867–1920	Steady economic development	Growing middle-class Asian population	Interest shown by Asians
1920–1965	Uncertainty over political future	Singaporeanisation or Malayanisation of sports	Dominated by locals equally willing to represent either country

Singapore on the offensive in the Malayan Cup game against Selangor, played at the Jalan Besar Stadium in 1963.

Up to this point in history, a model of the relationship between sports and society can be proposed:

It is clear that sports is woven into the fabric of social life, especially when social, economic and political factors inevitably find their way into the sporting arena. An interesting question can be posed at this point: Did sports in Singapore ever promote nationalism among the population? Nationalism, the feeling of national pride, is a notoriously difficult concept to measure. However, it is evident that the sporting event which elicited the greatest amount of national pride was the Malaya Cup, capturing the imagination and arousing the passion of a large cross-section of Singaporeans. This football tournament was conceived by British servicemen from the battleship, H.M.S. Malaya, in 1920. After a series of matches against various states, they raised the money for a silver cup and started the inter-state competition in 1921. Singapore was the first winner of the Cup, with a 2–1 victory over Selangor. The match was played at the Selangor Club in front of around 3,000 spectators (Robert 1991:3). That game was not without controversy, as Malayan states had complained that the Singapore team fielded too many European players. Since then, the competition has occupied a special place in the hearts and minds of Singaporeans and Malaysians alike.

Some indications of this include the loyalty supporters had towards their state-teams; bands of travelling supporters were a common sight even in the early days of the competition. Many Singaporeans still treasure memories of their favourite footballers and Malaya Cup moments. If Singaporeans had ever perceived themselves as an 'us' before 1965, it was usually against the 'them' of any Malayan state teams. This was particularly evident in the intense rivalry between Singapore and Selangor, which were usually the most powerful teams in the competition throughout its history. The Malaya Cup competition was also interesting because for once in Singapore's social life, the composition of the team was multi-ethnic. The roster of Singapore's teams from 1900 to 1950 had Chinese, Eurasian, European, Malay and Indian players at one time or another (see Robert 1991). It is also believed that the spectators at inter-state football games would be multi-ethnic, although this is much harder to verify.

While there was indeed loyalty and support for Singapore as a team, this could not in any way be referred to as the origins of nationalism. Nationalism requires loyalty not just to the nation, but also to its values, ideals and symbols. This therefore would not apply to the Singapore's team support. The dual process of uniting and dividing is evident once more. Conflict theories account for the fervent support for Singapore as the symbolising of the 'othering' process, where extra-sporting rivalries were embodied on the field of play. In this case, as far as Singaporeans were concerned, Selangor — the team, the state and its supporters — had become the designated 'old enemy.' As a result, those who pledge their support to the Singapore team are drawn closer to each other.

Conclusion

As can be seen in Singapore's sporting history, sports and sporting competitions have the ability to unite and divide people. Sports institutions were also able to use sports to consolidate one group against others, along class, race and gender lines. Singapore's history shows that sports was a part of social life and not an autonomous

Supporters at the stadium during the Malayan Cup game between Singapore and Selangor, 1963.

sphere. Sports was closely intertwined with other social, demographic, economic and political currents. At this point in time, we may ask: What is the social role of sportspersons and teams that represent Singapore in international events, such as the Southeast Asian Games, the Asian Games, the Olympics or specific tournaments such as the World Cup in soccer or the Thomas Cup in badminton? Do they participate out of a sense of national duty or for individual glory? Do they foster a sense of pride among other Singaporeans through competing? How does 'Team Singapore' affect the collective mood of the population when they do well or badly at these international events? And finally, what would happen if and when sports becomes fully professional and more commercialised in the future?

Appendix: Milestones in the history of Singapore sports (1819–1965)

1837: Cricket was first played at the Esplanade

1843: Horse-racing at the Serangoon Road Race Course

1859: Singapore Cricket Club*

1862: Singapore Rifle Association*

1875: Lawn tennis at the Esplanade

1883: Singapore Recreation Club (SRC)*

1886: Athletics at SRC
Polo Club**

1889: Soccer at Tank Road

1891: Golf Club**

Golf at Serangoon Road Race Course (Farrer Park)

1892: Football Association of Singapore*
Hockey at the Esplanade

1894: Singapore Swimming Club*

1895: Singapore Rugby Union*

1896: Lawn bowls at the Esplanade

1899: Singapore Polo Club*

1909: Chinese Swimming Club*

1910: Singapore Malay Football Club*
1924: Singapore Billiards and Snooker Council*
1928: Singapore Indian Association*
1929: Singapore Badminton Association*
Ceylon Sports Club
1930: Singapore Women's Hockey Association*
Singapore Lawn Tennis Association*
Singapore Table Tennis Association*
Singapore Amateur Boxing Association*
1931: Singapore Hockey Association*
1934: Singapore Amateur Athletics Association*
Singapore Amateur Weightlifting Association
1939: Singapore Amateur Basketball Association*
Singapore Amateur Swimming Association*
1948: Singapore Olympic Sports Council*
Singapore first participated in the Olympics
1952: First defence of the Thomas Cup in Singapore
1960: Singapore's first Olympic medal (silver) by Tan Howe Liang (weightlifting)

* formation
** introduction of
(Source: Singapore Sports Council)

Acknowledgments

I would like to thank the Singapore Sports Council for assisting in the initial research for this chapter.

Endnotes

1. The distinction between the two concepts is that sports is highly organised and formalised, whereas play is more open-ended and free-flowing. See Frey and Eitzen (1991) and Luschen (1980).
2. Social capital refers to the amount of status and prestige individuals might have in society. Economic capital refers to the economic resources individuals own. Either form of capital can be used to influence others.
3. The same was mostly true for other sports competitions reported in both Makepeace *et al.* ([1921] 1991) and Buckley ([1902]1984).

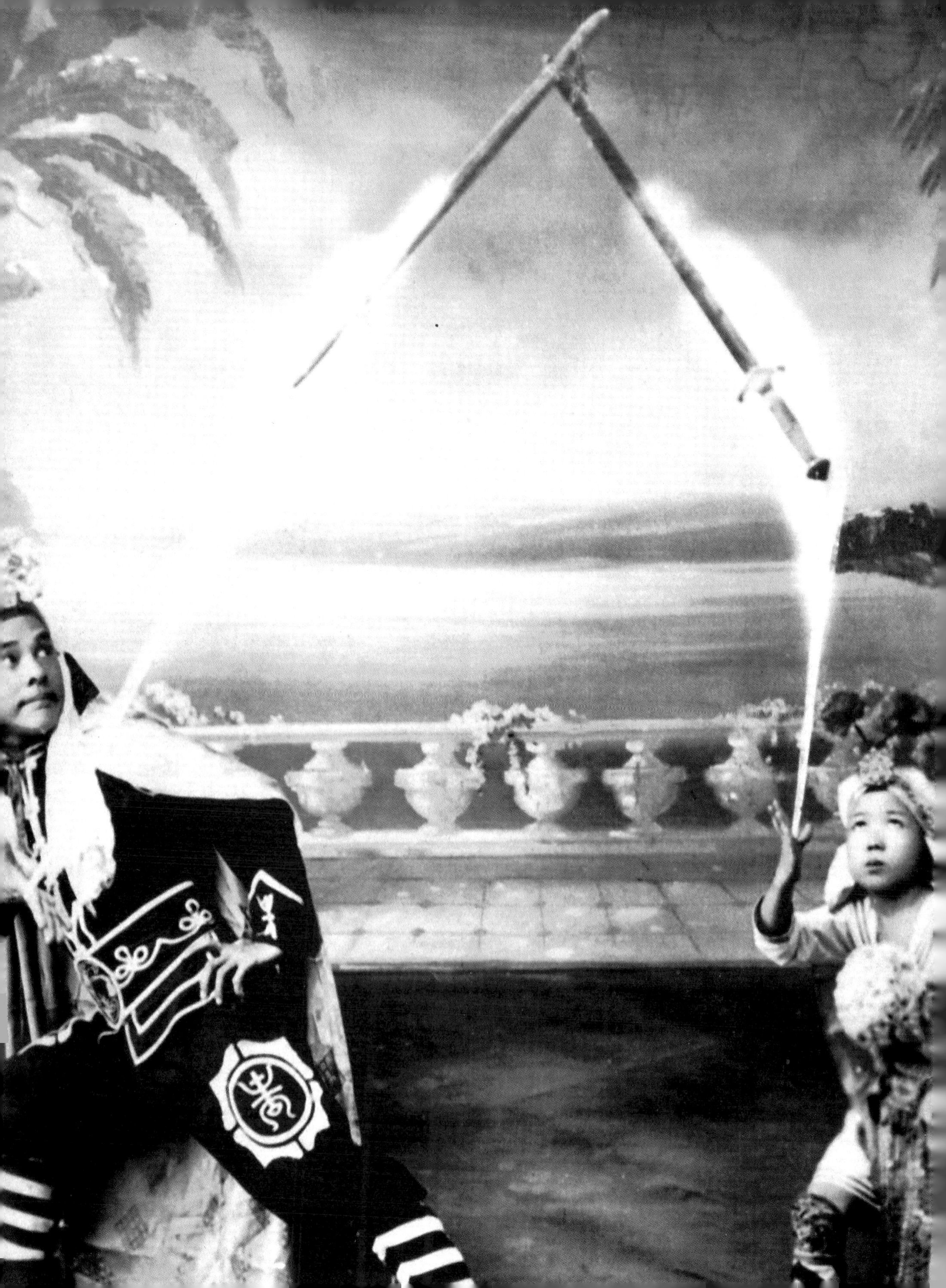

9 Leisure, Pleasure and Consumption: Ways of Entertaining Oneself

Yung Sai Shing & Chan Kwok Bun

Opposite: Special effects from the Teochew opera "Flying Swords," circa 1930s.

Writers on the entertainment scene in Malay and Singapore societies in the late 19th and early 20th centuries noted a dazzling variety of ways in which people went about amusing themselves: flying kites, playing chess, cock-fighting, hunting, story-telling, rolling marbles, playing bubbles, theatre-going, dancing, listening to music, collecting sea-shells, riding bicycles, reading, going to the circus, and so on (Gullick 1987; Wilkinson 1910; Sheppard 1986 [1972]). These writings often took the form of foreigners observing the local people from the outside, constructing detailed and often graphic narratives of the various activities. Gullick noted that the bulk of these amusement activities had been imported into Malaya from India, Java, China and Europe and then adapted, and some transformed, to suit local taste and habits. This discovery of cultural hybridisation in leisure is indeed noteworthy. Gullick also noted that the early forms of entertainment were mainly associated with significant religious festivals and events such as weddings and state ceremonies when rituals and entertainment, as spectacle and display of skills, dexterity, and talents, could scarcely be separated. The element of recreation and drama was part and parcel of the ceremonial event itself. The onlookers or participants were eager to be attracted or even shocked. Performances of rituals on such religious occasions were often held in open spaces, in the streets, where people can easily gather together as collectivities, waiting to be charmed or excited.

The early Chinese society of Singapore was an immigrant society in that making a living was the preoccupation and amusements were crude and few and far between, confining themselves to what the sociologists call 'ethnic vices': gambling, smoking, drinking, prostitution, or even crimes and delinquencies (Chan 1991:171). The more organised, large-sized forms of entertainment were primarily religious events, celebrated with opera performances on make-shift stages in the crossroads of the streets. As it happened, entertainment had little to do with consumption, industry and capitalism, at least at the very beginning. An important feature of this Chinese immigrant society in Singapore, like many other immigrant societies elsewhere, was the desire to maintain cultural and religious linkage with the traditions of places of departure for reasons of nostalgia, identity maintenance, cultural nurturance or sheer recreation when life was hard and opportunities were scarce. The past was retrieved in order to make the present bearable and the future predictable — nostalgisation was adopted as a strategy of coping with the immigrant condition. One Chinese almanac opined that an active participation in cultural activities or performances was an important source of mental or even 'spiritual' health of the Chinese immigrants, who were mainly male bachelors far, far away from their homes in Southern China. Cantonese, Teochew and Hokkien opera troupes were brought into Singapore from Shanghai and parts of Southern China on many 'going South' tours where stops were made throughout Southeast Asia. The impact of such dialect-based travelling opera troupes on Southeast Asia remains unexplored in the history of the Chinese diaspora of the 'South Seas.' Infused with strong moral themes, such dramatic narratives about native heroes and emperors laid the cornerstone of a moral community among the Chinese immigrants.

The introduction of amusement parks from Shanghai in the 1920s — first the New World, then the Great World and the Happy World — marked the beginning of Singapore's entertainment going indoors and becoming consumptive. In these 'worlds,' one saw a fascinating array of entertainment genres and forms: dialect-specific operas, movies, dance and music halls, magic shows, restaurants, and so on. Early Singapore society was ethnically segregated, but once inside these multi-purpose, multi-ethnic worlds of entertainment, one saw, as one writer remarked, 'racial conglomeration,' a mixture of east and west, rich and poor, old and young, even entire families, who went there for 'laughter and happiness,' comedies and tragedies of life (Rudolph 1996:21). The appearance of radio and then television put an end to all these worlds, one by one. People then began to acquire entertainment 'on the air' — listening to the radio and watching television quickly became national pastimes because they were cheaper. Science and technology ended it all. It was the eclipse of a golden era, the passing of a delightful, collective past. Singaporeans then began to make their ways into shopping centres, supermarkets, video arcades, and amusement parks. Modernity means people have choices, alternatives when entertainments are compartmentalised because each have taken on a specialised function, no longer multi-purpose. Singaporeans once had 'nowhere to go but these great worlds,' now they go everywhere, happily enjoying the wide options on offer. On the former sites of huge amusement parks now stand warehouses, condominiums, a Christian gospel hall and furniture stores. Places once enchanting and magical are now no more.

A social historical study of the everyday life of the Chinese in Singapore would remain incomplete had the analyst focused his or her sociological gaze at the work, production or economic realm only. One should also want to examine the production and reproduction of their social (and cultural) sphere, noting the transformation in it over time, whilst being mindful of its consequences for the kind of human condition in which the individual and the community will conduct themselves. The social sphere, as concept *and* as social reality, is used here to denote the realm of non-labour, non-work, non-production — it loosely pertains to moments in spaces, delimited or otherwise, when people, alone or with others, 're-create' themselves for pleasure, physical or mental, because they are entertained, amused and being playful in interaction with others (Habermas 1975).

What was the recreational life of the Chinese in Singapore like in the 1900s? How did they amuse, 're-create,' occupy themselves to obtain pleasure upon daily completion of economic production when making a living was at the time a serious, if not the only, preoccupation in an immigrant society?

The Four Moments

Lii postulated four moments in the transformation of the social sphere in a given society: religious ceremonies, public festivals, recreation and consumption (Lii 1996). While religious rituals occur at a fixed time and in a fixed space and participation is somewhat obligatory, the same cannot be said about public festivals, where participation is voluntary. This voluntary participation perhaps marks the beginning of individual freedom and autonomy, a characteristic of modernity. In that sense, an understanding of the history of recreation or amusement in leisure is an important part of the larger modernity *and* postmodernity project. In an immigrant society like Singapore, both content and form of public festivals were traceable to various migrant-sending communities of Southeastern China. As it happened, festivities in Singapore were community-, place- and calendar-bound, reflecting visible boundaries of various subethnicities that divided the Chinese community deeply. Nevertheless, these festivities were communal events that took place in the streets. When amusements went indoors — obtained in the amusement parks after a migrant had purchased a ticket and entered the gates of the amusement park — one witnessed the beginning of recreation as consumption. This was a strictly personal affair since one was to relate only and directly to the spectacle on stage, be it dance, music or drama, and not to anybody else — only one-on-one, no more side-by-side. The simple act of buying a ticket suggested several things: that a choice was made, that consumption occurred, and that enjoyment was experienced alone. The idea of recreating oneself with others in a fixed time and place was thus completely dispensed with — one could go anywhere to do anything anytime, practically (Lii 1996:23). In addition, the onset of radio broadcasting, and then, the all-powerful and all-popular television, put entertainment 'on the air,' transcending everything. Although radio and television were first invented and introduced to the masses, one was gradually inclined to listen to radio or watch television alone in a privatised space, and one often did. Even when one did these with others, one enjoyed the activities as separate individuals. The invisible walls between them, the small space between bodies, and seats, divided, and they divided deeply. Pleasure has become less tactile than mental, an inward rather than an outward experience and, in a word, lonely.

This chapter attempts to construct a genealogy of social transformation of leisure and recreation which culminates in the moment of recreational consumption, or recreation as consumption — a unique moment of modernity when we posit, as ideal types, three places where recreation occurred: in the streets, in the parks, and on the air.

Leisure is, strictly speaking, about non-work. Yet, leisure often imitates work, or worse still, gets replaced and displaced by work in the sense that the condition of alienation and loneliness engendered at work spills over into the leisure realm and gets reproduced there time and again. There is thus the replication of work at play — the person is not only disembedded from work because it exploits, he or she is also disembedded from leisure, entertainment and pleasure because he or she must now, at this historical moment, consume and do so invariably through the mediation of technology, machines and science. The spectre of science and capitalism is felt at work *and* at play, and its grip is tightened.

In the Streets

In 1879, while describing the performance of Chinese operas on the streets of the colony, Vaughan wrote: 'There are theatres in Singapore occupied by Macao, Tay Chew [Teochew] and Hokkien actors. Besides these fixed companies there are itinerant companies who perform on hastily-erected stages, before audiences who stand in the open air unsheltered from wind and rain' (Vaughan 1971[1879]:86).

Leisure, Pleasure and Consumption: Ways of Entertaining Oneself

During the 19th century, immigrants from Southeast China arrived in Singapore and brought with them different genres of Chinese opera, including Hokkien opera, Teochew opera, Cantonese opera and Peking opera. Besides performing in opera houses, as was the case for the *Dan Gui Yuan* Theatre in Chinatown, most of these operas were staged on the streets on the occasions of celebrating, among others, the birthday of the Goddess of Mercy, the Jubilee of Queen Victoria, the Chinese Lunar New Year, the Lantern Festival and the Hungry Ghost Festival. For such street performances, a temporary stage was set up, typically on a main street, for some days, if not weeks; an opera troupe performed for the community as part of the festivities after which the stage would be dismantled.

These performances added colour to the street life of the colony. The photograph on this page shows the staging of a play at a street theatre, probably in the late 19th century. The stage was set up in the middle of the street, stretching across the alley between rows of houses on both sides. Supported by vertical pillars some 20 feet high, the stage was visible to the audience at the other end of the street. The middle section of the stage was the central performing area, while the two 'wings' on the left and the right served as 'side stages,' where the actors rested and prepared for their turns. The top part of the stage was decorated with lanterns, and a pair of lively painted dragons stretched out from the middle section of the theatre. On the upper front of the stage are the four Chinese characters *mei yan qi rui*. Originating from Chinese classical texts, these words mean: a combination of plum and salt brings good fortune. In contrast, the *attap* leaves (of the nipa palm, used especially for thatching) above it have a strong local Malay flavour.

The scene on stage seems to be of the imperial court. A male actor was sitting in the middle of the front stage and appeared to be an emperor or a high-ranking official. The other actors, acting as officials, were presenting themselves to the court. On the left was a backstage worker who was busy moving props. The performers on the stage did not seem the least bothered by this 'outsider.' Another actor was standing behind this worker, waiting to enter the front stage. In the left compartment was yet

Chinese street opera in the late 19th century.

another actor busy putting on his make-up.

The audience was in front of the stage, watching and standing very closely to each other. Instead of concentrating on the performance on stage, some of them at the back were attracted by the camera, the machine which perhaps heralded, at least symbolically, the beginning of technology as a medium of entertainment. The audience was predominantly males between twenty and forty years of age. Very few women were there. The male-female ratio of the Chinese population in Singapore during the nineteenth century was lopsided. In 1890, there were 3,820 females registered, only 4 percent of the total population of the Straits Settlements. In fact, Singapore's Chinese females never exceeded 6 percent before the twentieth century (Lim 1967:99). The audience in the photograph suggests that the Chinese community was predominantly a 'bachelor-immigrant society' during that era. Also, at the time, women were discouraged from attending outdoor public theatres. Traditionally, the locale of street theatres was typically a site where people gathered and mixed. It was also a site where deviant activities such as gambling, murders, fights and elopement took place — part and parcel of an early immigrant society where bachelors succumbed to so-called ethnic vices.

A street theatre near the Singapore River in the late 19th century.

The architectural form of the theatre shown on the facing page is similar to that in the preceding page: built in the middle of the street, stretched across rows of houses, composed of three compartments and decorated with lanterns on the roof. The background of the photograph should be the Boat Quay or the Clarke Quay area. In the late 19th century, the Singapore River was one of the most popular sites for Chinese street operas. On March 8, 1889, Chinese immigrants in the colony celebrated Chinese Emperor Guangxu's wedding and his accession to the throne. The late Song Ong Siang wrote: 'The Chinese made the event a gala season decorating and illuminating their houses, with theatrical performances in different parts of the town. Market Street was *en fete*, with masts erected on each side of the street, along and across which poles were suspended, bearing lamps and lanterns by the hundreds, while a canopy of red and white cloth extended along the whole length of the street. These celebrations closed on the March 23, with a display of fireworks on Hong Lim Green' (1984 [1902]: 251). Musical groups and opera troupes performed at different sites along both sides of the Singapore River. These opera sites extended from today's Ellenborough Street to Upper Circular Road, then further east to Circular Road, Chulia Street, Raffles Place and Change Alley. Different genres of opera were staged along the southern side of the river. Teochew and Peking operas were staged at the *Shisan Hang*; and a female troupe *Yushan Feng*, probably another Teochew troupe, performed at *Shanzai Ding* (*Lat Pau* 8 March 1889). Both places were in areas where the Teochew community concentrated. On the other hand, the *Qingbai Nian* troupe was staging Cantonese operas in Chinatown, the main locale of the Cantonese community at the time. The early Chinese immigrant community of Singapore was visibly demarcated on the basis of dialect groups and district origins. The sites of those opera performances also followed such demarcation — united among themselves, but segmented as a whole.

Viewed as such, streets and alleys in the town centre provided spaces for public entertainment in 19th century Singapore. Whenever and wherever street operas were performed, the site of the temporary stage became the focal point at which people met and gathered. To a Chinese immigrant, his attendance at a public operatic performance was not a mere matter of entertainment or pleasure. To him, the occasion was also of social, religious and cultural significance: it allowed him to meet his fellow clansmen, to pray to their common patron deity and to enjoy and re-live the sounds and sights of their home village in which operas have been a popular spectacle of tradition for many decades. For an immigrant toiling and sweating thousands of miles

A street opera during the Hungry Ghost Festival in the 1950s.

away from home, this could be a major event in his social calendar, being part of the ritual to consolidate with others his communal identity.

The photograph above displays a performance during the Hungry Ghost Festival, in the late 1940s or early 1950s. The primary intent of a Hungry Ghost Festival was a religious one: to feed the ghosts of people who had died violently and keep them from harming the living. In such a communal activity, participants could be neighbours or residents from nearby streets. Besides this geographical affinity, they could be members of the same dialect group. They spoke the same dialect, enjoyed the same opera and identified themselves with the same local culture. In the photograph, a temporary stage was set up in the middle of an alley, making use of the common space between two rows of houses. At the far end of the alley was a temporary shrine or a temple. The stage was a simple one: a table, two chairs and a small backdrop. In contrast to today's common practice, the music accompanists were sitting in the middle of the back of the stage. This arrangement allowed the audience to see all the musicians. Few musical instruments were used; just the bamboo flute, the *suona* (a double reed instrument with a metal bell) and some percussion instruments. The female character performing on the left was probably a male impersonator. Depicting this practice of male impersonation in the Chinese theatre of Singapore, Vaughan wrote: 'There are no female performers. Women are represented by young men who play their parts, capitally deceiving the Chinese themselves. The writer has been at plays where some of the spectators have declared some of the performers to

Leisure, Pleasure and Consumption: Ways of Entertaining Oneself

be women, but he has been assured by the proprietors of the theatre that women are not admitted into their companies' (1971[1879]:85-86).

The atmosphere and the mood of the performance at the Hungry Ghost Festival was very casual. Most of the audience watched from under the canvas shelters set up above the houses. Yet some audience were watching on the hill slope, or even from behind the backdrop. The audience composition in this photograph was quite different this time; although men were still the majority, more women and children could be found. The children looked rather enthusiastic; most of them were standing close to the stage or resting on the edge of it, whereas male adults were watching from behind. Most of the audience were undistracted by the photographer and his camera, which by then had become a common sight.

Puppet plays were popular among children. In the streets of Singapore, various genres of puppetry had been patronised by different dialect communities. String and glove puppets were the specialty of the Hokkien troupes. The Teochew community enjoyed the artistry of the 'wire puppet,' while the Hainanese troupes were skillful in playing the 'rod puppet.'[1] The photograph below shows a string puppet troupe performing one evening. In contrast to scenes in the preceding photographs, the audience were mostly children and only a few male adults. Standing on their stools or sitting on the shoulders of their elder brothers, the children were enticed by the lithe movements of the puppets on stage. The troupe in the photograph was called *Xindeyue*, a well-known string puppet troupe of the Xinghua community, then a minority group

String puppetry in the 1950s.

of the Chinese population in Singapore. Compared with other major dialect groups, such as the Hokkien, the Teochew and the Cantonese, Xinghua migrants arrived in Singapore relatively late (Cheng 1993:29–33). By the time these latecomers arrived, the more profitable trades and the more favourable jobs had already been taken up by other larger dialect groups. The Xinhua managed to find their own niche in the transport industry — from the earlier rickshaw and trishaw to the later tram, mini-lorry and taxi. In the first half of the 20th century, Xinghua people lived around Rochor Canal Road, Sungei Road, Weld Road, Arab Street and Queen Street, near the concentration of rickshaw lodging-houses in the area (Cheng 1993:29–35). It was also here where the puppet troupes built their stages, including the one shown in the preceeding photograph.

In its golden age, this small Xinghua community was able to support two puppet troupes and two amateur opera groups that routinely put on performances during various religious festivals. The most well-known performance of the Xinghua troupes was undoubtedly *Mulian Jiumu* (*Mulian Rescues his Mother from Hell*). Organised by the Kiew Lee Tong Temple, this internationally-known play has been performed every ten years since 1944 to deliver the souls of orphans from their torture in hell. As such, the function of the play was not merely to entertain; its performance was an integral part of the ritual of deliverance, performed to 'cleanse the community of all impurities, which drove away the menace caused by the malevolent forces of contagion, and which pacified the dissatisfied souls of those who had suffered violent and premature death' (cited in Johnson 1989:207).[2]

Besides Chinese operas, another traditional street entertainment was storytelling. According to the famous Cantonese storyteller Lee Fook Hung, more popularly known as Lee Dai Soh, street storytelling in Singapore was popular before World War II. Stories were told in different dialects to serve different communities. Every evening, the Teochew storytellers performed near Boat Quay; Hokkien stories were told in the Telok Ayer area; and Cantonese performers told stories to their fellow clansmen near the South Heaven Hotel on Eu Tong Sen Street and today's Kreta Ayer People's Theatre, both in Chinatown (Lee Fook Hung 000260/07).

To most Chinese Singaporeans, however, Boat Quay was a memorable place for storytelling. 'There was a *jamban* (public toilet) at the Boat Quay. Four to five storytellers performed there every evening,' recalled Tan Giak, a professional Teochew storyteller in the early 1960s (Tan Giak 001040/02). A storyteller usually performed between 6:00 pm and 7:00 pm, after dinnertime. Before he started, he would light up

Storytelling along the Singapore River in the 1950s.

an incense stick standing on a wooden box in front of him while his audience sat around him on straw mats or wooden planks. 'Most of the audience were male, from the ages of fifty to seventy,' recalled Tan, 'Children and women seldom attended.' Before starting a new episode, he would recapitulate briefly what had been told the day before. After twenty minutes, or so, the incense stick burnt out, signalling the end of the first session as well as the time to collect money from the audience. The fee for each session was five cents, and there were usually six or seven sessions each night. The performance usually ended at 10:00 pm. It could take ten to twenty days to finish the whole story. 'The most popular stories were the martial art stories, since they were more thrilling and exciting — they also revealed a theme of righteousness. Our audience did not favour love stories, like *The Dream of the Red Chamber*. A storyteller should know the taste of the audience,' said Tan. The storyteller always knew what his audience wanted to hear. As it happened, probably the same audience came back, night after night, all wanting to listen to the same story, being swept away by episodes of the drama serial by a storyteller they all admired. Thus, a temporary bond grew among them.

In the Parks

The emergence of amusement parks in the 1920s and 1930s ushered in a new concept of entertainment to the community. The New World amusement park and the Great World were opened in 1923 and 1931, respectively. The Happy World, situated between Geylang Road and Mountbatten Road, started to operate in 1935. (Rudolph 1996:21-33; Wang 1988:32-52) Originating from Shanghai, these 'Worlds' provided 'holistic,' culturally and ethnically integrated entertainment which 'created a unique mixture of Eastern and Western entertainments with multi-ethnic participation' (Rudolph 1996:21). Unlike the street operas and street storytelling, which hailed from Southern China and were predominately community-specific and spatially spread out, the entertainments in these new amusement centres tended to be centralised, westernised, commercialised and multi-ethnic. A diversified, multicultural variety of entertainments was concentrated in these 'Worlds,' where amusements were produced and consumed as commodities. It was a place designed for recreational consumption, arguably a first in Singapore.

A flyer for the Great World from the late 1940s (on the facing page) shows a wide range of entertainments housed in an amusement park. At the Great World, Cantonese, Mandarin and Western movies were shown in the *Qingtian* (Blue Sky) Theatre, the Globe Theatre and the Atlantic Theatre. To celebrate its 19th anniversary, admission into all the movie and drama theatres was free for two days. Hokkien, Cantonese and Han operas were staged by local amateur groups. In the *Xiaoguanghan* Theatre, the renowned professional actor, Phan Wait Hong, performed in a Peking opera. While a Malay dance troupe performed in the Vienna Theatre and a brass band and a harmonica group played Western music in the Garden Cabaret, a Cantonese storyteller performed in the Central Garden. In the same venue, the magician Dr Liang Tan performed his frightening magic act, 'Beheading,' with elaborate equipment made in England which cost 500 pounds. During these two days of celebration, the Great

Top: The New World amusement park in the 1960s.

Above: The Great World amusement park in the 1960s.

Leisure, Pleasure and Consumption: Ways of Entertaining Oneself

A flyer for the Great World from the early 1950s.

The Silver Moon Revue in the 1930s.

World Cabaret held special parties, announcing that 'all the musicians of the dance band will play extravagantly; all the dance hostesses will dance wildly; the whole atmosphere will be extremely hot; the guests will be entertained unrestrainedly.'

In the early 1930s, a new type of entertainment arrived in Singapore: the *gewutuan*. The term *gewutuan* literally means 'song and dance troupe,' and was usually translated into English as 'revue.' Originating from Shanghai in the late 1920s, this form of entertainment, not unlike a variety show, included music performances, dances, drama and occasionally magic acts and acrobatic displays. Some of the famous *gewutuan* troupes that had visited Singapore before World War II were the *Meihua* (Plum Flower), the *Zhonghua* (China), the *Yinyue* (Silver Moon), the *Tianma* (Heaven Horse), and the *Guofa* (Prosperous Country). The photograph on the right shows postures of the dancers of the *Yinyue* troupe.

When *Gewutuan* first arrived in Singapore in the 1930s, it was regarded as a genre of show business that was fash-

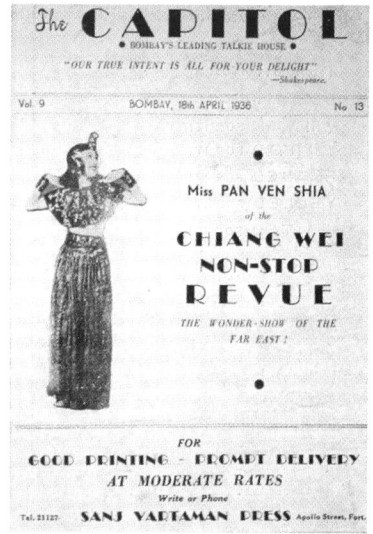

The Chiang Wei Non-stop Revue in 1936.

ionable, modern and trendy. Amusement parks provided the major venues for this popular entertainment (Bai Yan 1992:5). 'After performing in various theatres in Singapore and Malaya, we started to move into the amusement parks,' said Bai Yan, a renowned performer in Singapore and a core member of the *Yinyue* and *Jinxin* (Gold Star) troupes. 'At that time, amusement parks were the only place for Singaporeans to find their entertainment and to spend their money. They were extremely crowded, particularly during the weekends. We performed on an open-air stage, and visitors at the parks were free to watch by standing outside at a distance. But if one chose to watch closer and take a seat in the auditorium, one needed to buy a ticket. It cost between twenty and forty cents. After one had entered, the ticket would be stuck at the back of his seat. The ticket checker could then see it clearly' (Bai Yan n.d.).

A standard evening of a *gewutuan* performance began with music, followed by different programs of dancing. Between the dancing, there would be short skits or one-act plays. There were not too many singing programs: 'Microphones and amplifiers were still not popular at that time. It was not easy to find a well-trained vocalist who can sing in a big auditorium without a microphone,' explained Bai Yan.[3] When the performance started at 7:30pm, the lights of the auditorium dimmed. The band of the troupe kicked off by playing Western music for the first half hour. The band of the *Yinyue Gewutuan* consisted of about ten musicians, playing two pianos, one violin, three saxophones, one oboe and two trumpets. Bai Yan was particularly proud of the artistry of his musicians: 'Most of them were Filipinos who used to work for big

Leisure, Pleasure and Consumption: Ways of Entertaining Oneself

The "Leg Dance" from the 1930s.

cabarets and hotels in Singapore. During the War, they lost their jobs and joined our troupe. Their artistic standards were very high. At that time, each troupe had its own set of musical programs. The leader of the band kept the musical scores close to himself, a kind of trade secret; he would never reveal them to others.'[4]

After this prelude of Western music, the program would move on to a variety of dance performances, ranging from traditional folk dances to various styles of Western dance. The photographs on pages 167–168 reveal different scenes of dances by the *Yinyue* and *Jinxin* troupes in the early 1940s. In the picture above, the chorus girls of the *Yinyue* troupe were performing the sensational 'Leg Dance' (*Fentui Wu*). 'Blues' was a piece in which six men in tuxedo danced a waltz with women to 'blues music.' 'During war time, these tuxedo coats were not hard to find in an ordinary pawn shop,' Bai Yan joked, 'Life was difficult then. Even the foreigners needed to pawn their formal clothes.' In the *Jianli Wu*, 'Dance of Health and Strength,' the women dancers showed the beauty and strength of their bodies by striking glamourous poses. 'For our *Yinyue* troupe, three fifths of the troupe members were Shanghai ladies. All of them wore sexy costumes: dancing suits, short pants and brassieres. We really created a sensation,' said Bai Yan (1992:5). The *Jiaojian Wu*, 'Dance of the Foot

PAST TIMES: A SOCIAL HISTORY OF SINGAPORE

Tips,' was a popular name for ballet. In the following photograph, we see seven dancers performing. 'In fact,' explained Mrs Bai Yan, 'only Xu Lianmei in the middle had received proper training in ballet. The other six performers, including myself, were just making some poses or moving around her.' Mrs Bai Yan, then using her maiden name Ye Qing, was another major dancer of the *Jinxin* Troupe. Xu Lianmei, originally a member of the *Guofa Gewutuan* of Shanghai, joined the *Yinyue* troupe and became its lead dancer. One of Xu Lianmei's best-known pieces was the *Yinshen Wu*, 'Dance of the Silver Goddess.' For this piece, Xu danced with her whole body painted silver. A column writer recalled his experience in watching this performance in the New World: 'I saw a woman who wore, according to today's standard, a very conservative swimming suit and whose body was painted totally with shiny silver powder, dancing gracefully on the stage under dim light. In my impression, she danced like a water snake.'[5]

Top: The "Dance of the Foot Tips" in the 1930s.

Above: "Dance of the Silver Goddess" in the 1950s.

The highlight of the night was either a performance of *gewuju* ('dance drama'), or *huaju* ('spoken drama') for sixty to ninety minutes. *Gewuju* was a play that told a story through music and dance — without dialogues. Some of the well-known items included: *The Queen of the Snake Kingdom*, *Dance of the Spider*, *The Wizard of Oz*, and the sensational *The Market of Flesh*. The last, a four-act play, was also known as *A Night in Persia*. Set in the Middle East, it is a love story about two Persian slaves, and their struggle with a local tyrant. The following picture on the facing page shows a scene in which the Persian female slaves were being sold in the public market, exhibiting an exotic and sensuous world of the imagined Middle East.

Not all performances on the stage of a *gewutuan* appealed to sensuality. Being graduates from the academies of performing arts in Shanghai, some members of the *gewutuan* were eager to produce modern plays written by mainstream Chinese playwrights. Staged items included *Thunderstorm*, *Wilderness*, *The Ghost Buster*, and *The Abyss*. *The Abyss*, a three-act play written in Shanghai, was performed for the first time in Singapore by the *Yinyue* troupe in 1941. 'We attracted important people from the circles of art and culture, including the celebrated writer Xia Xian and the painter Xu Beixiong. *The Abyss* was a lengthy play of five hours. Our audience entered the theatre at 8:00 pm and stayed up watching until 1:00 am in the morning. Unlike today, they would not call a taxi. They all walked back home in the dark,' said Bai Yan.

Gewutuan in the amusement parks began to decline in the 1940s, and was gradually replaced by *getai*. *Getai* literally means 'song stage,' which emerged during the years of Japanese occupation. According to Shangguan Liuyun, a senior Chinese popular song writer, singer and movie star, one of the early *getai* in Singapore was the *Weiyang Gong* (Palace of Day and Night) of the New World. During the War, the *getai* in the New World was bombed and destroyed by the Japanese. The park then set up a new stage in the *Gongkai Tai* (Public Stage) for musicians. Some senior officers of the Japanese army were particularly fond of music. They brought scores of their favourite music to the *getai* and ordered the musicians to play.[6] Initially, the programs performed by the *getai* were very simple, mainly songs. Later, this burgeoning entertainment was enriched when the former members of the *gewutuan* joined the *getai* troupes as the former began to lose their popularity in the late 1940s. These newcomers quickly introduced new programs of dance, drama and acrobatics.

Getai reached its heyday in the 1950s, possibly because of the Korean War. As the demand for rubber increased drastically during the war, many Singaporean merchants benefited from the rubber trade and had more money to spend. In this golden era of the *getai*, there were four *getai* in the New World, and three in the Great World and the Happy World. The better-known *getai* were the *Bailemen* (Paramount), *Xianggelila* (Shangri-La), *Yehuayuan* (Night Garden), *Manjianghong* (Red Filling the River), *Xianle* (Heavenly Joy) and *Fenghuang* (Phoenix). 'At that time we were all paid well,'

The Market of Flesh (A Night in Persia), circa 1930.

Singers on the *getai* stage in the 1950s.

said Bai Yan, who joined the *Bailement Getai* of the Great World in the 1950s. 'Some of the performers were paid as much as $1,200 per month. This was the salary of a high-ranked manager.'[7]

The audience for *getai* came from different sectors of the society: businessmen, journalists, students and housewives. Upon arrival at a *getai*, one would be invited to sit at a table covered by clean white cloth. He would then be served a bottled soft drink, such as Greenspot, which cost him about eighty cents to a dollar. The performance would start at 8:00 pm. All the singers of the troupe would line up on stage to sing the opening song, usually a march, such as *Qiancheng Wanli* ('A Bright Future'), or *Boaige* ('Song of Universal Love'). It would then be followed by programs of singing, either in solo or duet. The most popular were traditional folk songs and Mandarin popular songs from Mainland China. When describing the behaviour of the singers on stage, Bai Yan said: 'In the 1950s, the singers sang seriously, without body movements. They came up the stage, stood there and sang with their eyes staring at the scores on the stand. Today's dance-cum-singing was introduced quite late.'

Drama was another genre of entertainment welcomed by the audience. As the competition between *getai* was very keen, the major *getai* all had their own dramatic masterpieces: *The Story of Ah Q*, *The Wild Rose*, *Beware of Fire* were some of the classical *huaju* ('spoken drama') frequently performed on the stages of *getai*. Probably influenced by Hollywood movies, *getai* troupes also produced popular plays adapted from Western stories. Shangguan Liuyun recalled how he revised the story of Samson and Delilah: 'Samson was blind and sang his miserable song while he was pushing the grinder. We put a big grinder on the stage. In the last act, Samson pushed down the city wall which was made of cardboard boxes.'[8] *The Great Dictator* was a skit written and performed by Bai Yan. Imitating the Hollywood movie by Charles Chaplin, this short sketch of about eight minutes parodied Adolf Hitler, dramatising the insanity and eccentricity of this malicious figure. 'It took quite some time to find the appropriate costume for Hitler,' said Bai Yan. 'Finally, I decided to use a police uniform.' Dramatic pieces like *The Story of Ah Q* and *The Great Dictator* continued to be popular. Watching *The Great Dictators*, the audience smiled, laughed and cheered, apparently bemused by the humour and the satire.

The Great Dictator in the 1950s.

On the Air

The introduction of radio broadcasting turned the history of amusement in Singapore to a brand new page. It represented the beginning of a modern entertainment that went beyond the boundary of a dialect-specific community or an amusement park. The mode of entertainment had changed from attending an immediate performance in a specific place during a specific time, to listening to air-transmitted programs through individual receivers. Physical space and time reduced themselves and collapsed, giving way to a new acoustic space produced by new technology, by new machines — a space that knows no borders.[9]

Bottom Right:
A couple listening to a radio broadcast in the 1950s.

Bottom Left:
A broadcaster in the studio in 1952.

171

Between 1936 (the year the British Malayan Broadcasting Corporation set up the first commercial broadcasting station in Singapore) and 1959 (when Radio Singapore was formed, having separated from the Radio Malaya), Cathay Building and Caldecott Hill were two places which had witnessed the history of Singapore broadcasting. Shortly after it had established its radio station in Caldecott Hill, the British government purchased the private British Malayan Broadcasting Corporation in 1940. It later amalgamated with the Ministry of Information, then operating as Malaya Broadcasting Corporation.[10] Before the outbreak of the Pacific War in 1941, the Department of Broadcasting was moved to the Cathay Building. Each day it broadcast twelve news bulletins in English, nine in Chinese, as well as bulletins in Malay, Tamil, Hindustani, Urdu, French and Dutch. When Singapore fell into the hands of the Japanese in 1942, the Japanese Military Administration took over the equipment left behind by the British and started to broadcast under the name of Syonan Hoso Kyoku. After the war, the British returned to the colony and reopened the radio station, resuming broadcasts on April 1, 1946. Popularly known as 'Radio Malaya,' it had branch stations in Kuala Lumpur, Penang and Malacca.[11] In 1952, the new broadcasting house in Caldecott Hill became the centre of wireless broadcasting in Singapore.

Since 1946, daily programs of classical and popular music, news, drama serials, storytelling, quizzes, sport commentaries, religious services, amateur talent shows, talks and documentaries were broadcast in English, Malay, Chinese and Tamil. In that year, there were only 1,000 hours of programs in English. The year after, it increased to 1,470, running from 1:00 pm to 2:00 pm and from 8.15 pm to 11:00 pm daily. In 1953, English early morning programs were extended to as early as 7.15 am. Since then, 'I was listening to a repeat broadcast of such-and-such program' became an excuse for late arrivals at the office.[12] The Chinese section of the radio station felt the need to cater to different dialect groups. Since the era of Radio Malaya, the Chinese section had been broadcasting in seven dialects: 'Mandarin for the younger generation; Cantonese, Amoy and Teochew for the commercial and industrial communities; Hakka for miners and farmers; and Foochow and Hylam [Hainanese] for coffee shops and eating-houses.'[13] Seven dialects were used in newscasts. Vernon Palmer, a program assistant of Radio Singapore,

An Indian musical group in the studio in 1953.

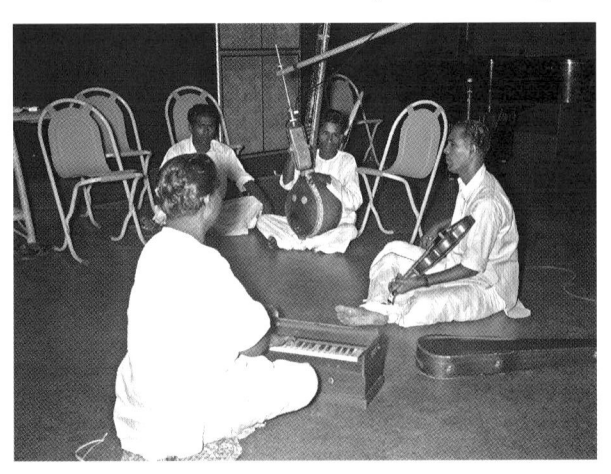

recalled that visiting foreign guests were fascinated when they saw a Cantonese news announcer passing his script to a Hokkien announcer and then to a Hakka announcer in the studio. They read off the same script but in their own dialects, thus not understanding each other.[14]

The most popular of the programs in Malay were the studio broadcasts of Malay music, old Malay folksongs and popular English and American hit songs, particularly sambas and rhumbas, arranged in a characteristic Malay manner.[15] For the Chinese, modern Mandarin songs and traditional operas were the most popular. Six types of operas were broadcast, and those in Cantonese and Teochew had the greatest following.[16] Amateur musical groups of different dialects were invited to the studio. 'To perform in the studio was really something,' said Foong Choon Hon, 'the musical groups of the clan associations treated it as a big event.'[17] The photographs above shows the performance of an Indian musical group and the Chinese Siong Leng Musical Association (a musical group which performed *nanyin* music) in the studio.

A majority of the music programs relied on commercial records. The picture at the bottom of this page shows the collection of gramophone records at the station. In 1953, the total number of records in the Gramophone Library of Radio Malaya amounted to about 50,000 pieces.[18] This collection included discs of Western music, Indian music (Hindustani, Tamil, Telugu and Malayalam), Malay discs produced locally, and Chinese discs in six different dialects (Mandarin, Cantonese, Hokkien, Teochew, Hainanese and Hakka) imported from Hong Kong. In the early 1950s, the station suffered from a shortage of commercial gramophone records in Foochow, Amoy, Hakka and Hainanese, which handicapped producers who wanted to present musical dramas in these dialects.[19] Partly due to a change in the political situation in China, Shanghai stopped being the centre of production of Chinese commercial records after 1949. Then a disaster was to strike: the broadcasting house caught on fire on June 15, 1967, and 94,000 records were destroyed or damaged. The station quickly built up the collection

The Siong Leng Musical Association playing *nanying* music in the 1950s.

The gramophone collection of Radio Malaya in 1954.

The "School Broadcast" in 1954.

again and has not stopped playing since.[20]

Children growing up in the 1950s still remember the 'School Broadcast,' the educational programs broadcast during school hours. In the late 1950s, these programs were broadcast 22 hours a week in English, Chinese, Malay and Tamil.[21] Yang Muxi, a producer of the 'Chinese School Broadcast,' explained the historical background of the program: 'At that time, schools in Malaya and Singapore were facing a lot of difficulties: insufficient teachers, lack of extra-curriculum readings, extreme scarcity of 'children's songs.' Music teachers were badly needed. The idea of a 'School Broadcast' was to help these schools out' (Yang 1996:90). Various subjects were produced, including music, dance, storytelling, English, history and geography. 'The facilities were rather limited and poor. In our studio, we only had one piano, two microphones, a sand-stone basin, a few broken bowls and plates and a door. Most of the sound effects were produced by the vocal imitation of the broadcasters themselves. We did not have any recording equipment. All programs were on live transmission.' But judging from the smiling faces of the children audience in the picture above, the programs appeared to be well received.

Besides this government station, the private Rediffusion started broadcasting in 1949. This new competitor to the government station operated on two channels, the Gold Channel in Chinese and the Silver Channel in Chinese and English. The photograph on the opposite page shows the Rediffusion Building on Clemenceau Avenue. 'Pay attention to the tree next to the building,' said Weng Shudao, a retired program director of Rediffusion, 'it has been there since Rediffusion started. It has grown up hand in hand with Rediffusion.' [22]

A columnist recalled the popularity of Rediffusion in the early 1950s: 'The age when broadcasting was affordable to common people began with Rediffusion...Their subscription fee was only four to five dollars, and they gave you a receiver free. People did not need to buy a radio set which would cost them a few hundred dollars. Seven to eight households sharing the same floor in a house in Chinatown usually subscribed to the service as a group. It cost each of them one dollar or less; in return, they were entitled to listen from day to night... Owners of shops and factories were also keen to install a set to allow their shopkeepers or workers to enjoy the delightful and colourful programs. Hence, listening to radio broadcasting was no longer a privilege for a small group of people only... Rediffusion had spread rapidly and became very popular in the community. Their Cantonese programs can be heard along the streets and alleys in Chinatown. Coffee shops would be full of listeners when the time came for the storytelling of Lee Dai Soh' (Si 1997:8). Radio was then a shared entertainment; listening to radio was a collective activity, building community, bonds and ties. There was something communal about a group of friends or neighbours gathering around a radio set at a certain time, listening, being informed, entertained and excited. Radio was once a binding force. It cemented relationships.

The Rediffusion building in the 1950s.

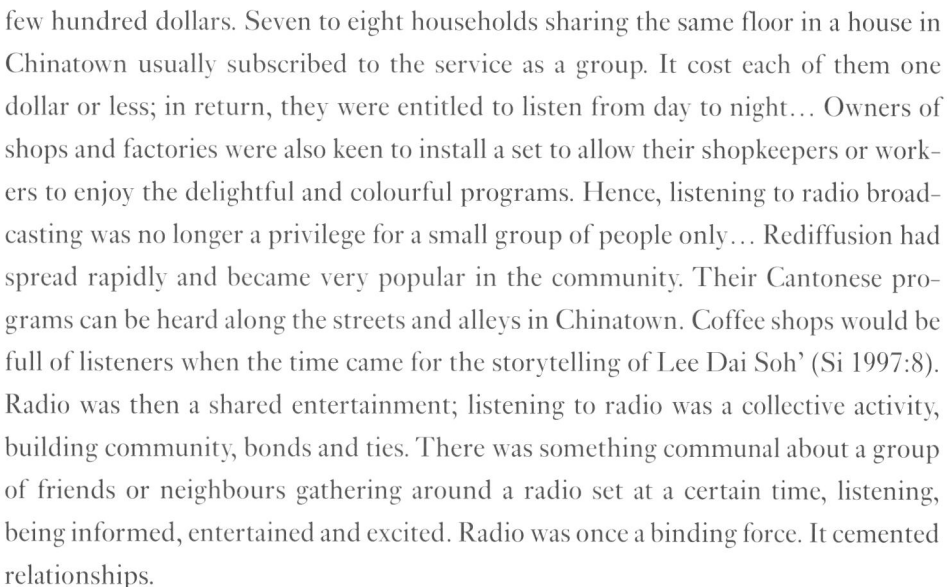

In the 1960s, Rediffusion was an inseparable part of the daily life of a family. Chew Kok Wei, a photographer, recalled his experience: 'The wooden box [the receiver] was set in my grandpa's room. He was the one to decide which channel we should listen to. My grandpa is a Hokkien. But both my granny and my mother are Cantonese, and we spoke Cantonese at home. Basically we all favoured the Cantonese programs. But we also listened to the programs of other dialects. We seldom turned the receiver off. We just let it run for the whole day. In the morning, Rediffusion was our alarm clock. Every morning we would be awakened by the morning prelude. I was then studying in a primary school near the Great World. The school day ended at 1:00 pm. It took about twenty minutes to walk back home. Everyday I ran home in order to be on time to listen to Lee Dai Soh's story. At night, we were very excited to listen to the program *Yeban Qitan* ('Ghost Stories Told at Midnight'). The lights in the house were turned off. In the dark, my brothers and sisters and I hid ourselves under a blanket. The sound was turned to a minimum. When the frightful music started, it was hair-raising.' [23]

Among the storytellers, the Cantonese storyteller Lee Dai Soh seemed to be the best known. He joined the Radio Malaya in 1938, telling 15-minute stories in a program called *Tantian Shuodi* ('From Heaven to Earth'). This started a lifelong career for this 'King of Storytelling.' 'Later I told serial stories,' said Mr. Lee, 'By that time, the Pacific War had started already. We needed to do propaganda [sic]. I told a story as part of a one-hour program from 5:00 pm to 6:00 pm everyday. My storytelling would be interrupted anytime by the latest news. This program was called *Nongcun Guangbo* ('The Rural Broadcast').' (Lee Fook Hung 000260/07)

Why was Lee Dai Soh's storytelling so fascinating? 'He tried to speak the ordinary language in a clear, slow and steady way. His stories were simple, not complicated at all. These folk tales were especially welcomed by the common people,' explained Foong Choon Hon. Speaking about his technique of storytelling, Lee said, 'I talk very fast in my daily conversation…However, once I was in the studio, sat down and began to perform [sic], quite naturally, I would slow down my speed of talking… The way to tell a story on the air is just like talking to a blind man. Although he cannot see you, he can still grasp your gestures through your voice. Then the storyteller is considered to be successful.' The photograph below shows Lee Dai Soh per-

Lee Dai Soh at work on his percussion instrument, *muyu* ('wooden-fish') in the early 1950s.

forming with the percussion instrument *muyu* ('wooden-fish'), telling a story based on the 'wooden-fish book,' a type of Cantonese vernacular narrative; the photograph on this page shows him telling his story in the studio.

Lee Dai Soh's favourite storyteller on the air was Li Wo, another Cantonese who had started to tell the *kongzhong xiaoshuo* (fiction on the air) in Guangzhou, Hong Kong and Macao (Wu Hao 1993:46- 64). 'It seemed that [Li] performed storytelling through a microscope. He went into the most minute details,' said Lee. 'There was a larger leisure class in Hong Kong (than in Singapore). They liked to lie down, relax and enjoy the stories slowly. Thus, Li Wo was very popular in Hong Kong. On the other hand, our Singaporeans found Li Wo too slow, too tedious' (Li Dasha [Lee Dai Soh] 1984:30-31).

Lee Dai Soh telling his story in the studio in the 1970s.

Another popular program on the Rediffusion was the 'dramatised story' (*xijuhua xiaoshuo*). The Cantonese masterpiece *Cimu Lei* ('The Tears of a Loving Mother'), told by the renowned broadcaster Ngai Mun, moved the hearts of housewives, *amah* (maids) and many, many other listeners. Rey Chow, the daughter of Ngai Mun, highlighted the distinction between this new genre and the traditional mode of storytelling: 'My mother's early work, then, consisted primarily in the instigation, through practice, of a transformation that was to become the way all radio dramas were conceptualised. Instead of using the single-person narration model, she created what was to become known as *hei kek fa siu suet / xiju hua xiaoshuo* ('dramatised fiction') — the presentation of which resembled a stage drama insofar as it introduced dialogue and used actors and actresses to play different characters in a story…there were now multiple voices and thus multiple personalities involved in the production of a single story' (Chow 1997:109–27). *Cimu Lei* became a hit on the radio and was subsequently made into an equally successful film. These programs played a decisive role in disseminating traditional values and ethics. Foong Choon Hon explained: 'Radio stories in those days were different from today's movies and TV dramas. Stories broadcast in that era always highlighted kindness, benevolence, filial piety, honesty and loyalty between people. Nowadays these traditional virtues are considered to be obsolete, gone with the era of radio story-broadcasting.'[24] Radio was thus inadvertently a moral force, building cohesive, moral communities out of an immigrant society.

Conclusion

A social history of leisure in Singapore, as attempted in this chapter, thus traces the transformation in the character and conduct of the social sphere, noting how individuals relate to the community and the cultural spectacle-performance itself. Early forms of entertainment or performance in the Chinese immigrant society of Singapore took the shape of festivals and festivities on special religious occasions. As such they took place in designated public places, usually main cross streets and alleys, and also at designated times, which could last for days, if not weeks — one thus marked down on the calendar dates during which one was being 're-created.' Celebration of festivals served religious, ethnic as well as moral functions, where values were reproduced and reinforced.

The sites of festive celebration being open and public, as in the form of a makeshift stage on which operas were performed, people of the same ethnicity gathered, concentrated, mixed, participated, had fun face-to-face, interacted and rubbed shoulders with each other. Ethnicity was produced when hundreds of people piled high on top of each other. Such festive events were as recreational as they were community-building and identity-bestowing. Such and such a person would go to such and such a street opera because he or she knows many others would be there — same time, same place, same people. The accent was on the body, the body of the other, on sensations, the physical. Entertainment during this period was a collective, multi-functional, many-faceted event. Part of the entertainment, of the pleasure, was seeing other people and interacting with them.

Leisure made an about face when entertainment moved out of the streets and went indoors, into amusement parks, cinemas, theaters, dance and music halls — when one had to decide when, where, why, with whom and at what price one was to be entertained. Entertainment became less communal, more individualistic, and therefore more voluntary. One had to pay a price, buy a ticket, to engage in a pleasurable activity. Entertainment was becoming consumption; or consumption was displacing entertainment, depending on how one viewed it. This was indeed a profound moment of social transformation because leisure took on a voluntary, individualistic, consumer, if not capitalistic, character. An individual had more of a choice at this point than before when he was once under the tight grip of the immigrant society which decreed how he conducted himself at work *and* at play. He would labour to pay for his leisure and pleasure; pleasure was commodified as recreational consumption or consumptive recreation. At this moment of history, whether he was watching a dance or listening to a song, he reduced himself to a passive, non-participative relationship with the object of desire. His sensations were by now becoming more audio-visual than bodily, maintaining a detached, distanced, and perhaps atomized and alienated relationship with all, just like at the realm of work. He had paid a price for being with himself, literally!

Unlike the earlier historical moment of festival celebration as collective entertainment, consumer leisure was obtained at scattered time, diffused space — anytime, anywhere, anything — thus the luxury of voluntarism and choice. Yes, one had a choice, indeed many choices. Recreational singularity contrasted with consumptive multiplicity. Now, one actually had to learn to pick and choose, to decide for oneself, so as to 're-create' oneself. One had to learn to make a choice to have fun.

The consumption of entertainment offered on the air through radio and television was made possible by the mediation of machines, equipment, technology, science and capitalism. Machines now came between the entertainer and the entertained, and created strangeness and anonymity; their extreme portability and manipulability meant a total annihilation of all things fixed by time and space. Streets, stages, audiences, community boundaries — all things material, physical — were gone. Increasingly, people listened to the radio, watched television, enjoyed a movie, a concert, a play, all on their own. The walls that divided the listener-watchers were invisible, but frighteningly real (Sennett 1978:217, cited in Lii 1996:26). The mass media transformed collectivities, cohesive or otherwise, into masses. A movie-goer faced the silver screen, alone, wrapped up in darkness and oblivious to anyone near and around him. Indeed a lonely experience. Admittedly, it was perhaps less so in the case of the radio and television when they were first introduced into Singapore. Being rather expensive technologies in those days, listening to radio and watching television were communal activities when families, peers and neighbours shared a radio or television set and were entertained, enchanted, and sometimes excited together. Radio was once known to extend the community, but no more. The spirit of communality began to disappear as technologies became more affordable. Separate radios for many, not one for all. A wide variety of electronic devices of entertainment went from streets to shops to homes to individual bedrooms. They are now smaller, lighter, all personalised and portable, thus a private property to be enjoyed only by oneself. One is now in his other own world, literally and metaphorically. The completion of privatisation of entertainment and leisure also meant the ascendancy of the individual and the demise of tribalism, community, tradition, history. One must now face the music, alone.

Acknowledgements

We would like to thank Mr and Mrs Bai Yan, Madam Xu Lianmei, Mr Shangguan Liuyun, Mr Foong Choon Hon, Mr and Mrs Wang Shudao and Mr Chew Kok Wei. We also thank Yee Wee Cheng, Julia Chee, Moey Kok Keong and Jason Lim for their help at the various stages of our writing.

Endnotes

1. Also known as *zhangtou muou* (staff-head puppet) or *shoutuo muou* (hand-supported puppet), the 'rod puppet' has been most popular in Guangdong and Hainan provinces. The size of a rod puppet measures about three feet in length and is composed of three parts: the head, the shoulders, and the arms. When performing, the puppeteer holds the puppet above his head and controls the mechanism of the puppet from the bottom by moving the central rod with his right hand and the other two arm sticks with his left hand. Locally known as *zhiyingxi* (paper shadow play), the 'wire puppet' is the dominant puppet theatre of the Teochew. The size of a wire puppet is about eight to twelve inches, with three major steel wires to control the movement of the figure body. Usually the puppeteers sit behind the backdrop of the stage, controlling the puppets from the back. See Tsao Pen-yeh, *Puppet Theatres in Hong Kong and their Origin* (Hong Kong: Urban Council, 1987), p. 83–89.

2. Piet van der Loon, 'Les origines rituelles du théâtre chinois,' *Journal Asiatique*, 265: 1–2 (1977), pp. 161–162. We are using the translation by Stephen Teiser. See van der Loon's 'The Ritual Behind the Opera: A Fragmentary Ethnography of the Ghost Festival, A.D. 400-1900,' in *Ritual Opera, Operatic Ritual: Mu-lien Rescues His Mother in Chinese Popular Culture*, ed. David Johnson (Berkeley: Chinese Popular Culture Project, 1989).

3. Personal interview with Bai Yan on February 21, 1997.

4. Ibid.

5. '*Tingge Kanxi De Na Duan Rizi*,' (*The Days of Song and Drama*), *Lianhe Wanbao*, March 26, 1984, p. 19.

6. Personal interview with Shangguan Liuyun on 28 May 1997. Guan Xinyi, a late *getai* performer, also postulated that *getai* was started during the Japanese occupation. He particularly mentioned the *Yinzuo* (Ginza) *getai* of the Great World in his talk entitled *Fengfeng yuyu yi getai* ('My Recollections of *Getai*'), 18 November 1995, *Qiongzhou Huiguan* (The Clan Assiciation of Qiongzhou), Singapore. See also *Xinjiapo zhinan* (*Directory of Singapore*), ed. Pan Xingnong, (Singapore: Nantao Publishing House, 1955; 5th edition), p. 83.

7. Personal interview with Bai Yan on February 21, 1997.

8. Personal interview with Shangguan Liuyun on 28 May 1997.

9. For a discussion on the concept of acoustic space, see Lee Tong Soon, "Technology and the Production of Islamic Space: The Call to Prayer in Singapore," *Ethnomusicology*, 43 (1), 1999: 86-100.

10. *Report of the Department of Broadcasting for the Years 1946-52* (Singapore: Government Printing Office, 1953), p. 1.

11. Foong Chong Hon, '*Da zhan qian hou de diantai*' ('Radio Broadcasting Before and After World War II'), in *Chengshi Huixiang* (Echoes in the City), ed. Zhang Liping et al. (Singapore: Radio Corporation of Singapore, 1996), p. 88.

12. *Report of the Department of Broadcasting for the Year 1953* (Singapore: Government Printing Office, 1954), p. 3.

13. Ibid., p. 8.

14. Singapore Broadcasting Corporation, *Radio Singapore, 4 January 1959*, c1988.

15. *Report of the Department of Broadcasting for the Years 1946-52*, p. 10.

16. *Report of the Department of Broadcasting for the Year 1953*, p. 8.

17. Personal interview with Foong Choon Hon on May 10, 1997.

18. *Report of the Department of Broadcasting for the Year 1954* (Singapore: Government Printing Office, 1956), p. 17.

19. *Report of the Department of Broadcasting for the Year 1953*, p. 8.

20. Singapore Broadcasting Corporation, *Radio Singapore, 4 January 1959*.

21. *Radio Singapore: A Story of Progress (1945-1959)* (Singapore: Government Printing Office, c1959), p. 10.

22. Personal interview with Weng Shudao on May 10, 1997.

23. Personal interview with Chew Kok Wei on June 4, 1997.

24. Personal interview with Foong Choon Hon on May 10, 1997.

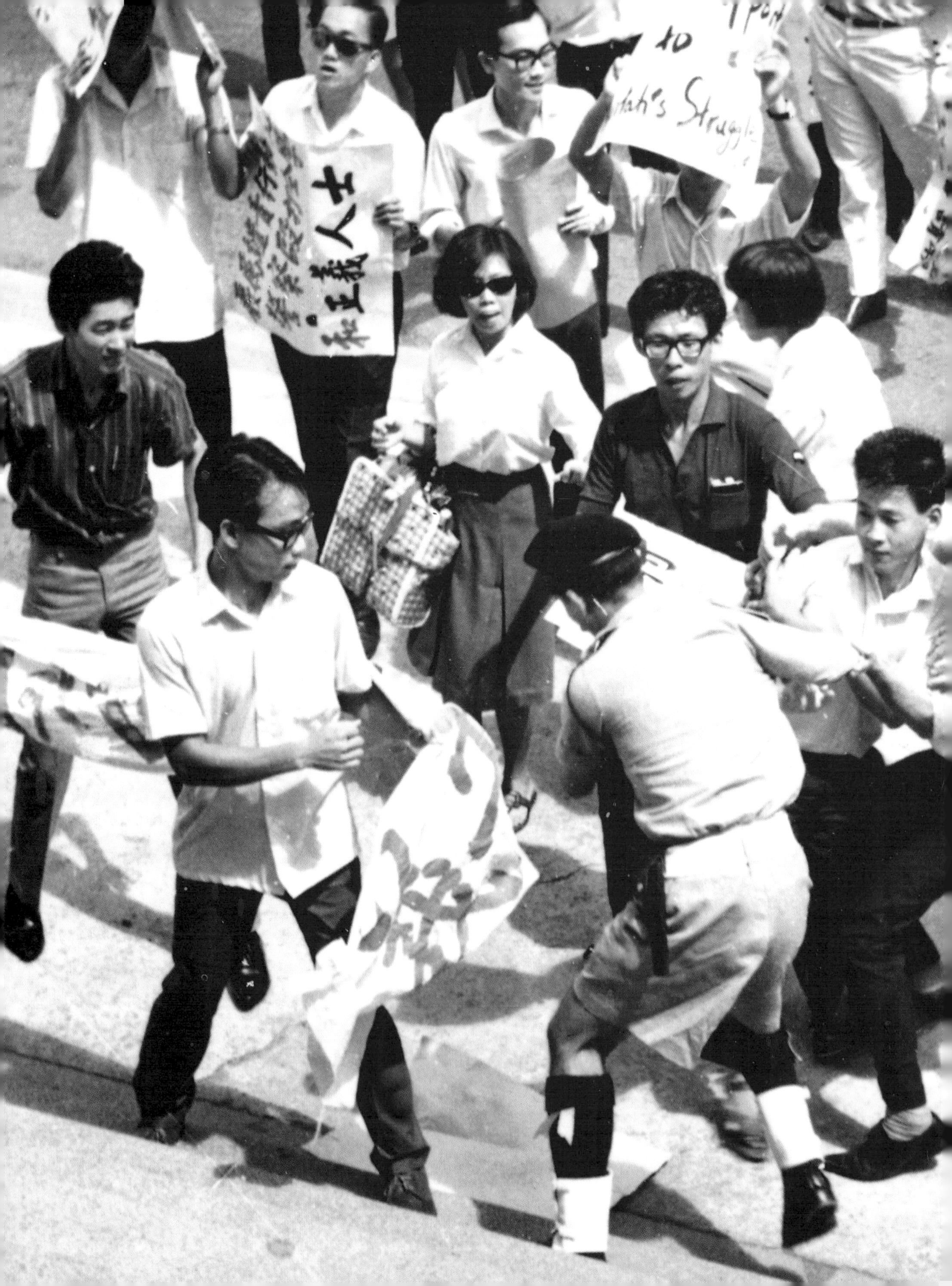
to
Struggle

10 Triads and Riots : Threats to Singapore's Social Stability

Alexius Pereira

Opposite: In November 1965, Nanyang University graduates were involved in several demonstrations against the government, which eventually turned violent (See pages 193–194).

This chapter examines two turbulent episodes in Singapore's history: the colonial period (1819–1942) and the post-World War II period (1945–1965). From the founding of Singapore to its independence, Singapore was not a safe or orderly society. Before 1942, the country was often described as a lawless 'frontier town' where the activities of criminal secret societies were rampant. Between 1950 and 1965, there were many riots and violent demonstrations. Why was social order difficult during these two periods? This chapter explores this question by using two sociological perspectives: the functionalist and the critical perspectives.

Social Order

One aspect of the functionalist perspective, based on the research of Emile Durkheim, presumes the presence of a set of customary beliefs or norms in every society that is accepted by its people. It is through the adherence and maintenance of these norms that social order is achieved. Durkheim, however, believed that while most people in a society generally subscribe to these norms, there are some who do not or cannot accept them (Chambliss 1976:3). This leads to a condition which Durkheim called 'anomie'—a state of normlessness. Although Durkheim originally used the term to understand suicide rates in France, Robert Merton argued that anomie could be the normal state of affairs for persons in certain segments of society when cultural goals (for example, economic success) are over-emphasised and legitimate opportunities to achieve those goals are blocked (Merton 1938). This leads to four possible outcomes: innovation, where new, usually illicit, means are adopted to achieve the goals; ritualism, where people renounce the goals only to focus on the means; retreatism, where they renounce both cultural goals and institutionalised norms; and rebellion, where they replace the established system of goals and means with another system (Rubington and Weinberg 1995:130–131). Another aspect of the functionalist perspective views social disorder as a result of rapid social change in society, leading to three types of disorganisation: normlessness (anomie), culture conflict and the breakdown of rules (Rubington and Weinberg 1995:57). Both aspects can be applied to Singapore's turbulent history.

The critical perspective offers an interesting and alternative means for analysing Singapore's history. Based on the works of Karl Marx, this perspective views social disorder as a result of the economic differences between different groups or classes in society. For example, in a capitalist economy, the capitalist class owns much of the essential economic resources whereas the working class does not. To survive, the working class needs to 'sell' itself as labour. This leads to the exploitation of the working class by the capitalists. Class struggle follows when the capitalists — the 'haves' — hold on to their possessions and maintain them at the continued expense of the working class — the 'have-nots' (Rubington and Weinberg 1995:234–235). Social conflict might arise when the inability of the subordinate class to achieve economic success results in frustration and anger. This may lead certain individuals to turn against the opposing class, and often to criminal activity. Both perspectives will be used in this chapter, sometimes in combination to account for the relatively high levels of social disorder in Singapore's history.

British Singapore: 'A Frontier Town' (1819–1942)

> A pioneer town of rootless immigrants, early Singapore was notoriously lawless, and there was little money to provide a police force. In May 1820, Farquhar established the first regular force, headed by his son-in-law, Francis Bernard, as Superintendent, with one constable, one jailer, one writer, one tindal and eight peons, at a total monthly cost of 300 Spanish dollars. In 1821, the leading European and Asian merchants agreed to contribute $54 a month as a night-watch fund to provide for an extra constable and nine peons.
> (Turnbull 1996:16–17)

Although Turnbull was describing Singapore during the 1820s, there were frequent reports of looting, rioting (or cases of *amok*), theft, brawls and murders right up to the onset of World War II. Why was crime so common? Singapore's social structure and composition of the population could provide answers to this question. As a laissez-faire entrepôt, the British colonial authorities provided only the basic economic

Sago Street in 1910, where a number of shophouses were used as brothels.

infrastructure, mainly for the benefit of British firms. It offered little else in terms of social services or welfare. Many migrant workers, mostly males, came from different parts of Asia to work as menial labourers. For example, there were those who came from China to escape the floods and droughts. Others came from the Indian subcontinent, the Malay archipelago and surrounding Indonesian islands to work on plantations. A large number of convicts from India was also posted to Singapore to build municipal buildings.

During this early 'lawless' period, there were many reports of murders, thefts and arson. Most of these crimes were committed by labourers. There are two possible explanations. From the functionalist perspective, these labourers, who formed the majority of the population, were facing a situation of conflicting norms, or a lack of norms. They came from diverse backgrounds and different cultures and faced difficulties in adjusting to life in Singapore, especially since many of these labourers were away from their traditional social structures and families. When this was compounded by a small and poorly-trained police force, social order became a problem. From the critical perspective, the problem was due to Singapore's class structure at the time. The population was divided into two categories: a very small community of administrators, merchants, businessmen and entrepreneurs, and a very large population of uneducated, lower-class menial workers. The labourers felt socially and economically marginalised because they were unable to achieve the wealthy lifestyle they saw the upper class enjoying. This could have led to feelings of frustration and alienation, which resulted in the disadvantaged class displaying anti-social behaviour.

The British authorities were also concerned about the proliferation of gambling houses (including cock-fighting arenas) and the rise of prostitution in Singapore, which were just pastimes for a group of marginalised workers. In other words, such activities were part of the norms for this group. However, this was in conflict with that of the British authority, which were perhaps tinted with a Puritan morality. The order was therefore given for the police to crack down on such activities, which only served to send them underground. This, along with a number of events that occurred outside of Singapore, led to the flourishing of criminal secret societies.

Secret Societies in Early Singapore

It is important to distinguish the differences between a regional or dialect-based clan association and a secret society, which is also known as a 'triad.' Clan associations were instrumental in helping immigrants, most of whom were from the southern parts of China and settled in Singapore. Turnbull wrote:

> Most Chinese immigrants to Singapore were illiterate youths, who had never been outside their home village, and when they moved to the bewildering new world of Singapore, they sought out familiar organisations among their own people. (1996:52)

From the mid-1830s, clan associations provided the necessary social structure for many new immigrant workers, who arrived in Singapore and saw the conflicting images of a society which appeared to be governed by European colonials, but in reality was in a state of lawlessness. Clan associations therefore served to alleviate the state of anomie that new immigrants experienced by reproducing the practices, norms and values the immigrants were familiar with. They performed five major functions: ancestral worship and worship of protector gods; observance of traditional festivities; helping destitute members; arbitration of disputes; legalisation of marriage; and promotion of education (Yen 1988). Certain clan associations also arranged for magistrates from China to mediate and arbitrate on affairs in Singapore.

The decay of the Ching (Manchu) dynasty in China saw the rise of triad gangs in the late 19th century, formed to overthrow the government in China. The term 'triad' was derived from Chinese, which referred to the links between the celestial, terrestrial and human (Song [1902] 1984:70). These triads soon infiltrated some of the clan associations in Singapore. Their activities, brought to Singapore by separate Fujian and Guangdong groups, extended beyond their original political platform. Many of these triads were identified by numbers and symbols. They functioned as organised criminal groups by operating illegal brothels, opium dens and gambling houses, and extorting 'protection money.' According to Turnbull, by 1840, around 6,000 persons were members of a triad and many people were killed as a result of clashes between competing or rival gangs (Turnbull 1996:52). There were frequent reports of riots, including the riots in 1846, after the police and gang members had a confrontation over the burial of a triad leader, and in 1854, which required the intervention of the British military who were stationed on three warships.

The *hoey*, as the triads were called in dialect, perceived themselves as a brotherhood and had a strict loyalty code, complete with initiation rites and rituals. These societies played an important, albeit criminal, function in Singapore. With the clearly dysfunctional norms in early Singapore society and the social structure divided along class lines, some of the marginalised uneducated working class labourers felt drawn

The Central Police Station at South Bridge Road in 1911.

towards secret societies. The lack of overall integration of this group with the top tier of society made joining the gangs more attractive. The immediate and tangible rewards for joining these *hoeys* clearly appealed to the workers: some menial labourers became relatively wealthy, due to their profits from criminal activities. While economic rewards might not be the only factors that appealed to these male labourers, the sense of solidarity among the brotherhood must have been very enticing. Therefore, when the norms and values of one segment of society become impossible for the marginalised population to follow, alternative activities that can satisfy them economically or socially become desirable (see Mak 1988).

Triads were officially outlawed in 1889 but it was commonly known that the British were helpless against the secret societies, not all of whom were Chinese. With a larger influx of immigrants from the coolie trade in the 1850s, some secret societies exploited prostitution rings as their main source of income. Many of these named themselves with numbers and had symbols and insignias which were often worn as badges or tattooed onto their members. There were also Malay and Indian secret societies functioning in a similar manner to the Chinese ones, only on a smaller scale. By 1867, there were several 'Mohammedan' secret societies, including the Red Flag and White Flag gangs who fought bitterly in Singapore and Penang. Some Indian and Malay secret societies had also collaborated or teamed up with Chinese gangs (Lee 1991:168–171).

The British were aware of the problem of the secret societies and tried to step up their campaign to control them. In 1857, Thomas Dunman was appointed as the first commissioner of the police and in 1881, European and Sikh contingents of policemen were introduced to bolster the small local force. It was only after the appointment of William Pickering as the Chinese Protectorate in 1877 that the British had more control over the secret societies in Singapore. Pickering was fluent in many Chinese dialects and familiar with Chinese culture, having worked in China for eight years. According to Turnbull:

> The Protectorate made a great impact from the beginning and with his strong personality, unique knowledge and flair for practical administration, Pickering rapidly extended his authority from the protection of immigrants to general supervision of the Chinese community.
>
> (Turnbull 1996:86)

The initiation ceremony of a secret society, circa 1860.

While he did not eradicate secret societies altogether, he did win the confidence of several *hoey* members, and even converted some headmen into government agents. He positioned the Protectorate as an alternative means of arbitration for the Chinese in Singapore, supplanting the *hoeys* in settling financial and domestic disputes (Turnbull 1996:87). Soon after, with the backing of the Colonial Office, Colonial Secretary Clementi Smith set up the Chinese Advisory Board in 1888 and passed the Societies Ordinance in 1890, which banned the societies. This ordinance, enforced by the large number of policemen in Singapore, broke the big *hoeys* into small bands of thugs who continued to extort 'protection money' from shops and operate gambling dens, opium houses and brothels. They were also a threat to the public when they fought among themselves for control of certain land areas (Turnbull 1996:88).

By the turn of the century, Singapore was known as the 'Chicago of the East in the 1920s…a haven of gunmen and street gangs, who carried out a reign of terror in Chinatown and the rural districts' (Turnbull 1996:131). Much of the blame could be attributed to the policies of the British administration. For instance, British police officers were required to learn Malay rather than Chinese although 90 percent of criminal activities involved Chinese people. Also, very few Chinese were recruited to join the police force at the time:

> The growing tendency of the ruling class to hold itself apart from Asians meant that the police leadership was remote from the realities of Singapore's underworld.
>
> (Turnbull 1996:131)

The proliferation of the secret societies highlighted two problems with early Singapore society: the lack of integration of the migrant workers into the main social structures, and the ineffectiveness of the police. These workers, who formed the majority of the population, were socially and economically marginalised. Compounded with the police force's relative lack of effectiveness, they sought to create their own set of social structures through joining the secret societies.

The Post-War, Pre-Independent Era

It may be argued that it was the onset of World War II that ended the influence of the triads rather than anything the British had done. After the Japanese left in 1945, Singapore faced the difficulties of Malayanisation, inter-ethnic strife, class struggle and communist insurgency. The problem of the secret societies was still present, although the gangs had shifted their focus towards extorting protection money. However, the problem of the triads paled in comparison to the many strikes, demonstrations and riots between 1950 and 1965. The country's main concern during that time was social integration, or the lack of it.

After World War II, relations between the various ethnic groups in Singapore became tense and worsened. The British announced that they would eventually withdraw completely from the region, but did not immediately decide the future political structure of Malaya, Singapore and East Malaya. This uncertainty over the impending statehood led to tension between several ethnic groups. Internal and external factors contributed to the tension: within the island, the ethnic composition posed a potential problem as the Chinese formed a substantial majority, even though they were a minority within the archipelago. Externally, the Communist take-over of China in 1947 was a cause for concern as both the British and the Malays were worried over Chinese nationalism in Singapore. The Malays were also harbouring anti-British sentiments both in Kuala Lumpur and Singapore.

In December 1950, a riot — later known as the Maria Hertogh Riot — broke out after a demonstration by radical Islamists turned violent. The British court had ruled that a Dutch girl, who was brought up a Muslim and had married a Muslim while her biological parents were interned during the war, should be returned to her Dutch (Christian) parents. It was unclear whether the Islamists demonstrating on the Padang

This picture was taken just before the demonstration in December 1950 by radical Islamists on the Padang in front of City Hall turned violent.

This scene from the Maria Hertogh riots (1950) shows a bus set on fire by rioters on North Bridge Road.

began the violence or were provoked by the European policemen into violence. However, within moments of the unrest in the city centre, many Malays, Muslim Indonesians and Indian Muslims took to the streets and attacked Europeans and Eurasians indiscriminately (Turnbull 1996:242). The majority of the policemen at the time were Malays; many were sympathetic to the rioters and therefore chose not to quell the fighting outside of the Supreme Court. This eventually led to two days of rioting in which 18 people were killed and 173 were injured, in addition to significant damages to property (Drysdale 1985:18). Order was not restored until the next day with the help of British troops and the participation of the 144-strong Gurkha Contingent, which arrived in Singapore the previous year.

Ethnic strife not only plagued Singapore, but Malaysia as well. There were more instances of rioting in 1964 — known as the Prophet Mohammed Birthday Riot — and in 1965 in Kuala Lumpur, which led to Singapore's expulsion from the Federation of Malaya. These cases showed how ethnic sentiments could become divisive factors in society.

From as early as 1929, the Communist insurgency was already present in Singapore and it was well known to many that the most active guerrilla force against the Japanese in Malaya was the communists. After World War II, the Communist threat remained. The political situation in China was just as bad, with the Communist Party waging war against the Kuomintang. Therefore, in the run-up to self-government around 1950, the various political and para-political factions — from the Communists to left-wing and right-wing sympathisers — were all struggling for political

These innocuous-looking photographs are believed to be Communist indoctrination sessions for the marginalised Chinese-educated youths, circa 1960.

power. In addition, the Chinese-educated working class had distinct anti-colonial feelings and this played into the hands of the communists. In 1948, the British declared a Malayan Emergency, which outlawed the Communist Party and its activities in the whole of Malaya. However, the communists' activities became more successful when driven underground. They infiltrated the Chinese-medium schools from 1952 onwards, and began their programme of 'indoctrination'. The results of these programmes could have led to the many pro-China anti-colonial demonstrations from 1953 onwards. A student protest against conscription into mandatory National Service in May 1954 spilled over into violence and the police had to use coercive tactics to control the crowd. Around the same time, pro-Communist student leaders began to work with labour unions to cause disruptions to essential public services, such as transportation, in their attempt to undermine local authority.

The local elections of 1955 became a focal point for more civil disorder. In May that year, students and workers turned a strike at the Hock Lee Bus Company into a violent demonstration which led to '…a night of terror and death' (Turnbull 1996:255). The Chief Minister of Singapore at the time, David Marshall, chose only to crack down on student leaders and threaten to close down the schools, which acted as the headquarters. This led to 2,000 students barricading themselves in Chung Cheng High School. Later that year, other unions such as the Singapore Factory and Shop Workers' Union, along with the extremist leaders of the Harbour Board, caused more labour disruption with the aim of bringing down the local authority. As Turnbull noted, of nearly 300 strikes in 1955, only one-third involved claims for better wages or working conditions. The rest were sympathy strikes or strikes calling for the release of union leaders (1996:256). From 1955 onwards, the police's barbed-wire barricades were seen along many of the major streets of the city centre and Chinatown.

In October and November 1965, undergraduates from the Nanyang University — a Chinese-medium university — took part in demonstrations which eventually turned violent. As part of the Malayanisation and later Singaporeanisation process, *Nantah*—as the Chinese-educated community called the university — was told by the Education Review Council to 'meet the needs of modern Singapore,' which ostensibly meant that *Nantah* should have a multi-ethnic student body and provide multilingual course studies (Bell 1972: 577–600). By that time, graduates of Nanyang University were facing difficulties in finding employment, and if employed, were paid a salary lower than that of graduates from the English-medium University of Malaya — later renamed University of Singapore. The economic marginalisation of the *Nantah* graduates and alumni was the main cause of these violent demonstrations, which were supported by pro-Chinese chauvinists in Singapore (Bell 1972). The Communists were also believed to be behind most of the actions of the student leaders (Lee 1996). There were serious clashes between the police and *Nantah* students only four months after Singapore's independence, and the riots occurred again in 1966. In the end, the demonstrations were forcefully suppressed and a wave of arrests followed.

The Hock Lee riots spilled over to the Chinatown area and the city centre in 1955. Here, members of the Police Reserve Unit faced a crowd of rioters at Cross Street.

Chinese-medium school students and Nanyang undergraduates in a violent confrontation with the police during their protest march in November 1965.

A casualty of the same 1965 incident at City Hall being taken aside by the police.

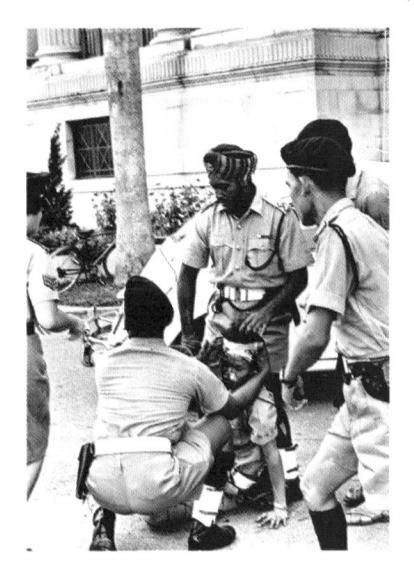

The roots of the civil disorder can be viewed from both the functionalist and the critical perspectives. From the functionalist perspective, due to the fragmented nature of post-war Singapore society, there were many different groups that espoused different sets of values, aspirations and norms. Ethnicity, ideology and language became highly divisive factors in Singapore. The case of religious and ethnic riots could be seen as groups fighting to protect their cultural integrity and defending their norms, values and practices. The same argument could be applied to the Communist or anti-Communist struggle, as well as the tension over English and Chinese languages. When people's norms or values were threatened, some took to violent means to protect themselves.

From the critical perspective, the source of social unrest is class struggle. Various groups jostled for position in the new order and the fear of losing out to another group (whose interests were different to one's own) was strong enough to lead to violent struggle, as seen in Singapore. The fear of marginalisation by various groups in pre-independent Singapore was a good example of class conflict — the competing interests (whether ethnic, linguistic or ideological) were directed at achieving political power. For example, the Nanyang University students' protests were an embodiment of the fear of economic marginalisation. The repression of their demonstrations was an attempt by the ruling elite — the English-educated population who dominated the economy — to protect and enhance their own interests.

Getting Tough

The transition from Singapore's history of social disorder to that of relative social stability can be attributed to two factors — the eventual independence of the island, and the improvements made in the police force. With independence in 1965, the political leaders of Singapore were very clear about their position in ethnic politics, political structures and future paths. The newly-installed government espoused an ideology known as 'multiracialism,' which safeguarded equal opportunity rights and the cultural heritage of the major ethnic groups (Hill and Lian 1995:5). They also maintained a strict anti-Communist policy and proceeded to successfully internationalise Singapore's economy, generating wealth for most of its population.

The problem of social order can once again be viewed from two perspectives. From the functionalist perspective, before full independence in 1965, social and civil order in Singapore was problematic because of a lack of social integration. Uncertainty over the island's future — particularly between 1950 and 1965, including a brief merger with Malaysia in 1963 — contributed to the instability of the period. During this time, different groups in Singapore were pulling in different directions. Ethnic, linguistic, ideological, religious and political differences were utilised by the extreme elements in society to divide the people. This was compounded by the short-handed police force, who were unable to control extreme elements in the various camps.

After independence, the police — now clear about its mandate, functions and

These two photographs collected by the Singapore Police Force in 1955 show some badges (*left*) used by secret societies, and a typical tattoo (*right*) on a triad member.

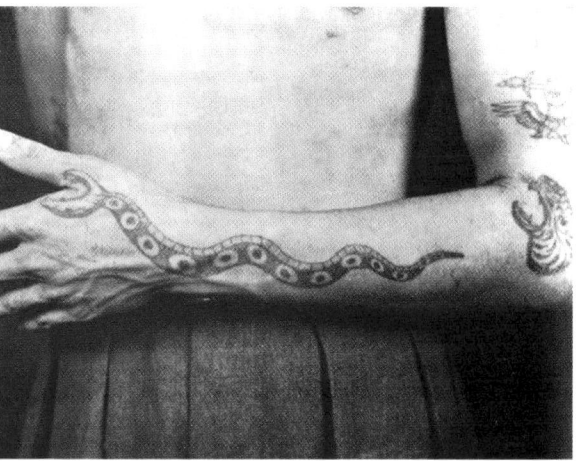

The late President Benjamin Sheares attending an exhibition on the 'Threat of Secret Societies' organised by the Singapore Police Force in 1971.

duties — could concentrate on maintaining order. Three special sections were created: the Special Branch (later renamed the Internal Security Department or ISD) addressed the problem of Communist insurgency; the Riot Squad (later reorganised as the Police Reserve Unit) was trained to handle public riots; and the Criminal Investigation Department would focus on secret society activities. The police also sought better qualified personnel and a more representative ethnic mix. The starting pay for new recruits was raised and attractive benefits were offered. This greatly attracted many people of different races, especially the Chinese who had stayed away from joining the police force in earlier times. Several were recruited on the basis of their fluency in dialects in which secret societies operated, and the Chinese-educated were targeted in the recruitment campaign to break the hold of the Communist Party or the secret societies.

From a critical perspective, Singapore's social stability after 1965 was due to the successful generation and relatively equitable distribution of wealth for the majority of the population through sustained economic growth until the mid-1980s. There was full employment and most citizens could afford public housing. Income differences, which were very wide during the colonial period, became less striking. As such, the motivation for class struggle was reduced significantly.

Looking Back

As we look back at history, we can see why there was disorder in the Singapore society. The lack of social integration was one of the main causes. There was also an absence or failure of norms, values and expectations, which were established only after independence and resulting in the recent relative social stability. The economic inequality caused by the capitalist and colonial system was the other main cause of social disorder. The British laissez-faire system had created two classes: an economically and politically dominant ruling class and a subservient working class. Throughout Singapore's history, economic marginalisation or the fear of marginalisation had been the reason why certain groups turned to crime, turned against the establishment or turned on other groups. Both perspectives offer warnings about the future. Should there be a situation where norms begin to fail, or a time when economic differences become marked, Singapore's social stability will once again be threatened.

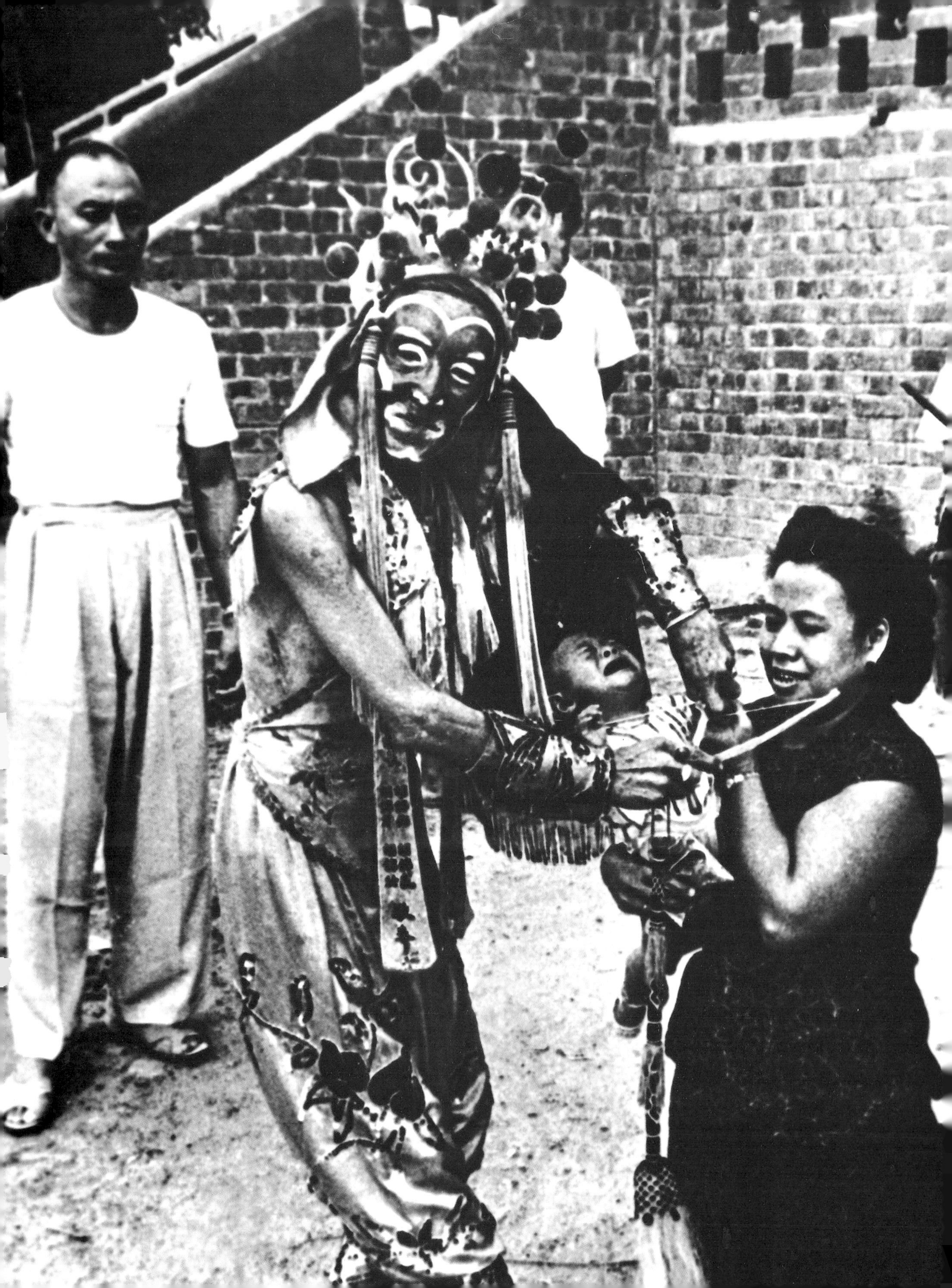

11 Believing and Belonging: Religion in Singapore

Lily Kong & Tong Chee Kiong

Opposite: One popular deity for Chinese religionists is the Monkey God. Seen here with a worshipper is a spirit-medium who has taken on the characteristics of the Monkey God, circa 1958.

Singapore is characterised by a colourful population that is at once multi-religious, multi-ethnic, multilingual and multicultural. In this essay, we examine religious life in Singapore from 1819 to 1965. We structure our discussion using two broad frameworks: believing and belonging. For each, we define a set of questions. In terms of believing, we identify the main religious belief systems in Singapore, characterising the main trends and tenets. We also explore how these belief systems began in Singapore and how they have burgeoned or declined through the years. We then examine how these beliefs are performed through rites and rituals, and how and why they have transformed over time — modified and adapted to suit local contexts. In terms of belonging, we examine the role of religion in creating and maintaining a sense of belonging and solidarity amongst adherents, and in bridging people of different religious orientations. We also give attention to how belonging to a religion may cause conflict between people, breaching races, classes and genders.

Believing

Identifying, characterising

For religious adherents, religion is anchored in faith; grounded in religious shrines, altars and temples; and manifested in rites and rituals. Yet, religious landscapes and rites and rituals change over time, as part of social change. Indeed, in Singapore, the history of religious change is a marker of the island's path towards modernity.

Records of religious adherence in Singapore have been kept only intermittently. Pre-independence municipal records are mostly silent about religion, even though details exist about other aspects of life, for example, sanitary conditions (*ARSM* 1893). This is perhaps indicative of a lack of concern on the part of the colonial rulers about the religious inclinations of the population, who were free to subscribe to whichever faith they chose as long as they did not create problems. This was in line with the

Table 1: Religious Profile of the Singapore Population (1849–1990)

RELIGION	1849	1911	1921	1931	1980	1990
Buddhism/ Taoism/ Confucianism	27,526 (52.0%)	216,501 (69.4%)	310,163 (72.8%)	411,665 (72.5%)	Buddhism: 529,140 (26.7%) Taoism: 580,535 (29.3%)	Buddhism: 707,885 (31.1%) Taoism/ Chinese religion: 510,382 (22.4%)
Islam	22,007 (41.6%)	53,959 (17.3%)	69,604 (16.3%)	86,827 (15.3%)	232,867 (16.3%)	350,520 (15.4%)
Christianity	1,861 (3.5%)	16,349 (5.2%)	21,386 (5.0%)	30,068 (5.3%)	203,517 (10.3%)	285,282 (12.5%)
Hinduism	1,452 (2.8%)	15,580 (5.0%)	19,772 (4.6%)	31,128 (5.5%)	72,401 (3.6%)	83,704 (3.7%)
Sikhism	—	146 (0.05%)	1,022 (0.2%)	2,988 (0.5%)	Subsumed Under 'Others'	9,545 (0.4%)
Judaism	22 (0.04%)	707 (0.2%)	623 (0.2%)	777 (0.14%)	Subsumed Under 'Others'	Subsumed Under 'Others'
Others	23 (0.04%)	14 (0.004%)	38 (0.009%)	306 (0.05%)	11,069 (0.6%)	12,525 (0.6%)
No religion	Not listed as a category	Not listed as a category	Not listed as a category	Not listed as a category	261,433 (13.2%)	326,436 (14.3%)
Not stated	Not listed as a category	62 (0.02%)	3,269 (0.8%)	3,694 (0.7%)	—	—
TOTAL	52,891 (100%)	311,987[1] (100%)	425,877[2] (100%)	567,453 (100%)	1,981,962[3] (100.0%)	2,276,734[4] (100.0%)

Sources: Census of Population, 1849, Marriott 1911; Nathan 1921; Vlieland 1932; Khoo 1981; Lau 1994.

[1] This total was calculated by adding the total population of each racial group. It left the religion of 8,669 unaccounted for. Some of these might have had no religion which was not a category captured in the data collection. Some of the discrepancy might also be due to inaccuracies in the data collection.

[2] This total is higher than the total calculated by adding up the total population in each racial group. This is presumably another case of inaccurate data.

[3,4] The totals here were taken from the respective Census reports. For the 1980 and 1990 figures, the figures refer to the resident population aged 10 years and over.

broader British ethos of not interfering with local life and customs. Although there were census reports produced more or less at decadel intervals during the colonial period, many of them did not reflect the religious profile. In the post-independence years, the first systematic record of religious adherence was taken only in 1980 and then at the subsequent census in 1990. Based on available data, the religious profile is constructed in Table 1.

While some of the religious groups are more easily characterised, others pose difficulties, requiring fuller elaboration. Singapore Muslims are primarily of the Shafii School of Law of the Sunni Islamic Sect. Adherents to this doctrine are commonly known as orthodox or Sunni Muslims and constitute over 90 percent of the entire Muslim community today (Farah 1994:170).[1] As with other Sunnis, Singapore Muslims follow a comprehensive system of community law, the Syariah. Christians are divided among the Catholic Church and a great variety of other Christian denominations, including, for example, mainline Protestants (Anglicans, Presbyterians, Methodists and Lutherans), neo-Calvinists (Baptists, Brethren and Bible Presbyterians) as well as other independent churches. Reflecting the South Indian bias in Singapore's Indian population, religious practice veer towards South Indian styles in the Republic. There is a predominance of South Indian temples which differ from North Indian ones in design and iconographic style, as well as in separate priesthoods and segregated patronage. Adherents to Islam, Christianity and Hinduism in Singapore sometimes also display evidence of infusion, where beliefs and practices are mixed with local tradition (for example, animistic beliefs), or are influenced by the practices of other religions. We will elaborate on these later.

'Chinese religion,' which we use here as a collective term to describe the myriad beliefs adhered to by the majority of the Chinese population, is by far the most difficult to characterise. It is also the religion of the majority of the Singapore population, and it is for this reason that we will give more space to characterising it here. The difficulty in characterisation is due primarily to the eclecticism (that is, the mixed character) of the religion.

One important element of Chinese religious practices is ancestor worship. It has sometimes been described as an extension of filial piety, an important value in Chinese society strongly rooted in Confucianist thought. In this practice of ancestor worship, ancestors, as with many of the other gods of the Chinese pantheon, have a role to perform in providing guidance and protection for the living descendants. In return, the latter will reciprocate by offering food and paper models of daily

Dead or alive, one is deemed to require a variety of necessities, which relatives and descendants burn as offerings. This picture was taken around 1985.

necessities (clothing, vehicles, money and more recently, television sets, video recorders, washing machines and even credit cards). Such is the manifestation of mutual care between generations — as much a part of the relationship between the living and the dead as it should be among the living. In another very important sense, ancestor worship also acts as a 'stimulus to morality' (Addison 1925:26). The consciousness that the ancestors are watching and will judge and reward or punish according to one's conduct heightens the moral sense of the community. Indeed, some scholars argued that ancestor worship is the most important religious phenomenon in the life of Singapore's Chinese (Addison 1925:83; Hinton 1985:44). However, it is seldom seen as composing a distinct religion, and is regarded more as a part of Chinese religious life in general (Tamney and Hassan 1987:4).

Apart from ancestor worship, Theravada and Mahayana Buddhism are also represented in Singapore, the latter far more so than the former. In addition, a Japanese branch of Buddhism, the Soka Association (formerly Nichiren Shoshu Association up till 1992) is also growing in significance (Clammer 1988:27). Furthermore, there is also Confucianism. Although it is sometimes argued that Confucianism is not a 'religion' but a moral code or philosophical system, Leo and Clammer noted that in Singapore, Confucius is regarded by some as a specific deity in his own right, worshipped apart from other deities and constituting the centre of a specific religious complex.

More common among Chinese religionists in Singapore are syncretic religions which incorporate elements of Confucianism, Taoism, and Buddhism as well as ancestor worship and other elements of animistic folk religions. As Hinton described it, 'the religion of the Singaporean Chinese Religionist is an ancient, rather animistic folk religion, infused, to a small degree, by a selection of often modified beliefs and practices from the so-called high religions…' (1985:31). *Shenism* has no canonical tradition. It is cultic, with each cult centred around a particular *shen* (spirit), whose chief mode of communication with this world is through spirit-mediums. It is syncretic, for the *shenist* pantheon can include Confucius, Buddhas and Bodhisattvas,

An elderly devotee at a Chinese temple in Kampong Alex Terrace, circa 1986. Devotees generally visit temples in the hope of obtaining blessings or answers to specific prayers.

alongside any other spirit, deified hero or emperor.[2] Even Jesus Christ and the Virgin are considered by some as *shen*. Indeed, as Wee pointed out, *shenists* have the habit of taking over deities of other religions and treating them as *shen* (1976:173).[3]

Beginning

How did the population in Singapore come to subscribe to the religions they do, and how did the different religions increasingly come to assert their presence? Although applicable only to some religions (for present purposes, Christianity and Islam), one of the key characteristics of belief is to proselytise and 'expand the flock,' so much so that one measure of success is the degree to which the particular religious population is burgeoning. In this section, we trace the origins and expansion of the key religions in Singapore as an indicator of the flourishing of belief or practice (or both).

When Sir Stamford Raffles landed in Singapore in 1819, it was believed that there existed an *Orang Laut*[4] population of no more than 150 (Song [1923] 1967). This community was believed to have 'long been converts to Islam' (Evans 1927).

Scholars who have attempted to trace the diffusion of Islam into Southeast Asia agree that, rather than being converted to the Muslim faith by the sword, Southeast Asians were won over to Islam through persuasion by Arab and Indian merchants who plied the Southeast Asian waters from the 12th century.[5] By the 14th century, Islam had become the principal religion of the region. Singapore, which was then a

Wak Hai Cheng Bio on Phillip Street, circa 1955, established in 1826. This was probably the first Chinese temple in Singapore established by the Teochews.

part of the Majapahit empire, also had a resident Muslim population. Despite the subsequent decline of the empire, at least a small Muslim population survived on Singapore island at the time of Raffles' arrival (Miksic 1985:33–34).

As with Islam, archaeological and historical evidence suggests that Buddhism and Chinese religion of some form existed in Singapore prior to Raffles' arrival. A Chinese temple, *Shuntian Gong* (Temple of Submission to Heaven), dedicated to the earth deity *Dabogong* (originally in Malabar Street, but currently settled, after several moves, in Geylang Lorong 29), was first built in 1796, according to an inscription inside the temple. It is believed to be the first Chinese temple in Singapore (Lee *et al.* 1994:149).

Chinese religion took root with the arrival of Chinese migrants, who came after Raffles and mainly from South China. A close alignment between temple construction and dialect affiliation soon became evident. Each dialect group began to establish its own presence and develop its own temples as the Chinese community grew in numbers (Lee *et al.* 1994:152). The Fujians established their own temples (for example, *Hengshan Ting* at Silat Road, built in 1828); the Teochews established *Wak Hai Cheng Bio* on Phillip Street in 1826; the Cantonese erected *Haichun Fude Si* in 1824; the Hakkas established the *Yinghe Guan* in 1823; and the Hainanese had a *Tianhou* temple on Beach Road in 1857.

Given the European appearance at the time of Singapore's founding, a Christian presence would soon become evident. In 1821, Reverend M. Laurent Marie Joseph Imbert of the *Société des Mission Etrangères* (the French Mission Society), visited Singapore, en route to China. The Bishop of Siam had asked him to gather information about the state of religion in this new settlement. His one-week stay in Singapore resulted in a letter to the Bishop, stating that 'there were only 12 or 13 Catholics in Singapore, who led a wretched life' (in Buckley 1902:242; Teixeira 1963:10). These were Malaccan Portuguese who were ministered to by a Portuguese priest from Malacca, Padre Jacob (Teixeira 1963:8, 10).

The Catholics were originally split between Portuguese and French jurisdiction. This acrimonious beginning arose because in 1824, the Catholics in Singapore wrote to the Bishop of Siam to send for a priest. Fearing that he might be said to have no jurisdiction over Singapore, the Bishop applied to the Sacred Congregation of the Propagation of the Faith in Rome in 1827. From there, Pope Leo XII sent a decree giving him jurisdiction. In the meantime, a Padre Francisco Da Silva Pinto e Maia arrived in Singapore from Goa in 1825, and established himself as the Catholic Pastor of the island by virtue of his rank (Knight of the Order of Christ), which had been bestowed on him by the Queen of Portugal (Buckley 1902:242). The whole dispute was settled only in 1886 when Pope Leo XIII and King Dom Louis of Portugal signed a new Concordat, agreeing that 'all the faithful living at Malacca or in Singapore Island and belonging to the old Portuguese Diocese of Malacca' would be passed to the jurisdiction of the Bishop of Macao, while the Diocese of Malacca would be restored and entrusted to the Foreign Missions of Paris (Teixeira 1963:16).

Aside from the Catholic Church, there are also a great variety of other Christian denominations in Singapore. The earliest non-Catholic Christian presence was the London Missionary Society (LMS), formed by laypersons and missionaries from various denominations in England (Sng 1993:26–35). Missionary work started as early as the founding of Singapore in 1819, with the arrival of Samuel Milton that year. He started a school for Malay and Chinese boys. Raffles contributed $150 on the condition that church services would be provided for the inhabitants. The next missionary to arrive was Claudius H. Thomsen in 1822. He started classes for both Malay boys and girls and by 1828, 12 Malays had been converted to Christianity. The East India Company granted a piece of land to LMS and a mission house and chapel was built in 1824 (Sng 1993:35). Apart from LMS, the main Protestant denominations established in the 19th century included four main groups — Anglican (1826), Brethren (1864), Presbyterian (1881) and Methodist (1885). Since the turn of the century, various other groups have taken root as well, such as the Seventh Day Adventists (1905), Assembly of God (1926), Lutherans (1927), Salvation Army (1935), Baptists (1937), Bible-Presbyterians (1952), Christian Nationals' Evangelism Commission (1952), and the Church of Jesus Christ of Latter Day Saints (1968).[6]

Left: The Sri Mariamman Temple (centre) is featured in a postcard from 1911.

Right: Sri Mariamman Temple at South Bridge Road (circa 1950) is the oldest extant Hindu temple in Singapore today.

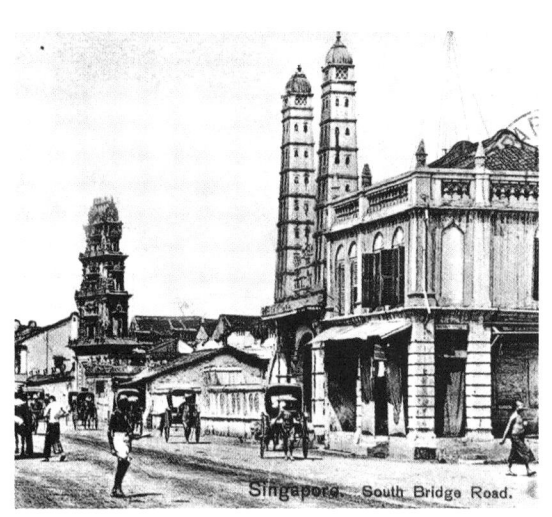

Hinduism was brought into Singapore by the Indian immigrants who came as early as 1819 as part of Sir Stamford Raffles' entourage. Although Southeast Asia had undergone a period of Indianisation from the second to the 10th century, migrations constituted a different migrant flow, and these contemporary Indian communities are descendants of the later flow (Hatley 1969:452). The later immigrants brought their religion with them and established temples very rapidly, propelled perhaps by an ancient Tamil adage: '*Kovil illa uril Kudiyirukka Vendam*,' or 'Do not settle in a land where there is no temple' (Sandhu 1969:223). Most of the early immigrants were convicts brought here for construction work, or labourers for the coffee and sugar plantations (Sandhu 1969; Mahajani 1960:96). In turn, 98 percent of the labour immigrants were from South India (Sandhu 1969:159). Given that about 80 percent of the early Indian migrants into Malaya were Hindus, it follows that the Hinduism in Singapore is essentially of a South Indian variety (Sandhu 1969:161). The remaining 20 percent of the migrants were Muslims, Sikhs and Christians. The first Hindu temple, located in Bras Basah Road, was believed to be founded by one Naraina Pillay from Penang, in 1819. But it was soon demolished (Tan 1962:31). Another temple was constructed in 1827, dedicated to the goddess Mariamman in South Bridge Road. It stands today as the oldest extant Hindu temple in Singapore.

Burgeoning

In some ways, the growth trajectories of the different religions are a function of the population growth of the different ethnic groups, although this alone is insufficient explanation for the changing religious profile over time. Because of the uneven level of historical information available, the contours of growth are presented below in different degrees of detail.

Catholicism is perhaps one of the best documented in this respect. While growth was evident in the 19th century, as outlined below, it was perhaps more pronounced in the 20th century. Be that as it may, there were 200 Catholics in Singapore in 1829 and 300 in 1832 (Teixeira 1963:20, 13). This presence was translated into an express desire for a formal place of worship. In 1832, therefore, the first stone was laid on ground granted by the government at the site of the present Singapore Art Museum (formerly St. Joseph's Institution). Construction was made possible through contributions from European and Chinese merchants, and the building was to be completed by 1833 (Buckley 1902:245). Completed during the time of the vicar, the Reverend Mr Albrand, the first chapel facilitated the growth of the congregation despite its small size, and Buckley recorded a rapid increase in the Chinese members of the congregation who reportedly had much respect for Rev. Albrand (1902:246). Between 1832 and 1839, the congregation witnessed 130 baptisms, 64 deaths and 20 marriages (Buckley 1902:247). By 1840, the congregation had grown to such an extent that the chapel became too small, and an appeal was again launched to seek financial support for a new building. The chapel was later converted to a school (St. Joseph's Institution) when a church was completed in 1847 (the Cathedral of Good Shepherd).

The growth of the Catholic population could not have been sustained if it had been confined to the European population alone. The Chinese became a majority in the Catholic profile although the majority of the Chinese population remained non-Christian. These Chinese Catholics were converted either before or after they arrived in Singapore. Chinese Catholic arrivals were usually the wealthier merchants rather than the lower class Chinese labourers (Tan 1988:58). Another group that converted to Catholicism in the 19th century was the Indian migrants, particularly the labourers and free immigrants (as opposed to the deported convicts and traders). Their presence in the Ophir Road area led to the establishment of the Church of Our Lady of Lourdes there in 1888, and a Catholic school of the same name next door.

Thomas and Manikam observed 'a strange character of the Church in Malaya,' that it had a presence among the immigrant population (the Chinese and Indians), but not at all among the Malays, the native inhabitants (1956:56). This need not be surprising, considering the monotheism of Islam and the pantheism of Chinese religion and Hinduism, which makes it much easier for the latter to embrace Jesus Christ, Mary and even the saints as part of the Chinese or Hindu pantheon of deities. Accepting Catholicism thus did not necessarily mean giving up their Chinese or Hindu practices. Certainly, one may then question why it is that conversion even took place if such syncretism could easily be accommodated. Here, reference may be made to Tamney and Hassan's explanation for religious switching. While their analysis was grounded in the context of post-independence Singapore, their argument is plausible for earlier periods as well. Essentially, they argue that colonialism and the concomitant domination of the British (politically and economically) created a situation in which the 'British/European cultural patterns [also] ascended to a position of dominance and superiority over the other main cultures' (Tamney and Hassan 1987:39). This cultural dominance was spatially manifested in the form of many cultural symbols: the centrality of churches, cemeteries, sports grounds, architecture and so forth. The cultural hierarchy also became institutionalised and embedded in the social consciousness of the people so much so that people would want to 'use' the symbols of 'Western' culture (for example, language and religion) for personal or social (or both) gratification and advancement. Language was more readily adopted than religion because it involved less of a redefinition of self, but religion was also adopted by some ethnic groups for whom the co-identification of

The Cathedral of the Good Shepherd, completed in 1847, continues to stand today as a landmark in the busy heart of the city.

Church of the Holy Family, as it was in 1923, along East Coast Road.

ethnicity and religion was not strong. Principally, this referred to the Chinese, unlike the Malays (Tamney and Hassan 1987:40–41).

What is perhaps more striking than the differential conversion of the various races to Catholicism, or Christianity in general, is Thomas and Manikam's observation that the different racial groups within the Catholic Church existed as separate entities, a fact underscored by their worshipping in different churches. For example, the Indians congregating at the Church of Our Lady of Lourdes. Indeed, even within the Chinese population, the different dialect groups had their own churches, often with masses conducted in their respective dialects. The Cantonese, for example, congregated at the Church of the Sacred Heart while the Teochews were primarily in the Church of St. Peter and Paul. Religion, therefore, was not necessarily the catalyst to bring different ethnic groups together.

Apart from the Catholic Church, histories of several Protestant denominations have been written, such as the Presbyterians (Harcus 1955; Greer 1956), the Anglicans (Loh 1963), and the Methodists (Doraisamy 1982; 1985). Recounting individual histories will entail writing several more chapters, so a brief overview of mainstream orthodox Protestantism will be presented instead. In this, Hinton is instructive. He divided this history into three periods (1985:14–28). The first, 1819–1930, was characterised as one in which Christianity grew slowly for a variety of reasons: Singapore's multiplicity of languages made missionary endeavour difficult; and immigrants expected to return to their homelands and were thus not prepared to make permanent and major religious changes. At the same time, the target of concern

St. Joseph's Institution, a beacon of LaSalle Brothers education, circa 1850. Across from it was the Convent of Our Holy Infant Jesus on Victoria Street.

for missionaries was really China, and when the British gained control in 1842, many missionaries were redeployed there. The second period from 1900–1950[7] was characterised as a period in which the 'seeds of hope' were sown, as immigrants began to settle down and the 'temporary immigrant' mentality shifted. This meant that some became more open to change and enjoyed greater freedom from traditional ties. It also meant that there was more marriage and child-bearing, contributing to a growing population that provided greater opportunity for conversion. At the same time, the Boxer Rebellion in China at the turn of the century caused many to flee the violence, including Chinese Christians who left with the 'deliberate intent of forming Christian colonies' (Hinton 1985:21). Singapore became one of the destinations. The third period, from the 1950s to the 1980s, or 'harvest time,' was a period in which new denominations were established. New congregations also grew among the older denominations. These may be attributed to a number of reasons. As English became more commonly used, not least because education became more widely available and the language became increasingly taught in schools, Christianity, with its English literature, agencies and missionaries from the West, became more accessible. At the same time, the post-1949 exit of missionaries from Communist China led to the entry of missionaries, including dialect-speaking ones, into Singapore. There was also a tide of missionaries from the United States. The consequence was a growth in the 'big four denominations' in Singapore (Anglican, Methodist, Brethren and Presbyterian), and the introduction of new dominations in the 1950s (the Southern Baptists, Lutheran Church of America, Christian Nationals Evangelism Commission and the Bible Presbyterians), adding to others which had already found little trouble in getting established (the Assemblies of God, the Seventh Day Adventists and the Evangelical Free Church). During this period, parachurch organisations were also introduced, including, for example, Overseas Missionary Fellowship (1952), the Varsity Christian Fellowship (1952), and Youth for Christ (1956), which increased interest and commitment, particularly among the young.

Today, the number of 'Christian' churches has grown tremendously since the establishment of the first London Missionary Society chapel in 1826 in Bras Basah Road. Although the Roman Catholic (37.7 percent of the total Christian population) and the Protestant population (63.3 percent) differ in strength, the difference is not reflected commensurately in the number of churches belonging to each group. While there are 29 Roman Catholic churches in all, there are about 300 Protestant churches. In part, this is because Catholics, with their sacramental approach, are not as free to use laity and house churches as Protestants are (Hinton 1985:109–110). In turn, Protestant groups have become distinctive in the post-independence years in their use of secular buildings for religious worship. For instance, the Methodist church has taken over the Metropole Cinema in Tanjong Pagar which had fallen into disuse. In contrast, certain places are used only periodically (such as over weekends) while generally fulfilling other functions at other times. The World Trade Centre auditorium is one example. Hotel rooms are also often used, as are school halls.

Post-independence growth in Christianity may be partly attributed to the decline of traditional Chinese religion and the fluctuating pull of Buddhism. Traditional Chinese religion has come to be viewed as superstition, particularly by the younger generation. Buddhism's prestige among Westerners as an abstract religion is also absent here (Tamney and Hassan 1987:42). In addition, there was, until the last decade or so, limited effort at proselytising by Buddhists. Topley noted in 1956 that there was only one full-fledged Buddhist monastery in Singapore (1956:70). Buddhism also did not require frequent ritual participation nor encourage regular contact between the religious and laity. It therefore did not perform, in a direct and visible way, the social function of some religions in bringing adherents together and offering opportunities for a sense of belonging. This has changed in the 1980s, with a form of 'Protestant' Buddhism emerging, characterised by the provision of a range of social services (indicative of a move to take Buddhism out of the temple), the establishment of Buddhist libraries offering books, lectures, forums and classes, and the introduction of forms of practices akin to Christian church services (for example, communal sessions in chanting and meditation, and personal counselling with the abbot by appointment). Buddhism in Singapore has also come to emphasise the 'text' more, with 'Sunday school' classes in Buddhist liturgy, talks and seminars by Buddhist monks and the emphasis on theology rather than ritual. This has resulted in the perception of Buddhism as more rational, systematic and intellectual than superstitious, which appeal to a younger set of Singaporeans. This process has been termed the 'intellectualisation' or 'rationalisation' of religion (Tong 1992).

The Convent of Holy Infant Jesus, circa 1910, was located in Victoria Street from 1854 to 1983; its grey walls offering protective education to the blue-pinafored 'Convent' girls over many generations.

Throughout the years of growth, whether gradual or more abrupt, one of the key characteristics of Christianity in Singapore, as elsewhere, is its active involvement in the provision of social services. Of its various involvements in Singapore, the most significant must be in the field of education (see Chapter 1). In 1852 and 1854 respectively, the de la Salle order and the Dames de St. Maur of the French Mission inaugurated Catholic mission school education, which has continued to this day. Beginning with St. Joseph's Institution in 1852, there are now 19 Catholic schools for boys (including pre-primary, primary and secondary schools, and vocational institutes). Catholic girls' schools total 31, the oldest being the Convent of the Holy Infant Jesus (established in 1854) that was re-located from Victoria Street to Toa Payoh in 1984. These girls' schools are spread amongst four orders — the Holy Infant Jesus order, the Canossian sisters, the Good Shepherd sisters and the Franciscan missions, and they also include schools of the various levels. In addition, there is also the Catholic Junior College, set up in 1974 for pre-university education.

The establishment of the earliest Catholic schools provides a lens into relations between coloniser and colonised in the mid-19th century. Father Beurel, founder of St. Joseph's Institution and the Convent of the Holy Infant Jesus, in a prospectus soliciting monetary support for the establishment of the schools, justified his call for support by referring to it as a 'most eminently Christian and civilising call' (quoted in Buckley 1902:261). He requested 'pecuniary assistance' to bring 'enlightened and disinterested teachers of youth' to this part of the world where 'Christianity and civilisation are yet so little diffused among the natives' (quoted in Buckley 1902:261). This found resonance in the *Singapore Free Press*, which, in its commentary, further embellished this view: Children who have the benefit of such education will be introduced to 'a higher state of civilisation' and be fit to spread it 'amongst their countrymen,' a mission that was viewed to be of 'the greatest importance to a proper civilisation and conversion of natives' (quoted in Buckley 1902:260).

Traditionally, the older established Christian denominations have also been involved in education and health, and this is reflected today in the schools and services which have been set up. The Methodists, Anglicans and Presbyterians have contributed particularly to education, with 17 schools of various levels among them. Similarly, the Church has been involved in the provision of health services through the St. Andrew's Mission and Orthopaedic Hospitals, Mount Alvernia Hospital, and Youngberg Memorial Adventist Hospital, for example. In 1969, counselling services for couples with marital problems and youths, for example, were initiated; in 1976, the Christian Anti-Drug Rescue Endeavour (CARE) was established as well.

Even while Christianity gained ground, albeit at an uneven pace, adherence to Islam held its own. Given the increase in the overall population, including the Malay population, it is no surprise therefore that the Muslim population has grown in absolute numbers since the early beginnings (refer to Table 1). This is partly reflected in the increased number of mosques constructed to serve the community. Even though a total of 25 mosques have been demolished since 1968 (18 on mainland Singapore and seven in the southern islands) this is not because of a decline in the Muslim population. Instead, bigger mosques have been built, particularly since 1975 (as part of the Majlis Ugama Islam Singapura's Mosque Building Fund Scheme) to meet the needs. Currently in Singapore, Muslims are well served by 74 mosques spread all over the country. The *surau*[8] however has declined in number as they face replacement by newer and bigger mosques. This change in the Islamic landscape is a significant

Sultan Mosque, built in 1928, is the oldest extant *masjid* in Singapore.

marker of Singapore's changing social and spatial structure. It is reflective of the growth of population, including Muslim population, as well as the reorganisation of the housing landscape, from *kampungs* to Housing and Development Board flats in new towns. The neighbourhood *surau* that served the needs of the *kampung* dwellers has given way to the large mosques that service a far larger hinterland and population.

Unlike Christianity which has grown in significance, and Islam which has principally held its own, our figures suggest a decline in the representation of Chinese religionists in the latter part of the 20th century. Some of the reasons have already been highlighted above. In addition, increasing urbanisation in Singapore had also led to the declining significance of some of the religious institutions and practices that had been prominent in China (Elliot 1955:22). In the case of scholastic Buddhism, there were not enough people of high intellectual attainment in early Singapore to maintain and expand its influence. Kinship networks in Singapore were not strong enough, leading to the decline of ancestral cults. Simultaneously, however, the fact that *caitang* (vegetarian houses) had increased in number in the 1950s may suggest conversely that there had not been a decline in the popularity of Chinese religious activities. These vegetarian houses — the center of a form of monastic organisation that started as a lay religion — were primarily residences for women, usually retired *amahs* (domestic helpers) who were often without family in Singapore (Topley 1956:105). They were in fact performing an important social role, perhaps more so than a religious one. In that sense, the fact that there were more *caitang* need not be an indication of greater adherence to religion at all, and Elliot's argument about a decline in Chinese religion may still hold, as the figures appear to bear out.

Hinduism is primarily the religion of Indians rather than of any other ethnic group, and the proportion of Hindus in the population over the years generally trails the proportion of Indians in the total population, as borne out in Table 1. Those Indians who are not Hindus are often of the Christian persuasion. In the last two decades, there has been a slower rate of growth of the Hindu population. Indeed, relative to the Indian population, the Hindu population has declined. This may be attributed to the spread of English, which has contributed to conversion to Christianity (Clammer 1985:61). Even those who remain as Hindus have begun to adopt what Clammer terms 'neo-Hinduism,' a reformist, less ritualistic orientation (1985:61). This further reflects the intellectualisation of religion in Singapore, a situation which we have discussed earlier in relation to Buddhism.

Performing

One visible manifestation of religious adherence is the performance of religious rituals, particularly in public places. Certainly, many rituals are also conducted in private places, particularly within one's dwelling. Some of these will be 'routine' rituals of orthodox worship while others will be those which depart from orthodox practice. The latter will reveal the prevalence of syncretism and the influence of local traditions.

Catholics are obliged to participate in congregational prayers once a week. This involves the worship of God through participation in mass every Sunday. Additionally, there are specific holy days of obligation in the church calendar, during which Catholics should attend mass. In Singapore, these include Ascension Day, Assumption of the Blessed Virgin Mary, All Saints' Day and Christmas Day. Catholics have a duty to receive Holy Communion frequently (at least once a year) as well as to receive the Sacrament of Penance (through confession) at least once a year. These two, together with baptism, confirmation, ordination, marriage and the anointing of the sick, are the seven sacraments through which it is believed Jesus Christ gives his spirit to his people. Rituals are an integral part of Catholic worship: many of the rituals are tied to the weekly mass, some of which have become abbreviated over time. Other rituals are commonly tied to cyclical calendrical events, such as the observance of Ash Wednesday (the day when ash is put on the forehead of believers to remind them that this is the state from which they came and to which they will return), and Maundy Thursday (the day before Good Friday when Jesus Christ died on the cross for the sins of humankind; foot-washing rituals are often conducted by priests on Maundy Thursday as a re-enactment of Jesus Christ's act of humility on the night before he died).

Baptism of baby G. John, circa 1949.

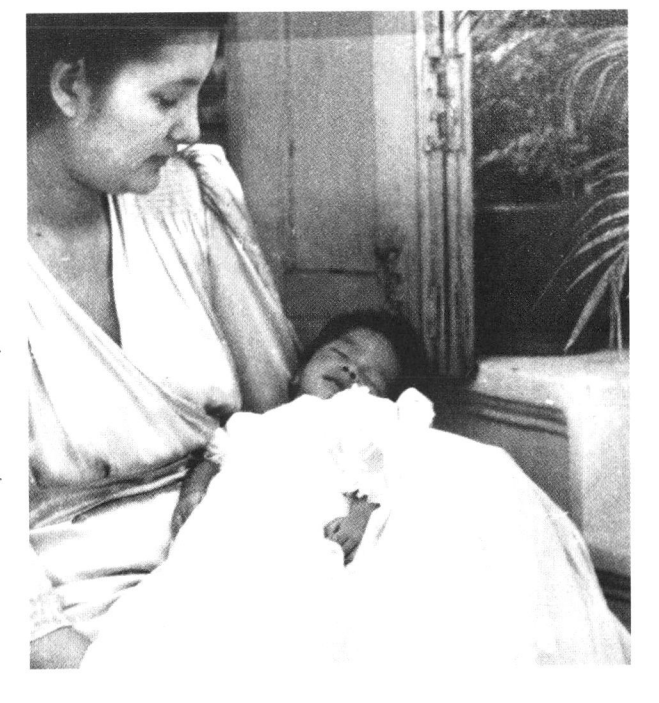

In Singapore, there is a certain degree of religious syncretism, for example, in the mixing of practices of Chinese religious traditions and Catholicism. This is evident in some practices of Chinese Catholics; for example, when holy water is sprinkled in homes to ward off evil spirits and when amulets with the engraving of Jesus, Mary or a saint are worn to protect the wearer from evil and accident (Low 1974). Churches also very often celebrate mass on the first day of Chinese New Year, and make traditional Chinese offerings, such as *nian gao,* melon seeds and Mandarin oranges. There is often also the blessing and distribution of oranges to the congregation. Similarly, in the ritual observances of at least some Catholic Vellala[9] in Singapore, it is possible to detect traces of the pre-Christian Hindu past. For example, Catholic Vellala marriage practices reflect this syncretism as well as change over time. Traditionally, the date for the wedding would be determined by consulting a Hindu astrologer — this is done only 'on the quiet' in more recent years (Stephens 1983:73). A major ritual of the traditional Catholic Vellala marriage ceremony is the *nalengu*, in which the groom stands in front of the family shrine. A happily married woman waves an incense-holder and camphor around him so that the incense wafts over him. The groom is then blessed by his parents. This is followed by prayers by happily married women, and then unrelated women. In modern times, the *nalengu* is often left out of the Catholic Vellala wedding ceremonies, or a moderated version is performed (Stephens 1983:75–77). While these are strictly not part of the orthodoxy of the Catholic Church, they continue to be practised by some adherents, illustrating the lasting power of rituals, which sometimes continue to be practised even when the symbolic meaning is no longer understood and when they strictly fall beyond the ambit of Christian teachings and beliefs.

Imam calling for prayers at the Harbour before embarking on the ship for Mecca, in 1952.

As with other members of the worldwide orthodox Muslim community, those in Singapore subscribe to the five 'pillars' of the faith; namely, *salat* or prayer, the payment of *zakat* (a religious tax), the *puasa* (fasting) during the month of *Ramadan*, the profession of faith *syahadat* ('There is no God but Allah, and Mohammed is His Prophet'), and the *haj* (pilgrimage to Mecca). As one of the five pillars, prayers are obligatory; and in Islam, they are both congregational and private. Strict orthodox Muslims pray five times a day: just before sunrise, at noon, around four o'clock in the afternoon, at sunset and just before bedtime. These prayers can take place anywhere: at work, in school, at home, in a *surau* or *masjid*.[10] Every Friday, all male Muslims who have reached puberty must congregate at a *masjid* for their noon prayers which are led by an *imam*.[11] These five pillars are also accompanied by a range of other orthodox practices. For example, circumcision or *sunat* is carried out in both females and males. According to Muslim law, circumcision is not compulsory, but is highly encouraged. In the past, circumcision was often carried out in one's own house by a *Tok Mudin*, often under *kampung* conditions. In more recent years, circumcision can be done in a hospital or a clinic where it is more sanitary. However, there are parents who still choose to circumcise their children in their own home.

The well-dressed Malay boy (centre) is surrounded by friends and relatives before his circumcision ceremony, circa 1960.

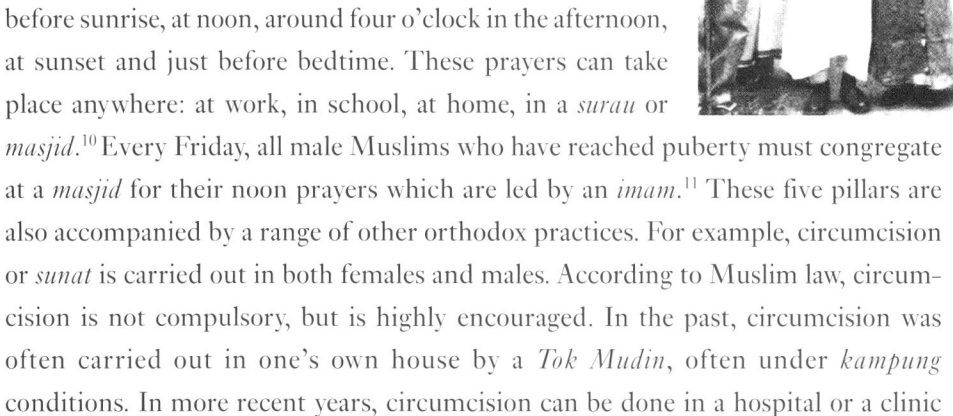

Orthodox worship aside, Islam as practised in Singapore is sometimes also blended with local cultural practices. One example is *keramat* worship in Singapore. To orthodox Muslims, this is a malpractice because they believe that God is providential and that any prayers should be directed to God rather than an intermediary. In the original Arabic context, *kerama* (*keramat*, plural) was used to refer to the 'marvels' performed by a *wali* (one who finds favour with God). These marvels are a gift bestowed by God and are not to be attributed to any innate miraculous power on the part of the *wali*. Orthodox interpretation would regard the miracles as deeds of the Almighty and *keramat* as the special gifts of persons of 'high

Devotees paying their respects at Keramat Habib Noh in the 1980s.

Worshippers at the Keramat Iskandar Shah in 1956.

religious esteem' through whom these miracles are performed (Van Donzel *et al.* 1975:615–616).

In Singapore, *keramat* worship is much more than the worship of persons of high religious standing for it incorporates elements of indigenous beliefs and Hindu influences. Mohamed Taib bin Osman classifies six different sets of *keramat* belief and practice prevalent among the Malays: worship at graves of persons said to have attained sainthood while alive or posthumously; worship at graves of kings, magicians, founders of settlements, and sometimes those of obscure and dubious history; belief in living saints and wonder-workers (*keramat hidup*); belief in invisible *keramat* inhabiting places or natural objects in specific localities; belief in *keramat* objects possessed of magical and wonderful powers, and belief in animal *keramat* (1967:188–89). Both Chinese and Malays are known to visit *keramat*, usually to pray for a wish to be granted, whether it be to heal an illness, to seek success in business or to bear children. Sometimes, small pieces of cloth may be tied to the branches of trees or to the railing near the *keramat* as markers (*petanda*) to the votary. Offerings may also be made at a *keramat* in fulfilment of a wish granted (Mohamed Nahar Ros 1985:40).

This form of worship has been subjected to forces of modernity in various ways. First, modernisation, concomitant with the provision of 'western education' has led to the 'subsequent inculcation of science, modern values and ideas,' which alters 'the environment suitable for old Malay traditions and beliefs.' Specifically, the ascension of rational science has enhanced the questioning of such 'old-world superstitions' which 'cannot be proved by any means of rational experiment or logic' (Mohamed Nahar Ros 1984: 68–69). This development is most evident in the younger generation of Malays. Indeed, there has been a general decline in the belief in *keramat*, and patronage to the more well-known *keramat*, such as the Keramat Sultan Iskandar Shah is sustained largely by older generation Malays. Second, a rise in Islamic fundamentalism in the last decade or so — evident in a clarion call for Muslims to 'return [to] the purity of Islam' — tends to undermine 'un-Islamic beliefs and customs' (Mohamed Nahar Ros 1985:72). *Keramat* worship is not consistent with such a resurgence in Muslim orthodoxy. Third, and related to modernisation, is the urbanisation (especially urban redevelopment) of Singapore. Inevitably, the acquisition of land by public authorities for urban renewal or housing projects would involve land where *keramat* are located. For example, the famous Keramat Bismilla-wali at Changi Road has made way for housing projects. Interestingly, such removal did not meet with any Malay objections. In fact, some segments of the Muslim community might even be supportive of the removal of such remnants of 'paganism'. Urbanisation and urban renewal have thus had a direct physical impact on the continued viability of *keramat* worship in Singapore.

Whereas weekly obligatory worship is a distinctive feature of Islam and Christianity, in Hinduism, temple attendance is not obligatory. While the temple was an integral part of Hindu life for the early migrants in a way reminiscent of life in India, it is argued that the influence of Hindu temples has declined after World War II for several reasons. One is urban renewal and with it the fact that people found permanent settlement and, increasingly, could perform most of the worship and rituals at home. In many Hindu households, it is common to find a separate room or space that is specially dedicated to the Hindu deities. These rooms or spaces are not exposed to nor visible from the public spaces in the house to avoid 'pollution' (that which is profane), an observance which was far less possible in the crammed living quarters of old. A second reason for the declining influence of the temple is a higher level of education and, concomitantly, the greater access to an increased number of secular and broad-based social institutions. This has meant that people can seek help and advice through other channels such as community or welfare associations, rather than the temple. However, in more recent years, there are pressures from temple-going Hindus as well as, less directly, from church and mosque-going Christians and Muslims respectively for Hindus to make regular temple visits (Sinha 1988:111). At the same time, in a modern context where both adult members of a nuclear family work full-time, there is little time to observe elaborate rituals at a home altar. For pragmatic reasons therefore, Hindus may prefer to go to a temple to pray —there is no need to tend to the paraphernalia of an altar at home (Sinha 1988:114).

Yet other effects of modernisation, including the living and work patterns of modern urban life, are evident in Hindu practice. The relatively long and fixed routine of work in Singapore, for example, has resulted in a reduction in the time available for ceremonial activity. As a result, many festivals are celebrated on a reduced scale in the evenings or on weekends (Babb 1976:166). Sunday mornings have become popular for temple-visiting. Consequently, a process of 'vicarious ritualisation' occurs, whereby the rich, especially, sponsor religious activity which is carried out by others on their behalf (Singer, cited in Babb 1976:166). One other phenomenon has also set in: compartmentalisation of a traditional home life in which Hindu practices are maintained, distinguished from a detraditionalised one which inhabits the public sphere of work and perhaps recreation (Singer, cited in Babb 1976:167). This affects Hindu men in particular who became 'traditional in diet, dress and behaviour at home; atraditional outside the immediate household setting' (Babb 1976:167). As more and more Hindu women also join the workforce, however, the compartmentalisation becomes less marked, as the traditions they previously maintained at home also recede in importance. The result is that the home also becomes an area of 'ritual neutralisation' (Singer, cited in Babb 1976:167).[12]

The temple, then, is still an important place of Hindu worship, festivals and ceremonies. For instance, *pujas* (prayers for universal good) are conducted at fixed times daily in some temples. Although devotees need not conform to these times, they nonetheless draw Hindus together in congregational worship. The temple is also the focal point of some festivals and ceremonies. The festival *Thaipusam*, for example, involves the procession of devotees carrying *kavadi*, in penitence or thanksgiving, from the Sri Srinivasa Perumal Temple on Serangoon Road to the Thendayuthapani Temple on Tank Road. The traditional *kavadi* is a wooden arch on a wooden base, decorated with peacock feathers and supporting various offerings such as flowers and fruits, and pots of milk (or sometimes sugar). In recent years,

A Hindu devotee, carrying *kavadi* during Thaipusam, circa 1960.

heavy metal *kavadi* have been used by some.

At Deepavali, another major festival in the Hindu calendar, the main temple activity is the fire-walking ceremony (*thimithi*) where devotees walk barefoot across a pit of heated granite chips. The heat from the pit is enough to burn. However, it is believed that a devotee who is strong in faith will be able to overcome this and emerge unhurt.

Many Hindu rituals such as those relating to birth, marriage and death, are also performed in the home. While many of these rituals were followed quite religiously in the past, we are now witnessing more shorthand versions, with families leaving out certain aspects deemed less important. One example is the set of rituals surrounding birth. For example, at the end of the period of confinement (for some, 28 days following the birth of a child, for others, 30 or 31, depending on the dialect group), ritual purification is practised, and this takes the form of house cleaning, prayers by a priest and the sprinkling of holy water. For some, until the ritual purification is performed, no family members may worship at a temple because of the pollution associated with birth.

These two photographs (above and below, taken in 1967) show Hindu devotees performing the fire-walking ceremony (*thimithi*) as enthralled spectators watch on.

Waterloo Street's *Kuan Yin* temple is transformed into a hive of activity on key days of the Buddhist calendar. This Vesak Day shot, circa 1985, reveals how devotees make their offerings cheek by jowl.

After confinement, a name-giving ceremony is held during which the baby is presented to the world for the first time. This is a ritual of integration. During the ceremony, gifts are presented to the mother and child. Friends and relatives are also invited to a vegetarian meal at home. Many also go to a temple to give thanks. Some also observe the ritual of hair shaving when the child reaches six months, but it is one of those rituals that some have dispensed with over time (Tham 1985:79).[13]

Like Hindus, Chinese religionists are not obliged to participate in weekly congregational worship. Indeed, they may visit temples at any time and as often as they please. One of the beliefs of Chinese religionists is that different gods have different powers, and to get a multiplicity of blessings, one would have to pray to many gods and visit many temples. These may be syncretic, Buddhist or Taoist ones. In addition, there are also ancestral temples, owned and run by associations of Chinese for the worship of ancestors (Topley 1956:95). There is also one temple dedicated to Confucius (Leo and Clammer 1983). Of all the temples, the syncretic ones were more popular than the others because they contained deities of all categories of Chinese religions (Lip 1983:6).

The list of deities worshipped by Chinese religionists is long. Some of the more common and popular ones are *Guan Gong* (God of War), *Dabogong* (Earth God), *Ma Zu* (Mother Goddess of the Sea) and *Kuan Yin* (Goddess of Mercy). They may be worshipped at home or in temples. Temple visits happen on an ad hoc basis, usually when one has a specific request, such as seeking help and advice when facing adversities or health problems. If the problem is solved, adherents will generally return to the temple to give thanks and make offerings of incense, food and the like. Adherents also visit temples on special festivals.

One of the most celebrated religious festivals in Singapore, by Buddhists and other Chinese religionists alike, is the birthday of *Kuan Yin*. This actually falls on three days, the 19th day of the 2nd, 6th and 9th month of the Chinese lunar calendar. Certain temples housing *Kuan Yin*, such as the one along Waterloo Street, become very crowded on such days. Chinese religionists also celebrate *Guan Gong's* birthday which falls on the 13th day of the 5th lunar month. Vesak Day is another important festival for Buddhists as it celebrates the birth of Buddha. This falls on the 15th day of the 4th lunar month. An important procession is usually held at the Bright Hill Temple in Sin Min Drive. Unlike other Chinese religions, Buddhism is 'simpler' in terms of the offerings made, the only ones being flowers and incense (joss sticks), which in some cases, are not even encouraged. Another well-celebrated event would be the birthday celebration of the Heavenly King, also known as the Jade Emperor. This event is known as *Tian Gong Dan*. This celebration is especially popular with the Hokkiens who perceive him to be the most powerful and influential of all gods.

Apart from birthdays of deities or Buddha, other calendrical events are also observed ritually. The 24th day of the 12th lunar month is the day when adherents send the deities back to Heaven. This can be done on the night itself or the night before. It is believed that every person's deeds will be reported to the Heavenly King when the deities return to Heaven. Based on this belief, sweet food such as cakes and sweets will be offered to ensure that these deities will not utter any bad things or report on misdeeds. When the deities return on the fourth day of the Chinese New Year, a lot of preparation also goes into welcoming them. On the last day of the lunar year, usually near midnight, offerings will be made to welcome *Cai Shen* (God of Prosperity), believed to bring wealth and prosperity.

The *Jiu Huang Ye* (Nine Emperor Gods) festival is another major event that is usually celebrated with a procession to welcome the deities. Some believe them to be the Nine Celestial Breaths of the Supreme One (the Lord Emperor *Taiyi*). Others believe them to be nine brothers, each taking care of a specific aspect of life and death (Cheu 1988:16). The festival is laden with rituals, the most common being the burning of incense-paper and the lighting of candles and joss sticks. It is believed that the more that are burnt (sacrificed), the more blessings will be returned (Cheu 1988:57). At the same time, vegetarian items are also offered during the festivals,

PAST TIMES: A SOCIAL HISTORY OF SINGAPORE

A *Jiu Huang Ye* procession along Upper Serangoon Road, circa 1947.

A public auction (photographed here in 1989) is always part of the events that mark the celebration of the Hungry Ghost Festival. Successful bidders are believed to enjoy prosperity.

while animals are sacrificed on the 10th day of the festival, after the nine deities have been sent off, to thank the non-vegetarian deities for their forbearance (Cheu 1988:55).

For many of these festivals, the standard rituals include the offering of incense (joss sticks), candles, food and paper money (incense-paper). The grander celebrations may even include performance by a Chinese opera troupe and feasting during which people bid for items that they think will bring them luck. Sometimes, a *ge tai* is put up with performances of songs and dance. Such celebrations are typical of *Zhong Yuan Jie*, better known as the Hungry Ghost Festival, which falls in the seventh lunar month. Throughout this month, offerings are made to appease the wandering ghosts and spirits. The profits generated from the bids and donations are used to organise a similar event the following year.

In *shenism*, spirit-medium possession is a popular way for people to seek solutions to their problems. The spirit-medium (*dang-ki*), when possessed, is said to have taken on the power of the spirit. In the past, spirit-medium performances were often spectacular. The spirit-medium would fall into a trance and use weapons such as spiked balls and swords to inflict torture upon himself or herself. This is symbolic of the power of the spirit which has rendered the medium invulnerable to pain and physical harm. Such acts of self-torture were common on special religious occasions but are not as common in recent years.

Certainly, the more gruesome forms of self-mortification have decreased significantly. However, if one visits a spirit medium temple, one may still see displays of some of these instruments of torture. Some spirit mediums do not go into any trance nor perform any acts of self-infliction. They merely prescribe 'cures' for people, usually in the form of a talisman or amulet that is deemed to have some 'magical' qualities. The popularity of the spirit medium is often dependent on the effectiveness of the cures that he or she prescribes. In the face of urban renewal, many of the smaller spirit medium temples have been evicted. They have nevertheless relocated to Housing and Development Board (HDB) flats and some remain quite popular, with queues of followers awaiting their turn outside these flats in order to seek advice.

The spirit-medium (centre) wields a sword while performing acts of self-immolation, circa 1962. Notice her pierced cheeks and arm.

A Hainanese opera at which the audience receives blessings from 'gods' and 'goddesses,' circa 1986.

Belonging

Even as religious adherents of different persuasions participate in various rituals — often (though not invariably) as manifestations of belief — we would do well to recall Emile Durkheim's thesis that religion is really an expression of group solidarity, and that, more than a matter of individual belief, participation in religious rituals is about maintaining social relations. In some ways, such a view is borne out in intra- and inter-religious relationships in Singapore. At times, evidence suggests that religion bridges divisions by bringing people together, although it is equally true that religion has breaches. Several examples from across the different religions and through the passage of Singapore's modern history will be cited to illustrate such bridging and breaching.

Bridging

Harking back to Singapore's early modern Christian history, one of the remarkable distinctions about social relations was the inter-denominational support that existed, ironical given the jurisdictional tussle within the Catholic Church itself, highlighted earlier in this chapter. Inter-denominational support was most evident in the fact that donations for the construction of the first Catholic chapel and subsequently the Cathedral of the Good Shepherd did not just come from the Catholic community, but from the Protestants as well (Buckley 1902:248). This was true even decades later when significant sums were contributed from the Protestant community for the extension of the Convent of the Holy Infant Jesus (Buckley 1902:268).

For much of the 19th and 20th centuries, Chinese temples were where religious and social functions were held, and where disputes and other businesses were settled (Lee *et al.* 1994:152). Religious place was therefore crucial to the social functioning of the Chinese community. Likewise, the Hindu temple was not only a place of worship, but also the centre of social life (Tan 1962:30). The same may be said of the mosque in its traditional origins, although in Singapore, this has not always been the case. Indeed, Mansor Sukaimi, in studying 'new generation' mosques in post-independence Singapore, draws attention to the fact that mosques in Singapore have changed in character and function. While in the past, many were small and originally designed with facilities meant primarily for prayers, the new mosques, built under the Mosque Building Fund Scheme, are multi-functional and are now 'socio-religious institutions,' fulfilling more roles than just as places of worship, in recognition of the traditional role of mosques (Mansor 1983:3). They are at the same time educational institutions, spiritual centres, council chambers for the deliberation of community affairs, community-service centres, secretariat offices and so forth. There have also been significant changes in terms of establishment, management, funding, activities and functions. While serving as focal points for prayers, they are also usually equipped with a library, computer room, conference room, classrooms for religious studies, multi-purpose hall, and a room for the *jenazah* (corpse) where preparations are made for burial, so that the mosque fulfils a role as a 'community' centre where the affairs of community development may be deliberated upon, and where programmes which lead to 'the upliftment of the *ummah*'[14] may be organised (MUIS 1986:8). This is reflected in that the mosque also conducts regular activities such as marriage counselling courses and exhibitions on drug abuse. It also houses kindergartens. In this way, MUIS hopes that mosques in contemporary Singapore might approximate to the roles played by mosques in the early days of Islam as religious, social, cultural and political centres (MUIS 1986:11).

Breaching

Even while a sense of community and social solidarity at an intra-religious group level may be enhanced, sometimes, belonging to one group can lead to a breach with others. There is ample historical evidence of this. In the mid-19th century, the growth of the Chinese Catholic population was viewed with some displeasure from the non-Catholic Chinese population which continued to subscribe to clan associations and secret societies. They viewed conversion to Catholicism as a threat to their membership and survival because converts tended to sever their links with clans and societies. In 1851, Chinese Christians were attacked in the northern parts of the country in Punggol and Upper Serangoon by secret societies, and resulted in a massive riot lasting a week. The military finally quelled the riot, but already, 500 had been killed, all Chinese, including well-to-do Catholic converts (Song [1923] 1967:82–83). As Song pointed out, however, the Chinese Christians were to blame as well, 'for they regarded themselves as a distinct brotherhood' and 'any quarrel occurring between their members and outsiders was at once adopted by the whole body, and riots ensued' (1967:83). A century later, in 1950, inter-religious strife emerged yet again in what has come to be known as the Maria Hertogh riots (see Chapter 11). This time, the clash between Muslims and Christians, resulting in 18 deaths, 173 injured and considerable property damage, highlighted the serious social unrest that could arise between two exclusive religions, particularly when insensitively handled.

Chinese priests performing rites and distributing blessings and auspicious items, circa 1990.

While most visible, chasms need not always be violent, and need not be rooted in religious divisions only. Sometimes, the chasms and marginalisation that are caused by religious differences may also correspond with other rifts and biases. Examples include the race, class and gender biases that were perpetuated by Catholicism in the mid-19th century. As the Catholic population grew, it became evident how the community began to engage more and more in social and other non-religious activities in increasingly pronounced and formalised ways, extending beyond an existence as a religious community. In 1866, for example, the St. George Singapore Catholic Young Men's Society was established, involving monthly meetings in which papers were read on various subjects such as education and experiments on the environment. The Society provides an excellent lens into the gender, race and class relations at that time, for it was a society essentially for white educated males who would be interested to propound on various subjects. It therefore served to accentuate gender, race and class divisions in a quiet way. While the Society was quickly to become defunct — which is assumed as the minute book ends abruptly in June 1867 — a similar club was established in 1900, 'in very good premises,' no less. It provided billiard tables and 'other amusements for the young men in the evenings, which are much more likely to continue to call them together than reading very long and scientific papers' (Buckley 1902:255). There was no reason to believe that the gender, race and class biases had been removed in this new club even at the turn of the century.

Conclusion

For every development and issue discussed here, there are silences multifold. The richness, complexities and changes over time of the multiple religions in Singapore cannot be totally captured within these few pages. Nevertheless, several observations may be made. First, religion took root very early in Singapore's modern history (with the coming of Raffles) and indeed predated that in some instances, such as in the case of Islam and Buddhism. Perhaps some of the adherence to religion may be attributed to the stresses and uncertainties that accompany migration, wherein religion offered an anchor and relief in the belief that there are powers sympathetic and helpful to people on the move. The affiliation with a religious group may also stem from the social functions of the religious institution, and the sense of community and solidarity that the religious group provides, which is particularly important for early migrants who ventured forth with neither kith nor kin.

As migrants arrived and engaged in religious practice, orthodox worship often became modified as rituals, and became syncretised with other world religious practices or more localised, often animistic, traditions. Such syncretism of practice belied a syncretism of belief, a mixing and matching that allowed the individual to seek comfort in different deities and solidarity with different communities, as the occasion demanded. Yet, while offering a sense of community and belonging, religion also served to divide, sometimes culminating in riotous bloodshed.

Despite increasing modernisation in Singapore, the role of religion has not declined. In other words, the conventional argument that secularisation sets in with modernisation has not been borne out here. However, it is true that, with the advent of modernisation and urban living, certain religions have declined where others have grown. The former refers primarily to Chinese religion, viewed to be anchored in superstition and illogic, while the latter refers primarily to Christianity. Buddhism, in particular, and to an extent Hinduism, have also attempted to remain relevant and appealing by adopting some of the practices of Protestant Christianity and emphasising the text — in a process earlier highlighted as the intellectualisation and rationalisation of religion.

Modern living has also necessitated the modification of rituals and sometimes the abbreviation of practice. On occasion, it has entailed a privatisation of performance (such as participation in a simple ritual at home rather than an elaborate public ceremony). However, at other times, the reverse has taken place, when a private ritual requires more time and effort than modern living allows, and participation in a public (usually communal) ritual where preparations are seen to by a 'professional' becomes much more manageable. All this underscores the dynamics of ritual to suit local conditions, and the force of modernity in reshaping religion.

Acknowledgments

We would like to record thanks to our student assistants Chia Choy Wan, Isaac Kang and Harvey Neo, and our research assistant Evelyn Lee for their help.

Endnotes

1. The Syiah Muslims constitute the other 10 percent and are principally found in Iran.
2. This is reflected in the varied names adopted to describe 'Chinese religion.' For example, Elliott (1955) termed it *shenism*, which he derived from the fact that when asked for their religion, most Chinese would respond with *bai shen* (praying to the spirits). Topley, who has researched the various Chinese religious practices, institutions and associations in Singapore, termed it the 'anonymous religion' (1954; 1956; 1961). Comber, in turn, referred to it as the 'religion of the masses' (1954, 1955, 1958). More recently, Clammer's introduction to a volume of works on contemporary Chinese religious practices in Singapore and Malaysia characterised it as 'Chinese folk religion' (Clammer 1983). Nyce similarly adopted that terminology (Nyce 1971).
3. See also Elliott 1955; Heinze 1979, 1981; Ju 1983; and Cheu 1988.
4. Meaning 'sea people.'
5. However, other accounts exist. Bartley suggested that the population was larger, and certainly included Chinese, as there were already gambier plantations owned and cultivated by the Chinese prior to 1819 (1933:177). Bloom cited some estimated figures: a total population of about 200, consisting of a few *Orang Laut* families ('nominally Mohomedans, but really believing in a sort of fetishism like all untutored peoples' (Buckley 1902:30), about 100 Muslim Malay fisherfolk, thought to have settled on the island in 1811, and a community of about 40 Chinese pepper and gambier cultivators (Bloom 1986:349). The Chinese were likely to have adhered to a form of Chinese religion.
6. The precise dates of establishment cited for each denomination have varied from source to source, so the dates represented here are drawn from one of the two sources accredited.
7. The overlap between the first two periods (1819–1930 and 1900–1950) is found in the original text. Presumably, Hinton (1985) meant that the 30 years from 1900 to 1930 were years of change and transition.
8. *Surau* is the Malay word for a small prayer house, where prayers other than the Friday congregational prayers are held.
9. According to Stephens (1983:9), the Vellala come from 'a very small part of a large, predominantly Hindu, agricultural 'jati-cluster' of South India.' The first record of Vellala converting to Catholicism is that of a school teacher in Madurai by Roberto de Nobilli (1983:33). Most of the Catholic Vellala first arrived in Malaya in the 1880s and settled in towns like Penang, Ipoh, Kuala Lumpur and Seremban (1983:47).
10. Malay word for mosque; literally means 'place of prostration.'
11. Malay word for prayer leader.
12. Singer explained ritual neutralisation as a process whereby a neutrally public area such as the workplace in India becomes 'increasingly free from ritual and religious restriction,' and where 'traditional rites, norms, and sanctions are abbreviated and specialised or become inoperative' (1972:329). He also described this as a process of deritualisation.
13. See Chapter 4.
14. Arabic for 'community,' also commonly used in Malay.

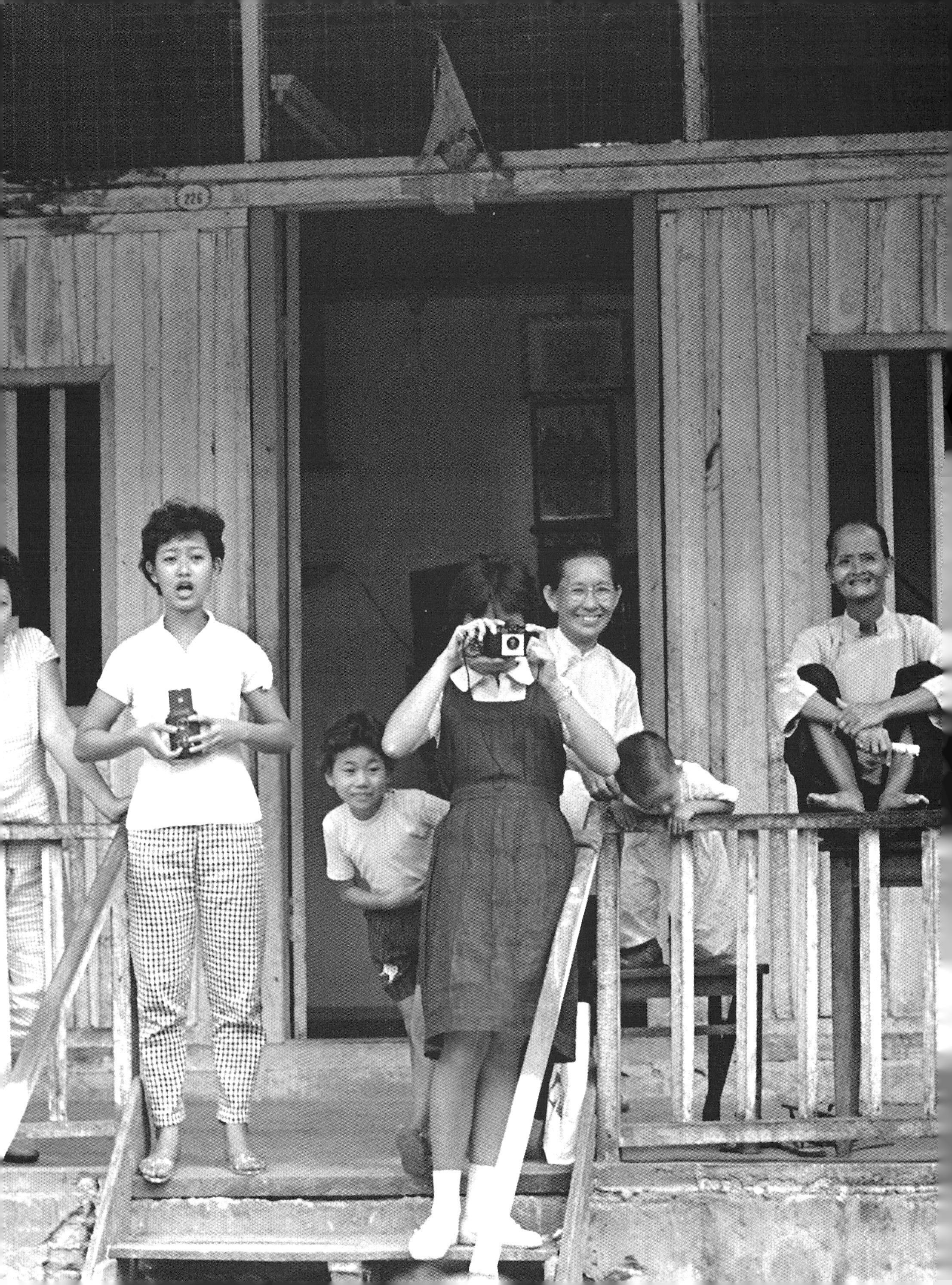
226

Theatre of Four Corners: Photographers, Subjects, Sociologists and Readers

Zaheer Baber & Chan Kwok Bun

Opposite: Residents awaiting with cameras outside their house during PM Lee Kuan Yew's 1963 tour of Kampong Kembangan constituency.

Photographers have studied anthropology and sociology and social scientists have studied photography.

Howard Becker[1]

Photography is a tool for dealing with things everybody knows about but isn't attending to. My photographs are intended to represent something you don't see.

Emmet Gowin[2]

If I could tell the story in words, I wouldn't need to lug a camera.

Lewis Hine[3]

The cliché, that a picture is worth a thousand words, has been deployed to good effect in journalism, but photographic images have not quite found their niche in serious social scientific research. This is in marked contrast to the prolific social commentary on and the analysis of images themselves and the practice of photography.[4] To be sure, photographic images have contributed significantly to the work of some social scientists; it has been well over fifty years since Gregory Bateson and Margaret Mead focused their Leicas on the inhabitants of Bali, resulting in the majestically-produced *Balinese Character* (1942). More recently, journals such as *Visual Anthropology* and *Society* publish sociologically-informed photo essays, and a regular section of the *American Ethnologist* is devoted to reviews of visual explorations of the human condition. The works of Howard Becker, John Berger, Berger and Mohr, Said and Mohr, Pinney, and Lalvani have demonstrated the dramatic enhancement of the power of critical social analysis and commentary when words are combined with photographic images. However, these studies are exceptions to the generalised absence of photography in social science, except as data or as 'illustrations'; for example, most ethnographies include at least a few photographs, but sociological writings do not. It is in this context that the present volume seeks to contribute to the desire of integrating visual representation with words.

Photography as 'Reality'

The deployment of photographic images in social analyses conjures up a host of specific issues. The most immediate of these is the assumption that photographic images provide, or have the potential for providing, *unmediated* access to reality. After all, among all other visual media, photography appears to come closest to 'reality.' It is precisely this *apparent* connection between photographic images and situations that were 'actually out there' that has led some commentators to accord a different kind of aesthetic standard to photography as opposed to, for example, painting, which has often been compared to photography. While few theorists would support the position that photographic images are identical to the settings or events they seek to represent, the association between photography and representational realism has found support in some unexpected quarters.

Roland Barthes, among others, initiated the process of loosening the connection between 'the signifier' and 'the signified,' a project that has been stretched to its limits and beyond by Jean Baudrillard who appeared to endorse such a position (Baudrillard 1981; 1994). In his posthumously published volume of essays, *Camera Lucida: Reflections on Photography*, Barthes argued that there is an essential connection between 'the necessarily real thing which has been placed before the lens' and the photographic image (1981). Contending that 'every photograph is somehow co-natural with its referent,' he underscored his conviction that photographic images serve to establish the fact that 'the thing has been there' even though the reality represented by such images is 'a reality one can no longer touch' (Barthes 1981:76–81). 'The important thing,' Barthes argued, 'is that the photograph possesses an evidential force, and that its testimony bears not on the object but on time' (Barthes 1981:88–89). Later on in this chapter, we will return to Barthes' conception of the connections between photography, evidential force and authenticity.

Barthes was surely not the first to draw attention to the authenticating role of photographic images. Along very different lines and writing in a radically different context, Peter Henry Emerson, an important photographer of the nineteenth century, wrote *Naturalistic Photography for Students of Art* where he urged budding photographers to produce images that would be 'as much as possible, identical with the visual impression an observer would get at the actual spot from which the photograph was made' (cited in Snyder and Allen 1987:62). Emerson's program of 'naturalism' was, in some ways, a continuation of the wish — dominant in the West at least since the Reformation — to overcome subjectivity as much as possible, to the point of obliterating human agency from the act of producing images. In this quest, photography was the natural candidate for delivering what traditional arts could not — a necessary, linear connection between the image and the objects it sought to represent. Reflecting on the differences between painting and photography, some commentators have pointed out that the latter 'overcame subjectivity in a way undreamed of by painting, one which does not so much defeat the act of painting as escape it altogether by *automatism*, by removing the human agent from the act of reproduction' (Cavell 1971:21–23). Photography presumably finally promised the practical realisation of the general artistic ideals of objectivity and detachment (Snyder and Allen 1987:63).

The search for an intrinsic connection between the photographic image, authenticity and representational realism was not restricted to the earlier generation of art critics and historians such as Siegfried Kracauer, Andre Bazin and E. H. Gombrich. In attempting to distinguish between painting and photographic images so as to claim artistic status for the latter, the contemporary theorist of photography Rudolph Arnheim emphasized the 'fundamental peculiarity of the photographic medium: the physical objects themselves print their image by means of the optical and chemical action of light.' He went on to argue that photographs 'have an authenticity from which painting is barred from birth' and while looking at photographs, 'we are on vacation from artifice' (Arnheim 1974: 155–157, cited in Snyder and Allen 1987: 65–67). As a consequence, for Arnheim, the issues of authenticity and the documentary value of photographs are unavoidable in a way that cannot be the case with paintings. While not going to the obviously problematic extreme of arguing that the 'photographic image is nothing but a faithful copy of the object,' and readily acknowledging that the photographer is 'part of the situation he depicts' and therefore 'upsets the facts on which he reports,' Arnheim nevertheless sought to retain the notion that, unlike other visual arts, photographs are not entirely 'made and controlled by man' but are 'mechanical deposits of light' that reflect as no other media can: they have the ability to embody 'the manifest presence of authentic physical reality' (Arnheim 1974: 159). Of course, Arnheim's view is not confined to a small circle of specialists. As Snyder and Allen pointed out, most people, if asked, would reason that whereas a painter can paint whatever he wants, the photographer must depict 'what is there' (1987: 66). It is hardly surprising then that a weak version of 'representational realism' continues to underpin photography as a genre.

Photography and Power

On the other side of the spectrum, the argument that photographs do not constitute a neutral transcription of the real is, despite vigorous claims to the contrary, hardly a latter-day theoretical innovation. Well over fifty years ago, Walter Benjamin categorically rejected the idea that photographic images mirror reality by arguing that 'less than ever before does a reproduction of reality tell us anything about that reality and therefore something has to be *constructed*, something artificial, something set up' (Benjamin 1980:119). Benjamin's contestation of the notion that documentary photography represents self-evident truth was informed by his understanding of the limits of photographic transcription and of reality as necessarily constructed, negotiated and actively produced in interaction with specific interpretive and ideological contexts. Clearly his understanding was premised on a recognition of the inadequacy of the single un-manipulated photograph to represent the contending real relations of power and interest that are themselves constitutive of the image. In a series of critical essays, especially 'The Author as Producer,' Benjamin insisted that the institutional conditions and power relations that contribute to the production of photographic images are inseparable from their formal intent (Benjamin 1978). For Benjamin, lack of reflexivity about the institutional apparatus and the actual conditions under which images are produced leads to collusion with authority and power, irrespective of the photographers' actual intentions (Benjamin 1978). Although Benjamin was not discussing documentary photography in particular and his own analysis did not actually connect photographic images to their institutional conditions of production, his formulations can be and indeed have been extended in this particular direction by scholars such as John Tagg.

Deriving his framework largely from Michel Foucault, the contemporary photography theorist John Tagg has been particularly influential in providing an explicitly sociological framework for locating the production of photographic images. In particular, his argument that the 'emergence of a modern photographic economy in which the so-called medium of photography has no meaning outside its historical specifications' has contributed to a particularly fruitful perspective (Tagg 1988:63). In his own empirical analyses, Tagg has deftly analysed the role, in nineteenth century England, of documentary photography in representing specific urban areas such as ghettos, slums, scenes of crime, etc., that could be targeted as objects of intervention and thus transformed into idealised spaces that require supervision and discipline. In such large-scale projects of state intervention involving specific techniques and strategies of normalisation and discipline, the production and deployment of photographic images were implicated at various levels. For Tagg, photography as practice and culture is tied to the institutions and agents that define it and set it to work. Photography is a mode of cultural production, and as such it is embedded in specific institutional and historical conditions. Photographic images are meaningful and legible only within the particular currencies they have. Like the state, 'the camera is never neutral…and the representations it produces are highly coded, and the power it wields is never its own…[because] it arrives on the scene vested with a particular authority to arrest, picture and transform daily life; a power to see and record' in highly specific ways (Tagg 1988:64). Specific institutional conditions and power relations are not to be treated as 'the externals of photography' but are implicated 'with the very conditions which furnish the materials, codes and strategies of photographic images, the terms of their legibility, and the range and limits of their effectiveness' (Tagg 1988:65).

The Infamous Farm Security Administration (FSA) Project

The role of photographic images in simultaneously representing and constituting social settings and creating the conditions for the exercise of power in a specific way was of course not limited to the nineteenth century. Photography and photographers were dramatically implicated in the expansion of the networks of state power in the United States under President Roosevelt's New Deal programmes of the 1930s. The Farm Security Administration (FSA) was set up in 1935 with the objective of documenting the consequences of the Great Depression on the land and agricultural labour force. The objective of this project was not simply to document the situation, but to create an ideological climate of support for the policies of the New Deal. Headed by Roy Stryker who had taught economics and sociology at Columbia University, the historical section of the FSA was responsible for supplying sociologically relevant pictures to the New Dealers in various government departments. Indeed it was Stryker who personally issued the directives, made clear what kind of pictures he wanted and indicated the types of moods and expressions the FSA was interested in. Dramatic images of hitherto unrepresented destitute Americans struggling in the aftermath of the Depression were made possible by the creative energies of photographers such as Walker Evans, Dorothea Lange, Arthur Rothstein, Jack Delano, Russell Lee and others, who played a very significant role in creating support for Roosevelt's New Deal policies.

The instructions from the FSA to its photographers were quite specific. The images were to be framed with the objective of visually impressing the fact that the victims of the Depression were not just poor but deserving poor. Thus images of the 'worthy' as opposed to the 'unworthy' poor were promoted in the pictures that were ultimately selected for use, not just by the FSA in its campaign but also for dissemination through newspapers and other mass-media forums (Solomon-Godeau 1991:169–70). In a set of specific instructions issued in 1936 to all the photographers in the project, Roy Stryker suggested the following subjects: 'Relationship between density of population and income of such things as: pressed clothes, polished shoes and so on…the wall decorations in homes as an index to the different income groups and their reactions' (Tagg 1988:170). Sometime after the pictures influenced by these guidelines were taken, under criticism from the Department of Farm Security Administration and the U.S. Congress in the period following Pearl Harbor, Stryker was calling for 'pictures of men, women and children who appear as if they really believed in the U.S. Get people with a little spirit. Too many in our file now paint the U.S. as an old person's home and that just about everyone is just about too old to work and too malnourished to care much about what happens.' Under dramatically changing social circumstances, Stryker demanded images of 'more contented-looking old couples — women sewing, men reading' (Tagg 1988:170). The department responsible for commissioning photographers for the FSA folded up after eight years of existence, and the stock of images produced was eventually supplied to various government departments, newspapers, magazines, exhibits and outlets. During the eight years of the existence of the FSA, over 270,000 images were created, out of which about 100,000 that were at odds with the specific ideological orientation of the organization were simply destroyed (Tagg 1988).

Imaging the Community and Nation

The role of these images in the creation of an ideologically favourable climate for the enactment of New Deal policies cannot be overestimated. But the influence of the labours of the photographers associated with the project extended far beyond the specific goals of the FSA and the New Dealers. The mass circulation of photo magazines such as *Life*, *Look*, etc. had certainly made a difference, while images produced by photographers such as Evans and Lange, though not as widely diffused as one would like, played a role in influencing how Americans saw themselves, their society and, ultimately, their nation. In a period of transition from a largely rural to an industrial society — a transformation which probably had begun a generation earlier — the images captured by the FSA photographers, as well as independent documentary photographers like Lewis Hine, played a significant role in the visual apprehension of this dramatic transition. If, as Benedict Anderson has argued, print capitalism played a significant role in the constitution of the 'imagined community,' in the American context at least, the unprecedented circulation of photographic images via newspapers, magazines, and coffee-table books, dramatising the more mundane aspects of the social life of the average American, were essential ingredients that made possible the visual imagination of the post-war American nation (Anderson 1983). The photographic images produced by Walker Evans in his *The Hungry Eye* (1960) and *Let Us Now Praise Famous Men* (1993) and other photographers of that period were as important in imagining the American nation as the evocative novelists such as Steinbeck and Faulkner. It should be added that Hollywood films and weekly newsreels were also potent visual sources — which scholars who wrote about documentary still photography continue to underplay.

The FSA photographs clearly had a large measure of success in legitimising New Deal initiatives, through creating specific interpretations of the diverse texture of the social life of the period. As such, the creation and circulation of the FSA images raise a number of questions: Who made these pictures? Why? Who was subjected to the gaze of the camera? What categories of people and social situations were excluded? How were the images circulated and consumed? What were the consequences of accepting the images as meaningful, truthful, or real? These questions, as John Tagg reminded us, are questions about the very conditions that furnish the materials, codes and strategies of photographic images, the terms of their legibility, and the range and limits of their effectiveness (1988:119).

The Specificity of the Visual

While the issues and questions raised by Tagg are indeed important from a sociological point of view, the significance of images, photographic or otherwise, cannot be confined only to the ideological and structural conditions of their production and the intended modes of circulation and consumption. This was certainly the case with the FSA photographs. Although they were used within the government departments and publications, their currency and influence extended far beyond the narrowly-defined mandate of the Historical Section of the FSA, and on to the reflexive constitution of the imagined community of the American nation, although the mediating influence of a host of elements — material, historical, social, psychological, ideological — cannot be discounted. As Roland Barthes pointed out, meanings generated by photographic meaning are not entirely stable and the same images can be interpreted in diverse ways and even mobilised for ideological projects at variance with the original context of production. Even though the specific structural and ideological conditions of production leave their traces on images, the consumption of these images is not a passive process. Images are consumed through specific interpretive grids constituted by complex articulations of class, race, gender, age and many other elements. As well, images circulate through complex and contradictory trajectories of production and consumption that contribute to the specific ways in which they ignite the viewers' imagination.

This book on Singapore's past provides evidence of the possibilities inherent in photography's power of authentication. Although the story of the transformation and evolution of Singapore has been told many times before, the interweaving of written and visual accounts captures the social history, or the details of the daily routines of individuals and institutions, the nitty-gritty of daily life and experiences with an efficacy that is not likely without the possibilities opened up by visual images. The texture of daily life and its momentous transformations are represented in all their intricacy and detail in the images reproduced here.

The production of these images was most probably mediated by a wide variety of institutional and power relations, as they range from the colonial period through the development of the modern post-colonial nation-state. These institutions of power — whether it was the state or the many organisations associated with it — had their own specific agendas and intentions in deciding which categories of people, events and monuments deserved to be photographed, to be included in or excluded from the visual record of the daily lives of Singaporeans. Indeed, these images played a significant role in the discursive construction and objectification of social life over which the grid of surveillance and disciplinary colonial and post-colonial power could be exercised. In the pre-photography era, non-visual representations such as the organised statistical and other social surveys created their own discursive realities that served as the foil for the exercise of disciplinary and other forms of power for the state and other institutions (Appadurai 1993; Hacking 1990). As we have seen, the infusion of the visual element into these modes of reality construction opened up other possibilities for the exercise of power. They did so through the pictorial articulation of ideological positions. Some of the chapters of this book, such as those by Erb, Waterson, Pereira, and PuruShotam, seek to extricate the imprint of these institutional and power relations on the images that were produced. Despite institutional influences, the 'relative autonomy' of the images themselves, or what Roland Barthes referred to as their 'authenticating power,' also makes possible their deployment for the critique and contestation of the hegemonic discourses.

Theatre of Four Corners

The photographs in this book were often arranged according to the wishes of the chapter authors. The intentionality of authorship thus lies in the choice of images, their juxtaposition to each other and their serial arrangement on the printed page, as well as to the words in the text. As sociologists, the authors' desire to inform, impress or even infect prevents them from allowing the photographs to merely speak for themselves; the authors are less interested in reproducing or representing the reality 'out there' than in revealing or unmasking or even changing the status quo. It is often said that the sociological promise lies in its ability to demonstrate that things are not what they seem or can be other than what they are, and this opens the door into a magical, dream-like world of 'makeability,' negotiability and changeability. The sociologist thus lives in a world of fantasy and would very much like to offer an invitation to others to step into this plausible world to experience the ecstasy of it all. One steps out of a pre-existing social structure (because it is confining) — first in mind, then in body, to experience the joy of liberation. In this way, the sociologist hopes to escape the confinement of the pre-existing social structure, and find a better way to live. As much as institutions deploy data, whether statistical or visual, to express or exert their power (since 'knowledge is power'), sociologists as 'authors' feel that it is their job, their promise to themselves and society, to go out and launch a counter-attack in this power game. Many sociologists are too involved in contesting the social construction of reality to simply tell things the way they are or were.

On the other hand, people being photographed are rarely at the complete disposal of the photographer. As much as the photographer wants to take snapshots of people in a particular way, meticulously arranging the subject's pose and posture, the to-be-photographed decides whether or not to hold his head high, whether to sit close to or far away from someone, how to wear a smile or a look, how to 'act' in front of the era to resist being manipulated or controlled. The tension between the photographer and the photographed is the fountainhead of politics, democracy and equality. There is thus always an element of surprise, of the unexpected, for both parties. As much as the photographer is intent on constructing 'reality,' the photographed is counter-constructing, thus transforming the shooting session into a moment of theatre, drama, suspense and novelty. When the photograph comes into the hands of the sociologist, as in this book, a third party joins this game of construction and counter-construction, and triangulates the tension. The full intentions of all three parties may not be entirely conscious, and the cross-currents between them open up all kinds of possibilities. Finally, the readers of a book add their own interpretations, transforming a three-cornered triangle into a four-cornered square that is always shifting, contorting, or even distorting itself. To give one example: what if the reader does not know the English language at all and looks at the photographs without reading the text? How will the person experience the book? What does he see? How does he feel? What fires up his imagination? What makes him sad, happy, moody, tearful?

Is it Art, or Science?

There is something not adequately discussed in photojournalism, visual anthropology and sociology: the aesthetic experience of seeing photographic images which are displayed here or there on the printed pages simply because they are beautiful, touching, arousing, inciting, emotive, evocative. In this instance, the sociologist-author desires to communicate a soulful moment, a moment that is critical because somewhere and somehow a heart is touched — thus connecting author with reader. When this kind of magic occurs, we ordinarily do not call it (social) science because it does not deal with information, with data — which is supposedly objective and therefore verifiable. Instead we call it art, literature, poetry, music, watercolours, oils, cinema, theatre because it is subjective and personal. Are art and science that separate? As Becker pointed out, it is conventional wisdom to insist that 'the two aims —social analysis and aesthetic expression — were necessarily contradictory, as though you could only satisfy one at the expense of the other' (1981:9). Does not art, being the artefact of one single person's impulse to capture what is beautiful, go straight to the heart of truth, which after all is the goal of science? Does not science, in the process of discovering what is true, verifiable and reproducible, often produce something that is profoundly pleasing to the eyes? Poetry of physics at one moment, and physics of poetry at another? Sort of art and science becoming one. As Becker said: '…so many artists' visions are of the truth about the world, and scientists' discoveries of that truth contain as strong an element of personal vision' (1981:9). This being the case, one wonders why sociologists and anthropologists do not use photographs, film, drawings and prints more often. One possible explanation is a certain distrust of the visual. The sociologist is used to dealing in the word, and the word only. The chasm and schism, between the word and the visual image has become a gulf, one that guarantees the poverty of many a sociologist's imagination. The modern-day sociologist should reach deeper into his toolbox to find arguably his two most powerful tools, his emotions and his imagination, because the postmodern world is unsettled and unsettling. He must now learn how to picture the world, to see the world in pictures, literally. It is more important than ever that sociologists use their eyes, both outer and inner.

The Aesthetic and the Narrative

There is no shortage of evocative photographs in this book to afford readers an aesthetic experience that is also informative. In Erb's chapter on education in early Singapore, one sees a stunning photograph of rows of pupils spreading their arms at the Church of Zenana Missionary School, as if in collective aerial flight, stretching their wings to take off. This photograph is a contrast to another placed right above it on the same page: girls posing, sitting on the lawn, in front of a majestic building of the Convent of the Holy Infant Jesus; people and architecture are in temporal suspense, frozen, motionless, adding form and solidity to a classical still photograph. In PuruShotam's chapter on the 'woman' in the photograph, the reader encounters arguably two of the most poignant images of the book. The first image portrays a mother and her young children, begging on the street. The second photograph shows another mother with her seven young children, yes seven. Who can forget the emotions of frustration but also determination to make it which the mother wears on her face? Her eyes tell all. Where is the husband-father? He is conspicuous in his absence. There are many, many other such images. In Erb's chapter on birth, one sees a newborn baby staring at a midwife. The baby's gaze is so full of life. A few pages later in the same chapter, one sees a row of babies lying on mats. Human beings, when together, doing the same thing, somehow always manage to catch the eyes of the artist and the sociologist. And then the reader will chance on the Malay houses in Chua's chapter

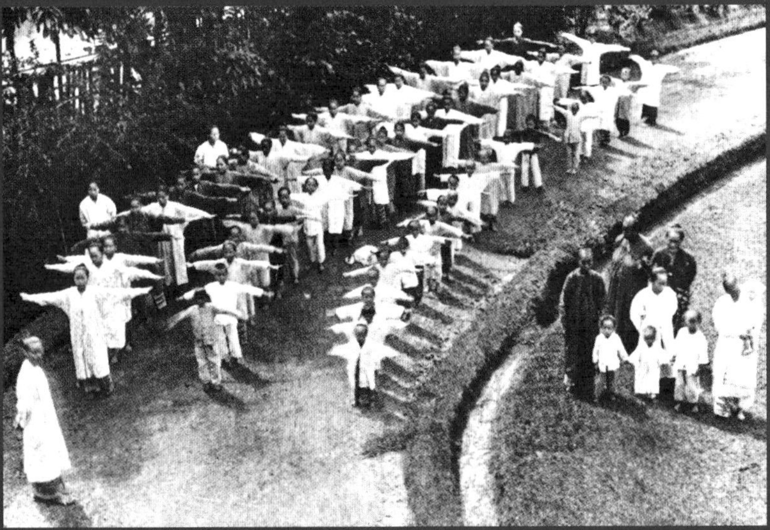

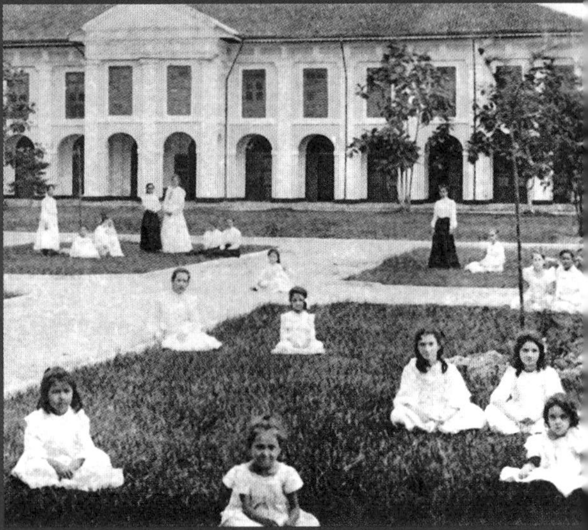

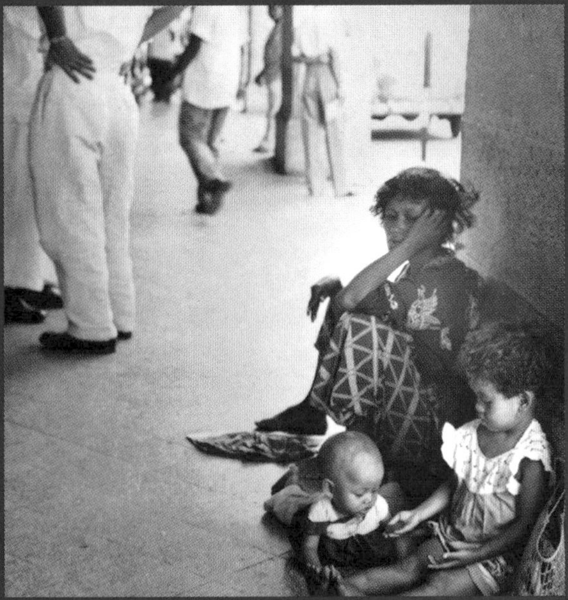

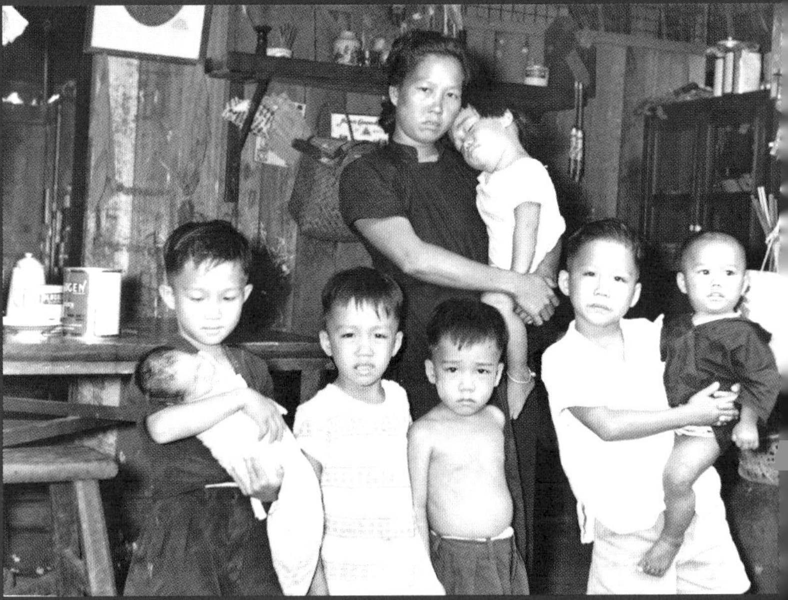

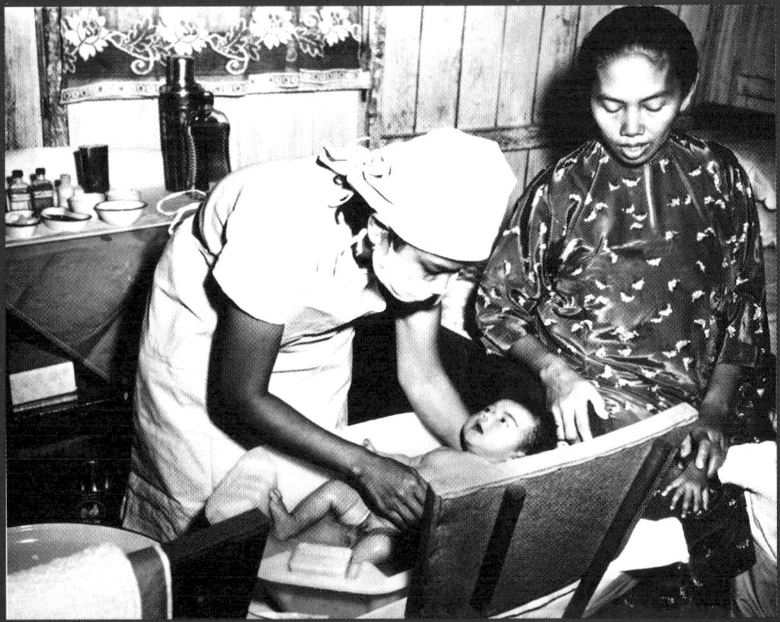

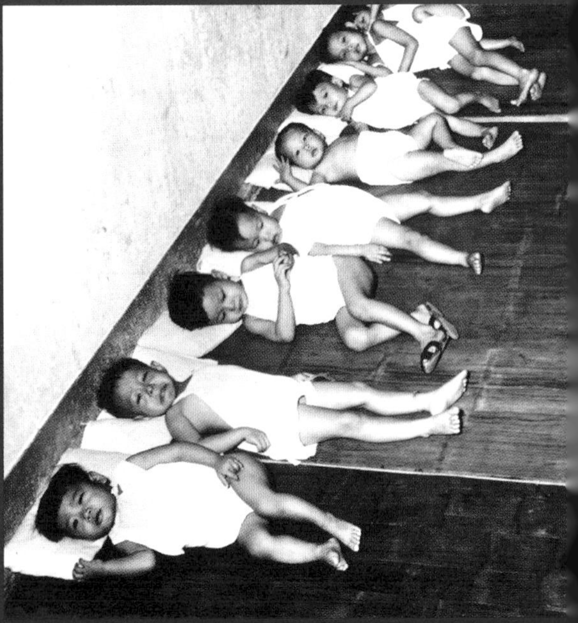

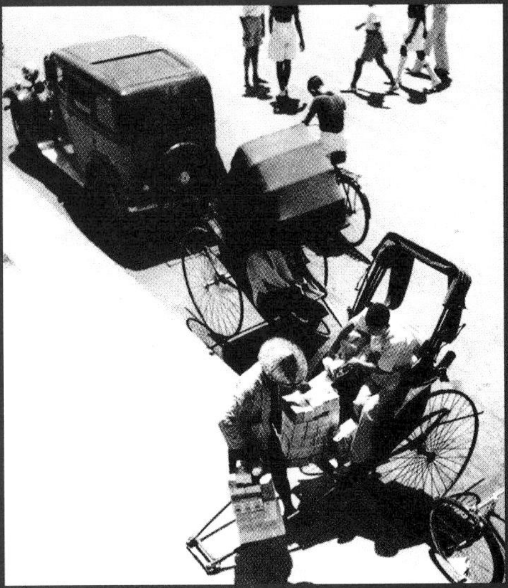

Magnolia
CERTIFIED PURE
ICE CREAM
COLD STORAGE
CREAMERIES LTD
S
1202

on housing and architecture, the kind of houses many urbanites will fly thousands of miles to see. Then, how about the full-page photograph of a rickshaw puller in Waterson's chapter on transport? So nostalgic, so Chinese. The photograph of a Straits Chinese family in Selina Chan's chapter on the family seems to be an exercise in elegance, material comfort, balance, bonding, and hierarchy — approximating a family ideal. Then in her chapter on food, who can miss a smiling ice-cream man making his rounds and the barefooted boy consumed by desire? Or the one portraying the comfort of a teahouse? Finally, in one photograph in Yung and Chan's chapter on Chinese entertainment, the reader is greeted by fresh-faced, young school girls sitting on the floor and paying rapt attention to a technological invention, the radio; and a Chinese opera on a makeshift street stage, fronted by hundreds of clansmen who seemed torn between the spectacle on stage and the presence of another technological marvel, the camera. In every instance, the photographers and the sociologists who have chosen the photographs and written about the world they evoke are 'seriously interested in understanding society and making art at the same time' (Becker 1981:11). Both scientist and artist 'leave us knowing more about some aspect of a society than we did before we absorbed their work. They all leave us with the thrill of appreciating a fresh vision' (Becker 1981:11). Scientist and artist are united by one and the same goal: *to change our vision, our usual way of seeing the world.*

Photography, Sociology and Society

Society exists as long as it can be conjured up by the individual in his mind and then in the minds of others through communication, excitement, or even incitement, in words and in images. Sociology, like art, aims to awaken us to an appreciation and understanding of life; and offers alternatives to suffering. The vulnerability and sham and shambles of the status quo can only be grasped by a mind (and an eye) that can invoke a picture of the world, both as it is and as it could be. This idea of option which is 'makeable' and therefore possible can be a potent force of liberation, even emancipation. Sociology has a moral commitment to making society a better place for us all to live in that goes back to its founding fathers. To do the job well, sociology is art is photography, and photography is sociology is society. When will sociologists turn to the artists and listen to them for insights, and vice versa? Aren't sociologists and artists after the same thing? Isn't it that children make no distinction between science and art — because they are curious about the same thing, which is experience, self, truth, nature, truth or consciousness — until society and socialisation teach them to discriminate? Is a child asking a question of science, or of art, when he marvels at rain in spring, waves on the beach, a tree that gives shade, a river that runs on and on, the smile on a baby's face, stars that fail to fully shine tonight? When shall we learn a thing or two from children? Have we forgotten our childhood? Did we have one?

Endnotes

1. Howard S. Becker. 1981. *Exploring Society Photographically*, Chicago: University of Chicago Press, p.9.
2. Quoted on p.200 in Susan Sontag, 1977, *On Photograph*. Harmondsworth: Penguin.
3. Quoted on p.185 in Susan Sontag, 1977, *On Photography*, Harmondsworth: Penguin.
4. See Barthes 1981; Berger 1972, 1980, 1982; Sontag 1977; Bourdieu 1990; Price 1994; Clarke 1997; Pulz 1995; Solomon-Godeau 1991; Wells 1997; Jay 1996; Mirzoeff 1998.

References

Chapter 1

Alatas Syed Hussein. 1971. *Thomas Stamford Raffles: Schemer or Reformer*. Sydney: Angus and Roberson.

Anderson, Benedict. 1983. *Imagined Communities: Reflections of the Origin and Spread of Nationalism*. London: Verso.

National Archives of Singapore. 1985. *The Japanese Occupation: Singapore 1942-1945*. Singapore: Singapore News and Publications Limited.

Awang bin Osman. In *Communities of Singapore (Part 3)*. Accession number:319, S/No. 16–18. Singapore: Oral History Department, National Heritage Board.

Bazell, C. (1921) 1991. "Education in Singapore," in *One Hundred Years of Singapore* vol.1, edited by Walter Makepeace, Grant E. Brooke and Roland St. J. Braddell. Singapore: Oxford University Press.

Bell, David Scott. 1972. *Unity in Diversity: Education and Political Integration in an Ethnically Pluralistic Society*. Ph.D. diss., Indiana University, Ann Arbor: University Microfilms.

Bloodworth, Dennis. 1986. *The Tiger and the Trojan Horse*. Singapore: Times International.

Bloom, David. 1986. "The English Language and Singapore: A Critical Survey," in *Singapore Studies: Critical Surveys of the Humanities and Social Sciences*, edited by Basant K. Kapur,. Singapore: Singapore University Press.

Chelliah, David D. (1947) 1960. *A History of the Educational Policy in the Straits Settlement*. Singapore: G.H. Kiat.

Chew, Melanie. 1996. *Leaders of Singapore*. Singapore: Resource Press.

Doraisamy, Theodore Royapan, ed. 1969. *150 Years of Education in Singapore*. Singapore: Publications Board, Teachers' Training College.

Kannusamy s/o Pakirisamy. In *Communities of Singapore (Part 2)*. Accession number: 81, S/No. 22. Singapore: Oral History Department, National Heritage Board.

PuruShotam, Nirmala. 1989. "Language and Linguistic Policies," in *Management of Success: The Moulding of Modern Singapore*, edited by Kernial Singh Sandhu and Paul Wheatley. Singapore: Institute of Southeast Asian Studies.

Sim, Victor, ed. 1950. *Biographies of Prominent Chinese in Singapore*. Singapore: Nan Kok Pub. Co.

Ward, A.H.C., Raymond Chu and Janet Salaff, eds. and trans. 1994. *The Memoirs of Tan Kah Kee*. Singapore: Singapore University Press.

Chapter 2

Anderson, Benedict. 1983. *Imagined Communities. Reflections on the Origin and Spread of Nationalism*. London: Verse.

Barthes, Roland. 1981. *Camera Lucida: Reflections of Photography*. Trans. Richard Howard. New York: Hill and Wang.

Blessing, Jennifer. c.1997. *Rrose is a Rrose is a Rrose: Gender Performance in Photography*. New York: Guggenheim Museum.

Bourdieu, Pierre, Luc Boltanski, Robert Castel, Jean Claude Chamboredon and Dominique Schanapper. 1996. *Photography. A Middle-Brow Art*. Trans. Shaun Whiteside. Cambridge: Polity Press.

Clarke, Graham. 1997. *The Photograph*. New York: Oxford University Press.

Goh Keng Swee. 1956. *Urban Incomes and Housing. A Report on the Social Survey of Singapore, 1953-1954*. Singapore: Department of Social Welfare.

Kaye, Barrington. 1960. *Upper Nankin Street, Singapore. A Sociological Study of Chinese Households Living in a Densely Populated Area*. Singapore: University of Malaya Press.

Lau, Cynthia Shiueh Chin. 1992. "Woman and Housework in a HDB Estate.". Academic exercise, University of Singapore.

Naipaul, V.S. 1979. *India: A Wounded Civilization*. New Delhi: Penguin Books.

National Heritage Board. c.1995. *From the Family Album: Portraits from the Lee Brothers Studio, Singapore, 1910-1925*. Singapore: Landmark Books

P.A.P (People's Action Party). 1959. *The Tasks Ahead. P.A.P.'s Five Year Plan, 1959-1964*. Singapore: Petir.

PuruShotam, Nirmala. 1992. "Woman and Knowledge/Power: Notes on the Singaporean Dilemma," in *Imagining Singapore*, edited by Ban Kah Choon, Anne Pakir and Tong Chee Kiong. Singapore: Times Academic Press.

PuruShotam, Nirmala. 1998. "Between Compliance and Resistance. Women and the Middle Class Way of Life in Singapore," in *Gender and Power in Affluent Asia*, edited by Krishna Sen and Maila Stivens. London and New York: Routledge.

PuruShotam, Nirmala. 2000. *Negotiating Multiculturalism. Disciplinג Difference in Singapore*. Berlin and New York: Mouton de Gruyter.

PuruShotam, Nirmala. "Constituting 'The Family': Normalizing Contestations" (work in progress).

Report on the Census of Population, 1957. Singapore.

Siddique, Sharon and Nirmala PuruShotam. 1982. *Singapore's Little India. Past, Present and Future*. Singapore: Institute of Southeast Asian Studies.

Wong, Aline K. and Leong Wai Kum. 1993. *Singapore Women. Three Decades of Change*. Singapore: Times Academic Press.

Chapter 3

Braga-Blake Myrna. 1992. *Singapore Eurasians: Memories and Hopes*. Singapore: Times Editions.

Chang Chen Tung. 1979. "Nuptiality Patterns among Women of Childbearing Age," in *Contemporary Family in Singapore*, edited by Eddie Kuo and Aline K. Wong. Singapore: Singapore University Press.

Clammer, John. 1980. *Straits Chinese Society: Studies in the Sociology of the Baba Communities of Malaysia and Singapore*. Singapore: Singapore University Press.

Djamour, Judith. 1965. *Malay Kinship and Marriage in Singapore*. London: Athlone Press.

Freedman, Maurice. 1957. *Chinese Family and Marriage in Singapore*. London: Her Majesty's Stationery Office.

——— 1961. "Immigrants and Associations: Chinese in Nineteenth-century Singapore," in *Comparative Studies in Society and History* 3:25–48.

Lim San Neo. 1997. *My Life, My Memories, My Story*. Singapore: Epic Management Services.

Png Poh Seng. 1969. "The Straits Chinese in Singapore: A Case of Local Identity and Socio-cultural Accommodation," in *Journal of Southeast Asian History* 10, no. 1: 95–114.

——— 1970. "Some Preliminary Observations of the Origins and Characteristics of Indian Migration to Malaya 1786–1957," in *Intisari* 3(4):22–40.

Saw Swee Hock. 1974. *A Collection of Reprint Articles on Population and the Labour Force in Malaysia and Singapore*. Singapore: University of Singapore.

Siddique, Sharon and Nirmala PuruShotam. 1982. *Singapore's Little India: Past, Present and Future*. Singapore: Institute of Southeast Asian Studies.

Sng Boey Kim. 1985. In Chinese dialect Groups. Interview. Accession number: 517, S/No. 26. Singapore: Oral History Centre, National Heritage Board.

Tan Chye Yee. 1986. In Chinese Dialect Groups. Interview. Accession number: 616, S/No. 7. Singapore: Oral History Centre, National Heritage Board.

Wong, Aline K. 1975. *Women in Modern Singapore*. Singapore: University Education Press.

Yao Souchou. 1987. "Ethnic Boundaries and Structural Differentiation: An Anthropological Analysis of the Straits Chinese in Nineteenth Century Singapore," in *Sojourn* 2(2): 209–30.

Chapter 4

Anniversary Edition. 1990. *Kandang Kerbau Hospital 1924-1990*. Singapore: The Hospital.

Bungar, J.B. 1991. "Sexuality, Fertility and the Individual in Singapore Society." Master's thesis, National University of Singapore.

Ebert R.V. 1959. "The Growth of Voluntary Social Services in Singapore." Acadmic exercise, University of Malaya.

Haniah Abdul Hamid. 1992. "Entering Life, Entering Death: The case of the Malays in Singapore." Academic exercise, National University of Singapore.

Lam June Ken-yin. 1959. "Family Planning in Ten Chinese Families." Academic Exercise, University of Malaya.

Lee Y.K. 1990. "A Short History of Kandang Kerbau Hospital and the Maternity Services of Singapore," in *Singapore Medical Journal* 30:599-613.

Lim Yien Yien. 1994. "Pregnancy and Childbirth: Interpreting the Experience." Academic Exercise, National University of Singapore.

Mohamed Hassan bin Haji Ngah Mahmud. 1967. "Patterns of Children Rearing Practices among the Malays." Academic exercise, University of Singapore.

Ng Jiak Lui. 1994. "Birth Rituals of the Chinese in Singapore." Academic exercise, National University of Singapore.

Raja, Mrs. "Indian Traditions," in *Communities of Singapore (Part 2)*. Interview. Accession number: 800, S/No. 013. Oral History Centre, National Heritage Board, Singapore.

Simmons, Ida M.M. 1939. "Pioneer Maternity and Child Welfare Work in Rural Singapore from 1927 to 1938," in *Health Talk on Maternity and Child Welfare* vol.1. Singapore: Government Printing Office.

SFCC (Singapore Federation of Chinese Clan Associations). 1989. *Chinese Customs and Festivals in Singapore*. Singapore: SFCC.

Tham Seong Chee. 1985. *Religion and Modernization: A Study of Changing Rituals among Singapore's Chinese, Malays and Indians*. Singapore: Graham Bash.

Valsiner, Jaan. 1989. *Human Development and Culture: The Social Nature of Personality and Its Study*: 117-162. Canada: Lexington Books.

Chapter 5

Chew, Daniel. 1989. "Towards a social history of Tanjong Pagar 19001940," in *Tanjong Pagar: Singapore's Cradle of Development*: 21–30. Singapore: Tanjong Pagar Citizens' Consultative Council.

Chua Beng Huat. 1995. "That imaginary space: nostalgia for the *kampong*," in *Portrait of Places: History, Community and Identity in Singapore*: 222–224, edited by Lily Kong and Brenda Yeoh. Singapore: Times Editions.

Edwards, Norman. 1992. "The Colonial Suburb: Public Space and Private Space," in *Public Space*: 24–39, edited by in Chua Beng Huat and Norman Edwards. Singapore: Singapore University Press.

Ho Kong Chong and Valerie N.E. Lim. 1992. "Backlanes as Contested Regions: Construction and Control of Physical Space," in *Public Space*: 40–54, edited by Chua Beng Huat and Norman Edwards. Singapore: Singapore University Press.

Kohl, D.G. 1984. *Chinese Architecture in the Straits Settlements and Western Malaysia: Temples, kongsis and houses*. Kuala Lumpur: Heinemann.

Lee Kip Lin. 1988. *The Singapore House 1819-1942*. Singapore: Times Edition.

Lim, Irene and Chua Chee Huan. 1989. "Opium Dens and Towkay Homes: the Social Mosiac," in *Tanjong Pagar: Singapore's Cradle of Development*. Singapore: Tanjong Pagar Citizens' Consultative Council.

Lim Jee Yuan. 1987. *The Malay House: Rediscovering Malaysia's Indigenous Shelter System*. Penang, Malaysia: Institut Masyarakat.

Savage, Victor. 1992. "Street Culture in Colonial Singapore," in *Public Space*: 11–23, edited by Chua Beng Huat and Norman Edwards. Singapore: Singapore University Press.

Chapter 6

Backhouse, Sally. 1972. *Singapore*. Newton Abbot: David and Charles.

Brown, Edwin Arthur. 1935. *Indiscreet Memories*. London: Kelly and Walsh.

Buckley, Charles Burton. (1902) 1984. *An Anecdotal History of Old Times in Singapore*. Reprint, Singapore: Oxford University Press.

Cameron, John. 1865. *Our Tropical Possessions in Malayan India*. London: Smith, Elder & Co.

Clutterbuck, Richard. 1973. *Riot and Revolution in Singapore and Malaya, 1945-1963*. London: Faber and Faber.

Collins, Dale. 1923. *Sea-tracks of the Speejacks Round the World*. London: Heinemann.

Earl, G. W. (1873) 1971. *The Eastern Seas: or Voyages and Adventures in the Indian Archipelago in 1823*: 33–34. Reprint, Singapore: Oxford University Press.

Hutton, Peter. 1981. *Wings Over Singapore*. Singapore: MPH, for Department of Civil Aviation and Ministry of Communications.

Kossak, Hans. 1873. *Professor Hildebrant's Reise um die Erde* (*Professor Hildebrant's Voyage around the World*). Trans. by Jill Easthope. Berlin: Vierte Auflage.

Makepeace, Walter, Gilbert E. Brook and Roland St. J. Braddel, eds. 1921. *One Hundred Years of Singapore*, vols. 1–2. London: John Murray.

Marvin, Bishop E. M. 1878. *To the East by Way of the West*. St Louis: Bryan, Brand and Co.

Peet, George L. 1985. *Rickshaw Reporter*. Singapore: Eastern Universities Press.

Reese, Albert M. 1919. *Wanderings in the Orient*. Chicago: The Open Court Publishing Co.

Scidmore, Eliza Ruhamah. (1899) 1984. *Java: The Garden of the East*. Reprint, Kuala Lumpur: Oxford University Press.

Siddique, Sharon and Nirmala PuruShotam. 1982. *Singapore's Little India: Past, Present and Future*. Singapore: Institute of Southeast Asian Studies.

Sidney, Richard John Hamilton. 1926. *Malay Land*. London: Cecil Palmer.

Singh, Reena. 1995. *A Journey Through Singapore*. Singapore: Landmark Books.

Song Ong Siang. (1923) 1966. *One Hundred Years' History of the Chinese in Singapore*. London: John Murray. Reprint, Kuala Lumpur: Oxford University Press.

Swettenham, F. A. (1906) 1948. *British Malaya: An Account of the Origin and Progress of British Influence in Malaya*. Reprint, London: George Allen and Unwin.

Warren, James Francis. 1986. *Rickshaw Coolie: A People's History of Singapore (1880-1940)*. Singapore: Oxford University Press.

York, F. W. and Phillips, A. R. 1996. *Singapore: A History of Its Trams, Trolleybuses and Buses, 1880s to 1960s* vol. 1. Croydon: DTS Publishing.

Yvan, Melchoir. 1855. *Six Months Among the Malays; And A Year in China*. London: James Blackwood.

Chapter 7

Chua Beng Huat. 1997. *Political Legitimacy and Housing*. London: Routledge.

Chua Beng Huat and Ananda Rajah. 1996. "Hybridity, Ethnicity and Food in Singapore," in *Working Paper Series, Department of Sociology* 133:1–24, National University of Singapore.

Douglas, Mary 1984. "Standard Social Uses of Food: Introduction," in *Food in the Social Order*: 1–39. New York: Russell Sage Foundation.

Fong Chiok Kai. In *Chinese Dialect Groups*. Interview. Accession number: 185, S/No. 32. Singapore: Oral History Centre, National Heritage Board.

Gennep, Arnold Van. 1960. *Rite de Passage*. Chicago: Chicago University Press.

Guide to Singapore and Spotlight on Malaya. 1960. Singapore: Andre Publications.

Guide to Singapore and Spotlight on Malaya. 1965. Singapore: Andre Publications.

Ong Siew Peng. In *Chinese Dialect Groups*. Interview. Accession number: 1210, S/No. 15. Singapore: Oral History Centre, National Heritage Board.

Singh, Reena. 1995. *A Journey Through Singapore: Travellers' Impression of a By-gone Time Selected and Arranged in a Complete Narrative*. Singapore: Landmark Books and Antiques of the Orient.

Chapter 8

Barth, Valerie. 1992. "Belonging," in *Singapore Eurasians: Memories and Hopes*, edited by Myrna Braga-Blake and Anne Ebert-Oehlers. Singapore: Times Academic Press.

Buckley, Charles Burton. (1902) 1984. *An Anecdotal History of Old Singapore*. Reprint, Kuala Lumpur: Oxford University Press

Frey, James H. and Eitzen, D. Stanley. 1991. "Sport and Society," in *Annual Review of Sociology* vol. 17: 503–22.

Luschen, Gunther. 1980. "Sociology of Sport: Development, Present State and Prospects," in *Annual Review of Sociology* vol. 6: 315-47.

Makepeace, Walter, Gilbert Brooke and Roland St. J. Braddell, eds. (1921) 1991. *One Hundred Years of Singapore* vols. 1 and 2. Reprint, Singapore: Oxford University Press.

Robert, Godfrey. 1991. *The Malaysia Cup*. Singapore: AAA Publications.

Seneviratne, Percy. 1993. *Golden Moments: the S.E.A Games 1959-1991*. Singapore: Percy Seneviratne.

Chapter 9

Bai Yan (Yan Bo Yuan) and Mrs Bai Yan (Yeh Qing). 21 Feburary 1997, 28 May 1997. Personal communication.

Bai Yan (Yan Bo Yuan). January 1992. "*Suxie gewutuan*" (A Quick Sketch of the *Gewutuan*), in *Xinming Ribao*, p.5

Bai Yan (Yan Bo Yuan). "*Gewutuan chu dao Xinjiapo*," (When the *Gewutuan* Just Arrived in Singapore), n.d.

Chan Kwok Bun. 1991. *Smoke and Fire: The Chinese in Montreal*. Hong Kong: Chinese University Press.

Chew Kok Wei. 4 June 1997. Personal communication.

Cheng Lim Keak. 1993. "The *Xinhua* Community in Singapore: A Study of the Socio-Economic Adjustment of a Minority Group," in *Chinese Adaptation and Diversity: Essays on Society and Literature in Indonesia, Malaysia & Singapore*, edited by Leo Suryadinata. Singapore: Singapore University Press: 28–56

Chow, Rey. 1997. "Playing on the Air: Recollections from a Hong Kong Childhood," in *Journal of Modern Literature in Chinese* 1.1: 109-27.

Foong Choon Hon. 1996. "*Da zhan qian hou di diantai*" (Radio Broadcasting Before and After the World War II), in *Chengshi huixiang* (Echoes in the City), edited by Zhang Liping et al. Singapore: Radio Corporation of Singapore: 88–89.

Foong Choon Hon. 10 May, 1997. Personal communication.

Gullick, J.M. *Malaya Society in the late Nineteenth Century: The Beginnings of Change*. Singapore: Oxford University Press.

Habermas, Jurgen. 1975. *Legitimation Crisis*. Boston: Beacon Press.

Johnson, David. 1989. *Ritual Opera, Operatic Ritual: Mu-lien Rescues His Mother in Chinese Popular Culture*, edited by David Johnson. Berkely: Chinese Popular Culture Project.

Lat Pau, 8 March, 1889.

Lee Fook Hung (Lee Dai Soh, Li Dasha). Interview. Accession number: 260, S/No. 07. Singapore: Oral History Centre, National Heritage Board.

Lee Toon Song. 1999. "Technology and the Production of Islamic Space: The call to Prayer in Singapore," in *Ethnomusicology* vol 43 (1): 86–100.

Li Dasha (Lee Dai Soh, Lee Fook Hung). 1984. *Li Dasha zizhuan: Jiang gu de yisheng* (The Biography of Li Dasha: a Life of Storytelling). Singapore: *Lianbang chubanshe*.

Lii Ding-Tzann. 1996. "Social Spheres and Public Life: A Genealogy of Modern Individualism and its Reactions to Cultural Performance." Unpublished mss., Institute of Sociology and Anthropology, National Tsing-Hua University, Taiwan.

Lim Joo Hock. 1967. "Chinese Female Immigration into the Straits Settlements, 1860–1901," in *Journal of The South Seas Society* (*Nanyang Xuebao*) 22: 1, 2 : 58-110.

Pan Xingnong. 1955. *Xinjiapo zhinnan* (Singapore Directory). Singapore: Nantao Publishing House.

Radio Singapore. 1992. *Radio Singapore: A Story of Progress (1945–1959)*. Singapore: Singapore Government Printing Office.

Report of the Department of Broadcasting for the Years 1946–52. 1953. Singapore: Singapore Government Printing Office.

Report of the Department of Broadcasting for the Year 1953. 1954. Singapore: Singapore Government Printing Office.

Report of the Department of Broadcasting for the Year 1954. 1956. Singapore: Singapore Government Printing Office.

Rudolph, Jurgen. 1996. "Amusements in the Three 'Worlds'", in *Looking at Culture*, edited by Sanjay Krishnan et al. Singapore: Artres Design & Communication: 21–33.

Sennett, Richard. 1978. *The Fall of Public Man*. New York: Vintage Books.

Shangguan Liyun. 28 May 1997. Personal communication.

Sheppard, Mubin. 1972. *Taman Indera: Malaya Decorative Acts and Pastimes*. Reprinted as *A Royal Pleasure Ground*. Singapore: Oxford University Press, 1986.

Si Jing. 15 December, 1997. "*Ting guangbo, tan jiushi: cong kongzhong xiaoshuo dao guangbo ju*" (Listen to Broadcast, Talk about the Past: From "Radio Story" to "Broadcast Drama"), in *Chaguan*, in *Lianhe Zaoboa*: 8.

Singapore Broadcasting Corporation. C.1988. *Radio Singapore, 4 January 1959*. Videorecording. Singapore: Television Corporation of Singapore.

Song Ong Siang. (1902) 1984. *One Hundred Years' History of the Chinese in Singapore*. Reprint, Singapore: Singapore University Press.

Tan Giak. 1990. Interview. Accession number: 1040, S/No. 02. Singapore: Oral History Centre, National Heritage Board.

"*Tingge kanxi de ne duan rizi*" (The Days of Songs and Drama), in *Lianhe Wanbao*. 26 March, 1984:19.

Tsao Pen-yeh. 1987. *Puppet Theatres in Hong Kong and their Origin*. Hong Kong: Urban Council.

Vaughan, J.D. (1879) 1971. *The Manners and Customs of the Chinese of the Straits Settlements, Singapore*. Reprint, Kuala Lumpur, Singapore: Oxford University Press.

Wang Zhengchun. 1988. *Gen de xilie* (*Roots: Series of Writings*). Singapore: Seng Yew Book Store.

Weng Shu Dao. 10 May, 1997. Personal communication.

Wilkinson, R.J. 1910. "Malay Amusements", in *Papers on Malay Subjects, Life and Customs, Part 3*. Kuala Lumpur: F.M.S. Government Press.

Wu Hao. 1993. *Xianggang dianying minsuxue* (An Ethnography of Hong Kong Movies). Hong Kong: Ciwenhua tang.

Yang Muxi. 1996. "*tan tan xuexiao guangbo*" (Some Remarks on the School Broadcast), in *Chengshi huixiang* (*Echoes in the City*), edited by Zhang Liping et al. Singapore: Radio Corporation of Singapore: 90.

Yu Shukun (ed). 1951. *Nanyany Nanjian*. Singapore: Nanyang Baoshe Co Ltd.

Chapter 10

Bell, David Scott Jr. 1972. "Unity and Diversity: Education and Political Integration in an Ethnically Pluralistic Society." Ph.D. diss., Indiana University.

Drysdale, John. 1985. *In Service of the Nation*. Singapore: Federal Publications.

Chambliss, William J. 1976. "Functional and Conflict Theories of Crime," in *Whose Law? What Order? A Conflict Approach to Criminology*, edited by William J. Chambliss and Milton Mankoff. New York: John Wiley and Sons.

Hill, Michael and Lian Kwen Fee. 1995. *The Politics of Nation Building and Citizenship in Singapore*. London: Routledge.

Lee, Edwin. 1991. *The British as Rulers: Governing Multiracial Singapore*. Singapore: Singapore University Press.

Lee Teng Hui. 1996. *The Open United Front: The Communist Struggle in Singapore*. Singapore: South Seas Society.

Mak Lau Fong. 1988. "Chinese Secret Societies in the Straits Settlements," in *Early Chinese Immigrant Societies: Case Studies from North America and British Southeast Asia*: 230–243, edited by Lee L.T. Singapore: Heinemann Asia.

Merton, Robert K. 1938. "Social Structure and Anomie," in *American Sociological Review* 3: 672–82.

Rubington, Earl and Martin S. Weinberg, eds. 1995. *The Study of Social Problems: Seven Perspectives*. Oxford: Oxford University Press.

Singapore Police Force. 1954. *Annual Report*. Singapore: Singapore Police Force.

Singapore Police Force. 1955. *Annual Report*. Singapore: Singapore Police Force.

Singapore Police Force. 1956. *Annual Report*. Singapore: Singapore Police Force.

Song, Ong Siang. (1902) 1984. *One Hundred Years' History of the Chinese in Singapore*. London: John Murray. Reprint, Singapore: Oxford University Press.

Turnbull, Constance Mary. 1996. *A History of Singapore: 1819–1988*. 3rd ed. Singapore: Oxford University Press.

Yen Ching Hwang. 1988. "Early Chinese Clan Organizations in Singapore and Malaya, "in *Early Chinese Immigrant Societies: Case Studies from north America and British Southeast Asia*: 186–229, edited by Lee L.T. Singapore: Heinemann Asia.

Chapter 11

Addison, John T. 1925. *Chinese Ancestor Worship: A Study of its Meaning and its Relations with Christianity*. London: The Church Literature Committee and S.P.C.K.

ARSM (*Administrative Report of the Singapore Municipality*). 1893. "Report on and estimates for, the disposal of night soil at Singapore and for the improvement of the surface drainage." Singapore: Singapore & Straits Printing Office.

Babb, Lawrence. 1976. "Patterns of Hinduism," in *Singapore: Society in Transition*: 189–204, edited by Riaz Hassan. Kuala Lumpur: Oxford University Press. (Page references are drawn from the reprinted version in *Understanding Singapore Society*, edited by Ong Jin Hui, Tong Chee Kiong, and Tan Ern Ser. 1997. Singapore: Times Academic Press.)

Bartley, W. 1933. "Population of Singapore in 1819," in *Journal of the Malayan Branch of the Royal Asiatic Society* XI: 177. Singapore: Printers Limited.

Blasdell, R.A. 1942. "How Islam came to the Malay Peninsula," in *Moslem World* 32: 114–21.

Bloom, David. 1986. "The English Language and Singapore: A Critical Survey," in *Singapore Studies: Critical Surveys of the Humanities and Social Sciences*: 337–458, edited by Basant K. Kapur. Singapore: Singapore University Press.

Buckley, Charles Burton. (1902) 1984. *An Anecdotal History of Old Times in Singapore*. Reprint, Singapore: Oxford University Press.

Census of Singapore 1849. 1950.In *Journal of the Indian Archipelago and Eastern Asia* 4. Reprint, n.p.: Kraus.

Cheu Hock Tong. 1988. *The Nine Emperor Gods: A Study of Chinese Spirit-Medium Cults*. Singapore: Times.

Clammer, John, ed. 1983. "Studies in Chinese Folk Religion in Singapore and Malaysia," in *Contributions to Southeast Asian Ethnography* 2. Singapore: Contributions to Southeast Asian Ethnography.

Clammer, John. 1985. *Singapore: Ideology, Society and Culture*. Singapore: Chopmen.

Clammer, John. 1988. "Singapore's Buddhists Chant a Modern Mantra," in *Far Eastern Economic Review*, 29 December: 26–27.

Comber, Leon. 1954. *Chinese Ancestor Worship in Malaya*. Singapore: Donald Moore.

Comber, Leon. 1955. *Chinese Magic and Superstition in Malaya and Singapore*. Singapore: Donald Moore.

Comber, Leon. 1958. *Chinese Temples in Singapore*. Singapore: Eastern Universities Press.

Doraisamy, Theodore Royapan. 1982. *The March of Methodism in Singapore and Malaysia, 1885–1980*. Singapore: Methodist Book Room.

———, ed. 1985. *Forever Beginning: One Hundred Years of Methodism in Singapore*. Singapore: The Methodist Church.

Elliott, A.J. 1955. *Chinese Spirit-Medium Cults in Singapore*. London: London School of Economics.

Evans, Ivor H.N. 1927. *Papers on the Ethnology and Archaeology of Malay Peninsular*. Cambridge: Cambridge University Press.

Farah, Caesar E. 1994. *Islam: Beliefs and Observances*. New York: Barron's.

Greer, R.M. 1956. *A History of the Presbyterian Church in Singapore*. Singapore: Malaya Publishing House.

Harcus, A.D. 1955. *History of the Presbyterian Church in Malaya*. For the 27th Annual Lecture of the Presbyterian Historical Society in England, London.

Hatley, R. 1969. "The Overseas Indians in South-east Asia: Burma, Malaysia and Singapore," in *Plan, State and Society in Contemporary South-east Asia*: 450–466, edited by R.O. Tilman. London: Mall Press.

Heinze, Ruth. 1979. "Social Implications of the Relationship between Mediums, Entourage, and Clients in Singapore Today," in *Southeast Asian Journal of Social Science* 7: 1–2, 60–80.

Heinze, Ruth. 1981. "The Nine Imperial Gods in Singapore," in *Asian Folklore Studies* 40, no. 2: 151–71.

Hinton, Keith. 1985. *Growing Churches Singapore Style: Ministry in an Urban Context*. Singapore: Overseas Missionary Fellowship. IRO. 1990.

Inter-Religious Organisation Singapore 40th Anniversary Commemorative Book. Singapore: IRO

Israeli, R. and A.H. Johns, eds. 1984. *Southeast and East Asia, Islam in Asia* 2. Jerusalem: The Magnes Press.

Ju S.H. 1983. "Chinese Spirit Mediums in Singapore: An Ethnographic Survey," in *Contributions to Southeast Asian Ethnography* 2: 3–48, edited by John R. Clammer.

Ke Zongyuan. 1984. "What was it Crawfurd saw on Fort Canning?," in *Heritage* 6. Singapore: National Museum.

Khoo Chian Kim. 1981. *Census of Population, 1980, Singapore; Release No. 9: Religion and Fertility*. Singapore: Department of Statistics.

Lau Kak En. 1994. *Singapore Census of Population, 1990, Release No. 69: Religion, Childcare and Leisure Activities*. Singapore: Department of Statistics.

Lee C.Y., Alan K.L. Chan and Timothy Y.H. Tsu. 1994. *Taoism: Outlines of a Chinese Religious Tradition*. Singapore: Taoist Federation.

Leo, J.B. and John R. Clammer. 1983. "Confucianism as Folk Religion in Singapore: A Note," in *Contributions to Southeast Asian Ethnography* 2: 175–78, edited by John R. Clammer.

Lip, Evelyn. 1983. *Chinese Temple Architecture in Singapore*. Singapore: Singapore University Press.

Loh K.A. 1963. *Fifty Years of the Anglican Church in Singapore Island, 1909–1959*. Singapore: University of Singapore Press.

Low, Sally Kim Lian. 1974. "*Teochew* Catholicism in Singapore: Some Impressions." Academic exercise, University of Singapore.

Mahajani, Usha. 1960. *The Role of the Indian Minorities in Burma and Malaysia*. Bombay: Vora.

Mansur Haji Sukaimi. 1983. *Dynamic Functions of Mosques: The Singapore Experience*. Singapore: Majlis Ugama Islam Singapura.

Marriott, H. 1911. *Census Report of the Straits Settlements 1911*. n.p.

Marrison, G.E. 1951. "The Coming of Islam to the East Indies." in *Journal of the Malayan Branch of the Royal Asiatic Society* 24: 1: 28–37.

McAmis, R.D. 1970. "Islam Comes to the Islands of Southeast Asis," in *Southeast Asian Journal of Theology* 12: 87–101.

Miksic, John. 1985. *Archaeological Research on the 'Forbidden Hill' of Singapore: Excavations at Fort Canning, 1984*. Singapore: National Museum.

Mohamed Nahar Ros. 1985. "Sacred Places: *Keramats* in Singapore." Academic exercise, National University of Singapore.

Mohamed Taib bin Osman. 1967. "Indigenous, Hindu and Islamic Elements in Malay Folk Beliefs." Ph.D. diss., Indiana University.

MUIS. 1986. *New-Generation Mosques in Singapore and their Activities*. Singapore: Majlis Ugama Islam Singapura.

Nathan, J.E. 1921. *The Census of British Malaya 1921*. London: Dunstable and Watford.

Nyce, R. 1971. "Chinese Folk Religion in Malaysia and Singapore," in *Southeast Asian Journal of Theology* 12: 81–91.

Sandhu, Kernial Singh. 1969. *Indians in Malaya: Some Aspects of their Immigration and Settlement*. London: Cambridge University Press.

Siddique, Sharon. 1990. "Singapore's Mosques: the Evolution of an Institution."

Siddique, Sharon. 1989. "Singaporean Identity," in *Management of Success: The Moulding of Modern Singapore*: 563–77, edited by Kernial Singh Sandhu and Paul Wheatley. Singapore: Institute of Southeast Asian Studies.

Singer, Milton. 1972. *When a Great Tradition Modernizes: An Anthropological Approach to Indian Civilization*. London: The Pall Mall Press.

Sinha, Vineeta. 1988. "Hinduism in Singapore: A Sociological and Ethnographic Perspective." Master's thesis, National University of Singapore.

Sng, Bobby E.K. 1993. *In His Good Time: The Story of the Church in Singapore, 1819–1992*, 2d ed. Singapore: Graduates' Christian Fellowship.

Song Ong Siang. (1923) 1967. *One Hundred Years of the Chinese in Singapore*. Reprint, Singapore: University of Malaya Press.

Stephens, Jacintha. 1983. "Catholic Vellala in Singapore: Origin and Identity." Academic exercise, National University of Singapore.

Tamney, Joseph B. and Riaz Hassan. 1987. *Religious Switching in Singapore: A Study of Religious Mobility*. Singapore: Select Books for Flinders University of South Australia.

Tan, Robert. 1962. "The Cultural Landscape of Singapore: A Study of the Growth and Distribution of Religious Institutions on the Island (1819–1961)." Academic exercise, University of Malaya.

Tan Khong Chew. 1980. "Church Architecture in Singapore since 1950." Academic exercise, University of Singapore.

Tan, Karen. 1988. "The Catholic Church in Singapore." Academic exercise, National University of Singapore.

Teixeira, Manuel. 1963. *The Portuguese Missions in Malacca and Singapore (1511–1958)*. Lisboa: Agencia Geral do Ultramar.

Tham Seong Chee.1985. *Religion and Modernisation: A Study of Changing Rituals among Singapore's Chinese, Malays and Indians*. Singapore: Graham Brash.

Thomas, W.T. and R.B. Manikam. 1956. *The Church in South East Asia*. New York: Friendship Press Inc.

Tong Chee Kiong. 1992. "The Rationalisation of Religion in Singapore," in *Imagining Singapore*, edited by Ban Kah Choon, Anne Pakir, and Tong Chee Kiong. Singapore: Times Academic Press.

Topley, Marjorie. 1954. "Chinese Women's Vegetarian Houses in Singapore," in *Journal of the Malayan Branch of the Royal Asiatic Society* 27: 1: 51–67.

Topley, Marjorie. 1956. "Chinese Religion and Religious Institutions in Singapore," in *Journal of the Malayan Branch of the Royal Asiatic Society* 29: 1: 70–118.

Topley, Marjorie. 1961. "The Great Way of Former Heaven: A Chinese Semi-secret Religion in Malaya," in *The New Malayan* 2: 9–13.

Van Donzel, E., B. Lewis, and C.H. Pellat, eds. 1975. *The Encyclopaedia of Islam* 4. Leiden: E.J. Brill.

Vlieland, C.A. 1932. *British Malaya: A Report on the 1931 Census and Certain Problems of Vital Statistics*. London: Crown Agents for the Colonies.

Wee, Vivienne. 1976. " 'Buddhism' in Singapore," in *Singapore: Society in Transition*: 155–88, edited by Riaz Hassan. Kuala Lumpur: Oxford University Press.

Winstedt, R.O. 1917. "The Advent of Muhammedanism in the Malay Peninsula and Archipelago," in *Journal of the Straits Branch of the Royal Asiatic Society* 77: 2: 171–75.

Conclusion

Agee, James and Walker Evans. 1960. *Let Us Now Praise Famous Men*. Boston: Houghton Mifflin.

Anderson, Benedict. 1983. *Imagined Communities: Reflections on the Origin and Spread of Nationalism*. New York: Verso.

Appadurai, Arjun. 1993. "Number in the Colonial Imagination," in *Orientalism and the Postcolonial Predicament*, edited by Carol A. Breckenridge and Peter van der Veer. Philadelphia: University of Pennsylvania Press.

Arnheim, Rudolf. 1974. "On the Nature of Photography," in *Critical Inquiry*, Vol.1:123–168.

Barrow, Thomas F., Shelley Armitage and William Tydeman. 1987. *Reading into Photography*. Albuquerque: University of New Mexico Press.

Barthes, Roland. 1981. *Camera Lucida: Reflections on Photography*. New York: Noonday Press.

Bateson, Gregory and Margaret Mead. 1942. *Balinese Character: A Photographic Analysis*. New York: New York Academy of Sciences.

Baudrillard, Jean. 1981. *For A Critique of the Political Economy of the Sign*. St. Louis, MI: Telos Press.

Baudrillard, Jean. 1994. *Simulacra and Simulation*. Ann Arbor: University of Michigan Press.

Becker, Howard. 1981. *Exploring Society Photographically*. Chicago: University of Chicago Press.

Benjamin, Walter. 1978. *Reflections*. New York: Harcourt, Brace and Jovanovich.

Benjamin, Walter. 1980. *Classic Essays on Photography*. New Haven: Leete's Island Books.

Berger, John. 1972. *Ways of Seeing*. Harmondsworth: Penguin.

Berger, John. 1980. *About Looking*. New York: Pantheon.

Berger, John and Jean Mohr. 1982. *Another Way of Telling*. New York: Pantheon.

Bourdieu, Pierre et al. 1990. *Photography: A Middle-Brow Art*. Stanford: Stanford University Press.

Cavell, Stanley. 1971. *The World Viewed*. New York: Metheuen.

Clarke, Graham. 1997. *The Photograph*. New York: Oxford University Press.

Evans, Walker. 1993. *The Hungry Eye*. New York: Harry N. Abrams.

Hacking, Ian. 1990. *The Taming of Chance*. Cambridge: Cambridge University Press.

Jay, Martin. 1996. *Downcast Eyes: The Denigration of Vision in Twentieth Century French Thought*. Berkeley: University of California Press.

Lalvani, Suren. 1996. *Photography, Vision and the Production of Modern Bodies*. Albany: State University of New York Press.

Mirzoeff, Nicholas (ed.). 1998. *The Visual Culture Reader*. New York: Routledge.

Pinney, Christopher. 1997. *Camera Indica: The Social Life of Indian Photographs*. London: Reaktion Books.

Price, Mary. 1994. *The Photograph: A Strange Confined Space*. Stanford: Stanford University Press.

Pulz, John. 1995. *Photography and the Body*. London: Calmann and King.

Said, Edward and Jean Mohr. 1993. *After the Last Sky: Palestinian Lives*. London: Vintage.

Snyder, Joel and Neil Walsh Allen. 1987. "Photography, Vision and Representation", in *Reading into Photography*, edited by T. Barrow, S. Armitage and W. Tydeman. Albuquerque: University of New Mexico Press.

Solomon-Godeau, Abigail. 1991. *Photography at the Dock*. Minneapolis: University of Minnesota Press.

Sontag, Susan. 1977. *On Photography*. Harmondsworth: Penguin.

Stryker, Roy and Nancy Wood. 1973. *In This Proud Land*. New York: New York Graphic Society.

Tagg, John. 1988. *The Burden of Representation*. Amherst: University of Massachusetts Press.

Wells, Liz. 1997. *Photography: A Critical Introduction*. New York: Routledge.

Index

Anomie 183, 185, 186, 187, 193, 197
aviation 118, 119
Aw Boon Haw 117, 118
Awang bin Osman 28

birth 69–85
    beliefs and rituals 70, 71, 72, 73, 74, 75, 76, 80, 81, 221, 222
    medical practices 76, 77, 78, 79, 80, 81, 82, 83
British Colonial Government 17, 18, 19, 21, 22, 23, 24, 26, 27, 29, 30, 78, 111, 138, 186, 187, 188, 189, 190, 199, 201
British East India Company 17, 19, 21, 22, 205
British Malaya Broadcasting Corporation 171, 172, 173, 176
Buckley, Charles Burton 105, 115, 116

Chan Choy Siong 47, 48, 49, 50, 51
China 24, 25, 26, 27, 29, 58, 59, 60, 63, 64, 102, 186, 210
citizenship 22, 46, 47
clan associations 65, 69, 186, 187, 228
coffeeshops 65, 92

early schools 17, 19, 20, 22, 141, 142, 143, 207, 210, 212, 227
education 17–31
    Chinese 18, 21, 24, 26, 27, 29, 30, 31, 48
    Japanese propaganda and 27
    Malay 18, 21, 26, 28
    Tamil 21, 23, 24
entertainment 153–181
    amusement parks 154, 155, 163, 164, 165, 166, 169, 178, 179
    celebrations and 153, 154, 157, 159, 160, 178, 179
    getai 154, 157, 169, 170, 171
    gewutuan 165, 166, 167, 168, 169

    operas 153, 154, 156, 158, 159, 160, 161, 164
    puppetry 163, 164
    radio 154, 171, 172, 173, 174, 175, 176, 177
    storytelling 162, 163
    technology and 154, 158, 179
    television 154, 179

family 56–67, 69
festivals 123, 124, 127, 134, 220, 221, 223, 224, 225
food 71, 73, 75, 123–135
    social cohesion and 132, 133
    social differentiation and 128, 129, 130, 131, 132

General Hospital 76, 77, 78, 79, 100

Hock Lee Bus Company 114, 192
housing and architecture 41, 87–99
    bungalows 97, 98, 99, 100
    five-foot-ways 94, 95, 96
    indigenous 42, 87, 88, 89, 90, 91, 92, 93, 97, 100
    shophouses 93, 94, 95, 96, 101

Japanese Occupation 27, 111, 112, 116, 169, 190

keramat 217, 218, 219

Lee Dai Soh (Lee Dasha) 175, 176, 177
Lee Kong Chian 29, 31
Little India 77, 101
London Missionary Society (LMS) 18, 19, 205, 211

Malaya 26, 27, 35, 59
Maria Hertogh Riot 190, 191, 228
marriage practices 58–66

Chinese 60, 61, 63, 64, 65, 66, 67
Indian 63, 64
Malay 61, 62, 63, 64
Straits Chinese 61, 62, 64
Mohammed Eunos 26

Nanyang University 25, 29, 30, 192, 193, 194, 206
National Archives 34, 36

People's Action Party (P.A.P.) 47, 50, 51
photography 41, 42, 158
Pickering, William 188–189
population 18, 22, 36, 57, 58, 60, 65, 69, 82, 83, 84, 95, 96, 185, 190, 199, 200, 207, 214

Raffles, Sir Thomas Stamford 17, 18, 19, 57, 102, 203, 205, 229
Rediffusion 174, 175, 177
religion 18, 22, 119–231
    Buddhism 211, 212, 214, 222, 223, 229, 230
    Christianity 19, 20, 200, 201, 203, 204, 205, 207, 208, 209, 210, 211, 212, 213, 214, 215, 216, 219,   227, 229, 230
    Hinduism 200, 201, 206, 208, 214, 219, 220, 221, 222
    Islam 200, 201, 203, 204, 207, 213, 217, 218, 219, 227, 228, 229
    shenist 199, 201, 202, 204, 214, 215, 222, 223, 227, 230
    spirit-mediums 224, 225
    syncretism 215, 216, 217, 218, 219, 230

Simmons, Ida 81, 82, 84
Singapore Bus Workers' Union (SBWU) 114
Singapore River 93, 94, 101
Singapore Traction Company (STC) 114, 115
social unrest 35, 49, 115, 183–197
    functionalist perspective 183, 185, 194, 196, 197
    critical perspective 184, 185, 194, 196, 197

class division and 184, 185, 186, 187, 188, 194, 197
communist insurgency and 191, 192, 193, 195, 196
sports 137–151
    badminton 138, 142, 144, 145
    boat racing 138
    conflict perspective 137, 139
    consensus perspective 137
    clubs 139, 140, 141, 142, 143, 144, 150, 151
    cricket 138, 140, 144
    football 138, 139, 140, 142, 148
    nationalism and 148, 149, 150
    women and 140, 142, 143, 144, 147

Sun Yat-Sen 25

Tan Kah Kee 25, 27, 29
Tanjong Pagar Dock. Co. 112
transport 102–121
    automobiles 106, 109, 116, 117, 118, 120
    bicycles 109, 111
    mosquito buses 113, 114
    rail 107
    rickshaw 106, 109, 110, 111, 112, 113, 120
    social status and 117, 118
    steam ships 104, 105
    trading fleets 102, 103
    trams 112, 113
    trolley buses 112, 113, 114

Winstedt, Richard O. 23
women 33–55
    civil society and 46, 48, 49
    education and 18
    employment and 37, 38, 39, 40, 45, 48, 60
    family and 43, 44, 45, 52, 53, 54
    marriage and 52, 53, 54, 60
    migration and 60
    Women's Charter 35, 34, 49, 51, 52, 64

Pictures

Alwee Alkaff Collection, courtesy of the National Archives of Singapore: 117.
Arshak C. Galston Collection, courtesy of the National Archives of Singapore: 23, 20 (top).
C.Y. Han Collection, courtesy of the National Archives of Singapore: 91.
Che Wil Collection, courtesy of the National Archives of Singapore: 192 (left), 192 (right).
Chu Sui Mang Collection, courtesy of the National Archives of Singapore: 97, 40 (bottom left).
Chuan Hui Tsuan Collection, courtesy of the National Archives of Singapore: 27.
Courtesy of Federal Press: 177.
Courtesy of Huzaimah Hamzah: 75.
Courtesy of KK Women's and Children's Hospital: 78, 80, 82.
Courtesy of Lily Kong: 222.
Courtesy of Mr Bai Yan: 169, 171, 165 (bottom), 166 (bottom), 167 (top), 168 (bottom), 168 (top).
Courtesy of Mr Chia Kah Mun, Andrew: 59.
Courtesy of Mr Y.H. Lim: 123 (left), 123 (right).
Courtesy of Sam King, author Tiger Balm, published by Times Editions Private Limited: 118 (top).
Courtesy of Siong Leng Musical Association: 173 (top).
Courtesy of the Chinese Newspaper Division, Singapore Press Holdings Limited: 182, 194 (bottom), 194 (top).
Courtesy of the National Archives of Singapore: 38, 68, 71, 84, 86, 88, 93, 99, 102, 107, 108, 111, 113, 119, 130, 131, 158, 170, 175, 176, 185, 187, 188, 190, 191, 196, 203, 209, 210, 213, 225, 226, 228, 104 (top), 106 (bottom), 115 (left), 118 (bottom), 126 (bottom), 144 (left), 145 (top), 164 (bottom), 164 (top), 171 (bottom right), 171 (bottom left), 173 (bottom), 174 (top), 206 (left), 206 (right), 217 (bottom), 221 (bottom), 24 (top), 224 (bottom), 37 (bottom), 40 (bottom), 44 (bottom), 44 (top), 89 (bottom), 94 (bottom), 95 (bottom), 96 (left).
Courtesy of the Singapore Police Force: 193, 195 (left), 195 (right).
Courtesy of Tong Chee Kiong: 202.
David Ng Collection, courtesy of the National Archives of Singapore: 92 (top).
Francis Lee Collection, courtesy of the National Archives of Singapore: 64, 66.
Gretchen Liu Collection, courtesy of the National Archives of Singapore: 56, 58.
K.F. Wong Collection, courtesy of the National Archives of Singapore: 134, 220, 126, 128, 163.
Ken Farm Collection, courtesy of the National Archives of Singapore: 126 (top).
Keppel Corporation Collection, courtesy of the National Archives of Singapore: 104 (bottom).
Lakshmi Hariram Collection, courtesy of Vineeta Singha: 76.
Lee Hin Ming Collection, courtesy of the National Archives of Singapore: 52, 53, 57, 60, 61, 62, 77, 116.
Lim Kheng Chye Collection, courtesy of National Archives of Singapore: 208, 212.
Margaret Clarke Collection, courtesy of the National Archives of Singapore: 215.
Ministry of Information, Communication and the Arts, courtesy of the National Archives of Singapore: 29, 32, 79, 81, 83, 148, 149, 172, 198, 216, 218, 232, 143 (left), 144 (left), 144 (right), 28 (bottom), 28 (top), 50 (left), 50 (right).
Mrs J.A. Bennet Collection, courtesy of the National Archives of Singapore: 115 (right).
Mrs Morgan Betty Basset Collection, courtesy of the National Archives of Singapore: 24 (bottom).
Nanyang University Collection, Ministry of Information, courtesy of the National Archives of Singapore: 30.
Oral History Centre Collection, courtesy of the National Archives of Singapore: 152.
Paul Piollet, courtesy of the National Archives of Singapore: 92 (bottom).
Paul Yap Collection, courtesy of the National Archives of Singapore: 19, 90, 109, 110, 112, 122, 132,., 106 (top), 20 (bottom), 89 (top), 95 (top).
Philip Gower Collection, courtesy of the National Archives of Singapore: 133.
Raffles Institution Collection, courtesy of the National Archives of Singapore: 16, 17.
Registry of Co-operative Societies Collection, courtesy of the National Archives of Singapore: 129.
Salbiah Sahat Collection, courtesy of the National Archives of Singapore: 63.
Sean Ip Puan Collection, courtesy of the National Archives of Singapore: 224 (top).
Shaw Organisation collection, courtesy of Mr Bai Yan: 165 (top).
Siglap Malay School collection, courtesy of the National Archives of Singapore: 37 (bottom left).
Singapore History Museum, courtesy of the National Archives of Singapore: 157, 160, 161, 136, 138, 139, 140, 141, 142, 147, 143 (right), 145 (bottom), 146 (bottom), 146 (top).
Tan Kok Kheng Collection, courtesy of the National Archives of Singapore: 25.
Terry Wright Collection, courtesy of the National Archives of Singapore: 96 (right).
The Straits Times Collection, courtesy of Singapore Press Holdings Limited: 39, 49 (right), 49 (left), 39, 40, 42, 43, 45, 37 (top).
The Straits Times, Singapore Press Holdings Limited, courtesy of the National Archives of Singapore: 124, 127.
Urban Redevelopment Authority Collection, courtesy of the National Archives of Singapore: 94 (top).
Wong Kwan Collection, courtesy of the National Archives of Singapore: 204.

Authors

Selina Ching Chan obtained her doctorate from Oxford University. Currently, she teaches in the Department of Sociology at the National University of Singapore. In addition to several publications on kinship structure and social identity in Hong Kong, she has also written on pawnshops in Singapore. Her articles have appeared in international journals that include *Modern China* and *Ethnology*.

Chan Kwok Bun is Head and Professor, Department of Sociology, and Director, David C. Lam Institute for East-West Studies, Hong Kong Baptist University. He is co-author of *Stepping Out: The Making of Chinese Entrepreneurs* (1994) and editor of *Chinese Business Networks: State, Economy and Culture* (2000) and of *Alternate Identities: The Chinese of Contemporary Thailand* (2001). He is presently editing a book on stress and coping among professionals in Singapore. He is co-editor of *Asian Journal of Social Sciences* and the *Asian Social Science* monograph series.

Chua Beng Huat is Professor in the Department of Sociology, National University of Singapore. He has written extensively on Singapore, including books on urban and housing policies, political development and the emergence of consumerism.

Maribeth Erb is Associate Professor in the Department of Sociology at the National University of Singapore. Her main research area is the western Flores in Indonesia, where she has been doing research on ritual ceremonies, mythology, and kinship and family since the early 1980s. Erb has written a book about western Florinese culture called *The Manggaraians: A Guide to Traditional Lifestyles* (1999), designed for a semi-popular audience. Recent work analysing tourism developments is found in *Annals of Tourism Research*, *Singapore Journal of Tropical Geography*, and *Journal of Southeast Asian Studies*.

Lily Kong is Associate Professor in the Department of Geography, National University of Singapore. She graduated with a B.A. (Honours) and M.A. from the National University of Singapore, and a Ph.D. from University College London. She is a social and cultural geographer with research interests in religion, music and cultural policy, urban heritage and histories, nations and national identities.

Alexius A. Pereira received his Ph.D. from the London School of Economics. His research interests and recent publications are in economic sociology, particularly in the fields of industrialization and entrepreneurship. Pereira has conducted fieldwork in Singapore, China and Ireland. He has also previously conducted research and published on the Eurasian community in Singapore.

Nirmala PuruShotam is currently attached to Department of Anthropology, Dartmouth College, New Hampshire as a Visiting Scholar. She has worked extensively in a variety of areas, including gender and race politics. Her numerous publications include the acclaimed *Negotiating Multiculturalism: Disciplining Difference in Singapore* (2000). She is currently working on a book on global culture and gender politics.

Tong Chee Kiong teaches in the Department of Sociology, National University of Singapore. He was the former Dean of the Faculty of Arts and Social Sciences and Director of the Graduate School. Tong completed his undergraduate training at the University of Singapore and his M.A. and Ph.D. at Cornell University. His research interests center on the study of the Chinese in Southeast Asia, religion and religious change in Singapore and Asian business networks. His publications include *Imagining Singapore* (1992), *Religion in Singapore* (1993), *Alternate Identities: The Chinese of Contemporary Thailand* (2001), and *The Making of Singapore Sociology: Society and State* (2002).

Roxana Waterson has been living in Singapore since 1984, and has taught in the Department of Sociology at National University of Singapore since 1987, where she is now an Associate Professor. She took her Ph.D. in Social Anthropology at New Hall, Cambridge (1981), and has done field research with the Sa'dan Toraja people of Sulawesi (Indonesia) since 1978. She is the author of *The Living House: An Anthropology of Architecture in Southeast Asia* (3rd ed., 1997), and numerous articles about aspects of Toraja society and culture. Waterson's current research interests include the study of social memory, life history, and visual anthropology.

Yung Sai Shing is Associate Professor in the Department of Chinese Studies, National University of Singapore. His research interest includes traditional Chinese drama, Chinese ritual theaters, Cantonese opera, and social history of Chinese opera in Singapore. He published his first book entitled *An Anthropology of Chinese Drama: Ritual, Theater, and Community* in 1997. Now he is completing his second book which studies the cultural history of gramophone industry of Cantonese opera and music since the 1900s.

Zaheer Baber is the Canada Research Chair in Sociology at the University of Saskatchewan. He is the author of *The Science of Empire* (1996) and has published research papers in journals such as *British Journal of Sociology*, *Theory and Society*, *Sociological Inquiry*, etc. His current research interests include science and technology studies, social theory, historical sociology and visual sociology. He is a Contributing Editor of the *Bulletin of Science, Technology and Society* and Associate Editor of *Asian Journal of Social Science*.